MW00388716

WILEY SERIES 66 SECURITIES LICENSING EXAM REVIEW 2020 + TEST BANK

WILEY SECURITIES LICENSING SERIES

This series includes the following titles:

Wiley Securities Industry Essentials Exam Review 2020

Wiley Series 3 Securities Licensing Exam Review 2020 + Test Bank: The National Commodities Futures Examination

Wiley Series 4 Securities Licensing Exam Review 2020 + Test Bank: The Registered Options Principal Examination

Wiley Series 6 Securities Licensing Exam Review 2020 + Test Bank: The Investment Company and Variable Contracts Products Representative Examination

Wiley Series 7 Securities Licensing Exam Review 2020 + Test Bank: The General Securities Representative Examination

Wiley Series 9 Securities Licensing Exam Review 2020 + Test Bank: The General Securities Sales Supervisor Examination—Option Module

Wiley Series 10 Securities Licensing Exam Review 2020 + Test Bank: The General Securities Sales Supervisor Examination—General Module

Wiley Series 24 Securities Licensing Exam Review 2020 + Test Bank: The General Securities Principal Examination

Wiley Series 26 Securities Licensing Exam Review 2020 + Test Bank: The Investment Company and Variable Contracts Products Principal Examination

Wiley Series 57 Securities Licensing Exam Review 2020 + Test Bank: The Securities Trader Examination

Wiley Series 63 Securities Licensing Exam Review 2020 + Test Bank: The Uniform Securities Agent State Law Examination

Wiley Series 65 Securities Licensing Exam Review 2020 + Test Bank: The Uniform Investment Adviser Law Examination

Wiley Series 66 Securities Licensing Exam Review 2020 + Test Bank: The Uniform Combined State Law Examination

Wiley Series 99 Securities Licensing Exam Review 2020 + Test Bank: The Operations Professional Examination

For more on this series, visit the website at www.securitiesCE.com.

WILEY SERIES 66 SECURITIES LICENSING EXAM REVIEW 2020 + TEST BANK

The Uniform Combined State Law Examination

The Securities Institute of America, Inc.

WILEY

Cover Design: Wiley
Cover Image: © Jumpeestudio/iStock.com

Copyright © 2020 by The Securities Institute of America, Inc. All rights reserved.

Published by John Wiley & Sons, Inc., Hoboken, New Jersey.
Previous editions published by The Securities Institute of America, Inc.
Published simultaneously in Canada.

No part of this publication may be reproduced, stored in a retrieval system, or transmitted in any form or by any means, electronic, mechanical, photocopying, recording, scanning, or otherwise, except as permitted under Section 107 or 108 of the 1976 United States Copyright Act, without either the prior written permission of the Publisher, or authorization through payment of the appropriate per-copy fee to the Copyright Clearance Center, Inc., 222 Rosewood Drive, Danvers, MA 01923, (978) 750-8400, fax (978) 646-8600, or on the Web at www.copyright.com. Requests to the Publisher for permission should be addressed to the Permissions Department, John Wiley & Sons, Inc., 111 River Street, Hoboken, NJ 07030, (201) 748-6011, fax (201) 748-6008, or online at http://www.wiley.com/go/permissions.

Limit of Liability/Disclaimer of Warranty: While the publisher and author have used their best efforts in preparing this book, they make no representations or warranties with respect to the accuracy or completeness of the contents of this book and specifically disclaim any implied warranties of merchantability or fitness for a particular purpose. No warranty may be created or extended by sales representatives or written sales materials. The advice and strategies contained herein may not be suitable for your situation. You should consult with a professional where appropriate. Neither the publisher nor author shall be liable for any loss of profit or any other commercial damages, including but not limited to special, incidental, consequential, or other damages.

For general information on our other products and services or for technical support, please contact our Customer Care Department within the United States at (800) 762-2974, outside the United States at (317) 572-3993, or fax (317) 572-4002.

Wiley publishes in a variety of print and electronic formats and by print-on-demand. Some material included with standard print versions of this book may not be included in e-books or in print-on-demand. If this book refers to media such as a CD or DVD that is not included in the version you purchased, you may download this material at http://booksupport.wiley.com. For more information about Wiley products, visit www.wiley.com.

ISBN 978-1-119-70397-6 (Paperback)
ISBN 978-1-119-70394-5 (ePDF)
ISBN 978-1-119-70402-7 (ePub)

Printed in the United States of America.

V99FD88C2-764C-4926-9E15-315E8E4E7B14_022820

Contents

CHAPTER 2
SECURITIES INDUSTRY RULES AND REGULATIONS   25

CHAPTER 3
ECONOMIC FUNDAMENTALS   **53**

CHAPTER 4
CUSTOMER RECOMMENDATIONS, PROFESSIONAL
CONDUCT, AND TAXATION

71

CHAPTER 5
VARIABLE ANNUITIES, RETIREMENT PLANS, AND LIFE INSURANCE 111

About the Series 66 Exam

Congratulations! You are on your way to becoming licensed to represent both a broker dealer and an investment adviser in all states that require the Series 66. The Series 66 exam will be presented in a 100-question multiple-choice format. Each candidate will have two-and-a-half hours to complete the exam. A score of 73% or higher is required to pass.

TAKING THE SERIES 66 EXAM

The Series 66 exam is presented in multiple-choice format on a touch-screen computer known as the PROCTOR system. No computer skills are required, and candidates will find that the test screen works in the same way as an ordinary ATM machine. Each test is made up of 100 questions that are randomly chosen from a test bank of several thousand questions. The test has a time limit of two-and-a-half hours and is designed to provide enough time for all candidates to complete the exam. Each Series 66 exam will have 10 additional questions that do not count towards the final score. The Series 66 is composed of questions that focus on the following areas:

Economic factors & business information	5 questions	5%
Investment vehicle characteristics	20 questions	20%
Client recommendations & strategies	30 questions	30%
Laws, regulations, & unethical business practices	45 questions	45%
TOTAL	**100 questions**	**100%**

HOW TO PREPARE FOR THE SERIES 66 EXAM

For most candidates, the combination of the textbook, exam prep software, and video class instruction proves to be enough to successfully complete the exam. It is recommended that the candidate spend at least 40 to 50 hours preparing for the exam by reading the textbook, underlining key points, watching the video class, and completing as many practice questions as possible. We recommend that candidates schedule their exam no more than one week after completing their Series 66 exam prep.

Test-Taking Tips

☐ Read the full question before answering.

☐ Identify what the question is asking.

☐ Identify key words and phrases.

☐ Watch out for hedge clauses, such as except and not.

☐ Eliminate wrong roman numeral answers.

☐ Identify synonymous terms.

☐ Be wary of changing answers.

WHY DO I NEED TO TAKE THE SERIES 66 EXAM?

In order to conduct fee-based securities business, most states require that an agent successfully complete the Series 66 registration, as well as the Series 7 registration.

WHAT SCORE IS NEEDED TO PASS THE EXAM?

A score of 73% or higher is needed to pass the Series 66 exam.

ARE THERE ANY PREREQUISITES FOR THE SERIES 66?

A candidate is not required to have any other professional qualifications prior to taking the Series 66 exam. However, the Series 7 is a corequisite to becoming registered to conduct securities business.

HOW DO I SCHEDULE AN EXAM?

Ask your firm's principal to schedule the exam for you or to provide a list of test centers in your area. If you are not with a FINRA member firm, you must fill out and submit Form U10 prior to making an appointment to take the test. The Series 66 exam may be taken any day that the exam center is open.

WHAT MUST I TAKE TO THE EXAM CENTER?

A picture ID is required. All other materials will be provided, including a calculator and scratch paper.

HOW SOON WILL I RECEIVE THE RESULTS OF THE EXAM?

The exam will be graded as soon as you answer your final question and hit the Submit for Grading button. It will take only a few minutes to get your results. Your grade will appear on the computer screen, and you will be given a paper copy at the exam center.

If you do not pass the test, you will need to wait 30 days before taking it again. If you do not pass on the second try, you will need to wait another 30 days. If you fail a third time, you must wait 6 months to take the test again.

About This Book

The writers and instructors at The Securities Institute have developed the Series 66 textbook, exam prep software, and videos to ensure that you have the knowledge required to pass the test and to make sure that you are confident in the application of that knowledge during the exam. The writers and instructors at The Securities Institute are subject-matter experts as well as Series 66 test experts. We understand how the test is written, and our proven test-taking techniques can dramatically improve your results.

Each chapter includes notes, tips, examples, and case studies with key information, hints for taking the exam, and additional insight into the topics. Each chapter ends with a practice test to ensure that you have mastered the concepts before moving on to the next topic.

About the Test Bank

This book is accompanied by a test bank of more than 150 questions to further reinforce the concepts and information presented here. The access card in the back of this book includes the URL and PIN code you can use to access the test bank. This test bank provides a small sample of the questions and features that are contained in the full version of the Series 66 exam prep software.

If you have not purchased the full version of the exam prep software with this book, we highly recommend that you do so to ensure that you have mastered the knowledge required for your Series 66 exam. To purchase the exam prep software for this exam, visit The Securities Institute of America online at www.SecuritiesCE.com or call 877-218-1776.

About The Securities Institute of America

The Securities Institute of America, Inc., helps thousands of securities and insurance professionals build successful careers in the financial services industry every year.

Our securities training options include:

- Onsite training classes.
- Private tutoring.
- Classroom training.
- Interactive online video training classes.
- State-of-the-art exam preparation software.
- Printed textbooks.
- Real-time tracking and reporting for managers and training directors.

As a result, you can choose a securities training solution that matches your skill level, learning style, and schedule. Regardless of the format you choose, you can be sure that our securities training courses are relevant, tested, and designed to help you succeed. It is the experience of our instructors and the quality of our materials that make our courses requested by name at some of the largest financial services firms in the world.

To contact The Securities Institute of America, visit us on the Web at www.SecuritiesCE.com or call 877-218-1776.

Definition of Terms

INTRODUCTION

In order to successfully complete the Series 66 exam, it is important to have an in-depth understanding of the terms used within the securities industry—specifically within the framework of the Uniform Securities Act (USA). The terms used by the USA, also known as The Act, may have broader meanings than we are accustomed to in everyday usage.

SECURITY

A security is anything that can be exchanged for value that involves a risk to the holder. A security also represents an investment in an entity managed by a third party. The Supreme Court used the Howey test to determine a security. The Howey test states that a security must meet the following four characteristics:

1. It must be an investment of money.
2. It must involve a common enterprise.
3. It must give the investor an expectation of a profit.
4. It must entail the management of a third party.

The following are examples of securities:

- Stocks
- Bonds

- Notes
- Debentures
- Evidence of indebtedness
- Transferable shares
- Warrants, rights, or options for securities

Oftentimes when you see the term *certificate*, you have a security that is a:

- Certificate of interest in a profit sharing or partnership agreement.
- Preorganization certificate.
- Collateral trust certificate.
- Voting trust certificate.
- Certificate of interest in oil or a gas mining title.
- Certificate of deposit for a security, such as an American depositary receipt (ADR) or an American depositary share (ADS).

The term *variable* will also identify a security, as in:

- Variable annuity.
- Variable life insurance.
- Variable contract.

The phrase *interest in* is another key to identifying a security on the Series 66 exam. All of the following are securities:
Interest in:

- Farmland and animals.
- Whiskey warehouse receipts.
- Commodity options (not futures).
- Insurance company separate accounts.
- Real estate condominiums or cooperatives.
- Merchandise marketing programs, franchises, or schemes.
- Multilevel distributorships, such as Amway.

The term *option* is also a good way to identify a security, such as:

- Stock option.
- Index option.

- Futures option.
- Commodity futures option.

The following are not considered securities:

- Real estate
- Retirement plans, such as IRAs and 401Ks
- Bank accounts
- Collectibles
- Precious metals
- Fixed annuities/fixed contracts
- Whole and term life policies
- Antiques
- Futures contracts (commodities)
- Trade confirmations
- Prospectuses

The term *future*, as it appears alone, is an indication that a security is not involved. If the question is asking about a commodity future option, however, then a security is involved. Also, the term *fixed* is a good indication that a security is not involved.

PERSON

The term *person*, as it is used in the USA, refers to any entity that may enter into a legally binding contract. Any entity that can enter into a legally binding contract may transact business in the securities markets. Agreeing to buy or sell a security represents a legally binding contract. For the Series 66, a person is any of the following:

- Natural person
- Corporation
- Trust
- Government organization
- Partnership
- Joint stock company
- Sole proprietor

- Association
- Unincorporated organization

A nonperson is an individual or entity that may not enter into a legally binding contract and therefore may not transact business in the securities market. A nonperson is:

- A minor.
- Someone deemed to be legally incompetent.
- A deceased individual.

BROKER DEALER

A broker dealer is a person or a firm that maintains a place of business and affects transactions in the securities markets for its own account or for the account of others. A broker dealer must be registered in its home state as well as in the states of its individual clients.

A broker dealer is *not*:

- An agent.
- A bank.
- A savings and loan.
- A person with no place of business in the state, who deals exclusively with financial institutions or issuers.
- A person who conducts business with existing clients who do not reside in the state and are in state for less than 30 days.

AGENT

An agent or registered representative may only be an individual (natural person) who represents the issuer or a broker dealer in the purchase and sale or the attempted purchase and sale of securities with the public. Agents are required to register in their home state, their state of employment, and the state of residence of their customers.

Agents are *not* required to register if:

- They represent the issuer or a broker dealer in an underwriting transaction.
- They represent a bank or a savings and loan in the issuance of securities.

Agents who represent exempt issuers are not required to register. Examples of exempt issuers are:

- U.S. government
- State and municipal governments
- Canadian federal and municipal governments
- Commercial paper with maturities of less than 270 days, sold in denominations exceeding $50,000
- Investment contracts associated with employee pension plans, profit sharing, stock purchases, or savings plans
- Foreign national governments recognized by the United States

ISSUER

An issuer is any person that issues or simply proposes to issue a security. Issuers include:

- Corporations.
- U.S. government and agencies.
- State and local governments.

In an issuer or primary transaction, the issuer receives the proceeds from the sale.

NONISSUER

A nonissuer is anyone who does not issue or propose to issue a security. All secondary-market transactions that take place on an exchange or in the over-the-counter (OTC) market are nonissuer transactions, and the selling security holder receives the proceeds from the sale.

INVESTMENT ADVISER

An investment adviser is any person who is actively involved in and receives a fee for any of the following:

- Issuing research reports or analysis
- Publishing a market letter based on market developments or conditions

- Advising clients as to the advisability of the purchase or sale of a security
- Providing investment advisory services as a complement to their services and claiming to provide such services for a fee
- Presenting him- or herself as an investment adviser, also known as the shingle rule
- Providing advice about selecting portfolio managers or asset allocation
- Nationally recognized statistical ratings organizations such as Moody's
- Serving as a pension consultant

PENSION CONSULTANTS

A pension consultant is anyone who advises employees on how to fund their employee benefit plans. A person would also be considered to be a pension consultant if he or she advises employees on the selection of asset managers or investment advisers for the plan.

An investment adviser is *not*:

- A bank or savings and loan.
- A broker dealer.
- An agent.
- A lawyer, accountant, teacher, engineer (LATE) whose services are incidental to his or her business and who do not receive a specific fee for such services.
- Any person exempted by the administrator or SEC.
- Individuals who only provide advice relating to government securities.
- Publishers of newspapers and magazines.
- Securities information processors.

INVESTMENT COUNSEL

The Investment Advisers Act of 1940 provides a strict definition as to which professionals may call themselves an investment counsel. An investment counsel must be principally in the business of giving continuous investment advice and must supervise or manage the accounts. The Act does not define how much of the professional's time must be dedicated to providing advice, just that the professional's principal business is giving advice. A key to meeting the definition of an investment counsel are the key words "continuous and regular supervisory or management services" A professional who provides a wide range of services indicates that the professional in question is not principally involved in giving investment advice.

FORM ADV

An investment adviser will begin the formal registration process by filing Form ADV, which provides detailed information regarding the investment adviser. Form ADV has four parts: 1A, 1B, 2A, and 2B. Form ADV Parts 2A and 2B are provided to clients.

ADV Part 1A includes general information about the investment adviser, including:

- The principal office address.
- Type of organization, such as corporation or partnership.
- How the adviser will conduct business.
- If the firm engages in other activities, such as that of a broker dealer.
- Biographical data on the officers, directors, or partners.
- Disciplinary history of the officers, directors, partners, and the firm.
- Location of books and records if other than the principal office.
- If the adviser has custody of customer assets.
- If the adviser has dictionary authority over customer assets.

ADV Part 1B provides details on the indirect owners of the firm and is filed with the state securities administrator for advisers registered at the state level. Advisers who are federally registered do not file ADV Part 1B.

Form ADV Part 2A is the adviser's narrative brochure and will disclose information relating to clients. ADV Part 2A includes:

- How and when fees are charged.
- The types of securities the adviser does business in.
- How recommendations are made.
- The type of clients the adviser has.
- The qualifications of officers and directors.

Form ADV Part 2B provides information relating to individuals who:

- Provide investment advice and who have direct contact with advisory clients.
- Have discretion over client assets regardless of whether the individual has contact with clients.

New rules have been enacted to further enhance the required disclosures by investment advisers. These enhanced disclosures are designed to provide more information to both clients and regulators regarding the adviser's business. Investment advisers must now also disclose the following on form ADV:

- The total number of offices and detailed information relating to the adviser's 25 largest offices.
- Detailed information regarding the adviser's separately managed account including the type of assets held, the use of derivatives, leverage and ownership or operation of private funds.
- Detailed information regarding the number of clients serviced by the adviser and amount of assets managed for each category of client, for example: individual, institutional.
- Advisers with over $1 billion in assets under management must report the value of their AUM within one of three ranges $1 to 10 billion, $10 to 50 billion and greater than $50 billion.
- Advisers who utilize social media must disclose all social media accounts such as Facebook, Twitter, LinkedIn and all websites operated for the adviser's business.
- If the chief compliance officer of the firm is employed at any other adviser the fact must be disclosed to but not approved by regulators.

INVESTMENT ADVISER REGISTRATION DATABASE (IARD)

Investment advisers will file Form ADV and all of the required parts based on their business profile and place of registration through the Investment Adviser Registration Database or IARD. The IARD is a centralized clearinghouse for all investment adviser registrations. Advisers electronically file all required registration documents, disclosures, and any required updates or amendments through the IARD. The IARD is used by the SEC and NASAA to review all investment adviser registration data. Advisers must file annual updates to their Form ADV within 90 days of the end of the adviser's fiscal year. It is at this time that the adviser will certify the value of the assets under the adviser's control. Advisers must promptly file any changes to the adviser's business and to Form ADV through the IARD. These changes include any:

- Change in the business location
- Name changes
- Changes in custody policy or location of assets
- Material changes to the adviser's brochure
- Change of contact information or personnel
- Change in legal structure (how the firm is organized, i.e., corporation, partnership, etc.)
- Changes to disciplinary history
- Change in location of books and records

INVESTMENT ADVISER REPRESENTATIVE

An investment adviser representative is a person who is under the control of the investment adviser and includes:

- Officers and directors
- Partners
- Solicitors
- Supervisors

Clerical employees are not considered investment advisory representatives and are not required to register.

SOLICITOR

A solicitor is any person who for compensation actively seeks new business for an investment adviser. A solicitor can also include professionals who refer clients to the investment adviser for a fee. All solicitors must be registered as investment adviser representatives. Investors who are introduced to an adviser through the use of a solicitor must be provided with the solicitor's brochure. The solicitor's brochure will provide the client with the details of the solicitor's relationship with the adviser and the compensation arrangement, including the amount of the management fee paid to the solicitor. If the client is paying a higher fee by being introduced to the adviser by the solicitor, that fact must be disclosed as well. The solicitor's professional background is not required to be disclosed in the brochure.

ACCESS PERSON

An access person is anyone employed by the investment adviser who has access to nonpublic information relating to activity and holdings in client accounts or in the investment adviser's portfolio account. A person will also be deemed to be an access person if that individual makes recommendations to clients or has access to recommendations prior to the release of such recommendations. All of the firm's officers and directors are deemed to be access persons at advisory firms where the primary business is providing investment advice. All access persons must report their personal transactions to the firm's chief compliance officer or duly designated compliance officer. The firm must maintain a list of all individuals who were deemed to be access persons in the last 5 years.

INSTITUTIONAL INVESTOR

An institutional investor is a person or firm who trades securities for his or her own account or for the accounts of others. Institutional investors are generally limited to large financial companies. Because of their size and sophistication, fewer protective laws cover institutional investors. It is important to note that there is no minimum size for an institutional account. Institutional investors include:

- Broker dealers
- Investment advisers
- Investment companies
- Insurance companies
- Banks
- Trusts
- Savings and loans
- Government agencies
- Employment benefit plans with more than $1,000,000 in assets

ACCREDITED INVESTOR

An accredited investor is an individual who meets one or more of the following criteria:

- Has a net worth of $1,000,000, excluding the primary residence,

  or

- Earns $200,000 per year or more for the last 2 years and has the expectation of earning the same in the current year,

  or

- Is part of a couple earning $300,000 per year or more.

QUALIFIED PURCHASER

A qualified purchaser must meet strict minimum financial requirements. Securities sold to qualified purchasers are not required to register in the state where the qualified purchaser resides. A qualified purchaser is:

- An individual with at least $5,000,000 in investments.
- A family-owned business with at least $5,000,000 in investments.
- A trust sponsored by qualified purchasers.

PRIVATE INVESTMENT COMPANY

A private investment company is an unregistered investment company or hedge fund that raises funds through the sale of securities to qualified purchasers for any business purpose.

OFFER/OFFER TO SELL/OFFER TO BUY

An offer is any attempt to solicit the purchase or sale of a security for value. An offer is considered to have been made in the state where the offer originated, as well as in the state where it is received or directed. An offer will not be considered to have been made if it was received through a television or radio broadcast originating outside the state. Additionally, an offer will not be considered to have been made if received by a newspaper or magazine published out of the state or by a magazine published in a state that has two-thirds of its paid circulation outside of the state.

SALE/SELL

To sell a security, its ownership must be conveyed for value. A sale is considered to have been made at the time of the contract (trade). A sale of a security that has warrants or a right attached is also considered a sale of the attached security. A sale of any security that is convertible or exercisable into another security is considered to include a sale of the security for which the security is convertible or exercisable. A gift of assessable stock is also considered a sale. Assessable stock is stock that may require the holder to make additional payments as a term of ownership. A sale does not include a dividend or the pledge of a security for a collateral loan.

GUARANTEE/GUARANTEED

The term *guarantee* means that another party, other than the issuer of the security, has guaranteed the payment of principal, interest, or dividends. Only three parties may guarantee something:

- U.S. government
- Insurance company
- Parent company (it may guarantee obligations of a subsidiary)

CONTUMACY

Contumacy is the willful display of contempt for the administrator's order. An act of contumacy may result in the agent's or firm's registration being revoked or other disciplinary action.

FEDERALLY COVERED EXEMPTION

A federally covered exemption provides for a full exemption from state registration for federally covered investment advisers and federally covered securities.

A federally covered investment adviser is one who meets the requirements for assets under management and is registered with the Securities and Exchange Commission (SEC).

A federally covered security is any of the following:

- A security listed on a centralized U.S. stock exchange or on the Nasdaq.
- An investment company security issued under the Investment Company Act of 1940.
- Securities sold to qualified purchasers.

ESCHEATMENT

In the event an account owner cannot be located after a significant effort by the broker dealer or investment adviser, the account will be considered to be abandoned and the state will claim the account through the escheatment process. The state will hold the account on its records as a bookkeeping entry. The former account owner or their estate may make a claim for the assets if they become aware of the existence of the account. The amount of time that must pass prior to an asset being deemed abandoned and being turned over to the state varies between asset classes and from state to state.

12B-1 FEES

Most mutual funds charge an asset-based distribution fee to cover expenses related to the promotion and distribution of the fund's shares. The amount of the fee will be determined annually as a percentage of the NAV or as a flat fee. The 12B-1 fee will be charged to the shares quarterly, reducing the investor's overall return on the fund. Because a 12B-1 fee reduces the return, it is a type of sales load. 12B-1 fees cover such things as the printing of prospectuses and certain sales commissions to agents. To start and continue a 12B-1 fee, three votes must initially approve the fee and annually reapprove it. The three votes that are required are:

- A majority vote of the board of directors.
- A majority vote of the noninterested board of directors.
- A majority vote of the outstanding shares.

To terminate a 12B-1 fee, only two votes are required. They are:

- A majority vote of the noninterested board of directors.
- A majority vote of the outstanding shares.

LIMITS OF A 12B-1 FEE

A mutual fund that distributes its own shares and markets itself as a no-load fund may charge a 12B-1 fee that is no more than .25%. If the fund charges a 12B-1 fee that is greater than .25%, it may not be called a no-load fund. Other funds that do not call themselves a no-load fund are limited to .75% of assets, and the amount of the 12B-1 fee must be reasonably related to the anticipated level of expenses incurred for promotion and distribution. All 12B-1 fees are reviewed quarterly.

POWER OF ATTORNEY

A power of attorney once given to an individual allows that person to make decisions on behalf of the grantor with the same force and effect as if the grantor had entered into the agreement himself. Most powers of attorney in the investment world are limited powers of attorney that allow an investment professional to purchase and sell securities without speaking to a client first. A full power of attorney will allow the individual to withdraw cash and securities from an account. A standard power of attorney will terminate upon the death or incapacitation of the grantor. A durable power of attorney will remain in full force during the incapacitation of the grantor and will only terminate upon the grantor's death. Discretion may not be exercised until the power of attorney has been received and approved.

OPTION CONTRACTS

An option is a contract between two parties that determines the time and price at which a stock may be bought or sold. The two parties to the contract are the buyer and the seller. The buyer of the option pays money, known as the option's premium, to the seller. For this premium, the buyer obtains a right to buy or sell the stock, depending on what type of option is involved in the transaction. Because the seller has received the premium from the buyer, the seller now has an obligation to perform under that contract. Depending on the option involved, the seller may have an obligation to buy or sell the stock. The Black-Scholes model is a popular option pricing model used by many investors to determine the value of options.

CALL OPTIONS

A call option gives the buyer the right to buy, or to call, the stock from the option seller at a specific price for a certain period of time. The sale of a call option obligates the seller to deliver or sell that stock to the buyer at that specific price for a certain period of time.

PUT OPTIONS

A put option gives the buyer the right to sell or to "put" the stock to the seller at a specific price for a certain period of time. The sale of a put option obligates the seller to buy the stock from the buyer at that specific price for a certain period of time.

FUTURES AND FORWARDS

Futures, like options, are a two-party contract. Many futures contracts are an agreement for the delivery of a specific amount of a commodity at a specific place and time. Futures were first traded for commodities such as wheat and gold, and over the years they have expanded to include financial futures, such as on Treasury securities, and, most recently, single stock futures. The specific terms and conditions of the contracts are standardized and set by the exchanges on which they trade. The contract amount, delivery date, and type of settlement vary between the different futures contracts. Most investors will use futures as a hedge or to speculate on the value of the underlying commodity or instrument. Forwards are privately negotiated contracts for the purchase and sale of a commodity or financial instrument. Forwards are often used in the currency markets by corporations and banks doing business internationally. If a corporation knows that it needs to make a payment for a purchase in foreign currency three months from now, the corporation can arrange to purchase the currency from a bank the day before the payment is due. The big drawback with forwards is that there is no secondary market for the contracts.

SECONDARY MARKET ORDERS

Investors who do not purchase their stocks and bonds directly from the issuer must purchase them from another investor. Investor-to-investor transactions are known as secondary market transactions. In a secondary market transaction, the selling security owner receives the proceeds from the sale. Secondary market transactions may take place on a centralized exchange or in the OTC market known as Nasdaq. Although both facilitate the trading of securities, they operate in a very different manner. We will begin by looking at the types of orders that an investor may enter and the reasons for entering the various types of orders. Investors can enter various types of orders to buy or sell securities. Some orders guarantee that the investor's order will be executed immediately. Other types of orders may state a specific price or condition under which the investor wants an order to be executed. All orders are considered day orders unless otherwise specified. All day orders will be canceled at the end of the trading day if they are not executed. An investor may also specify that an order remain active until canceled. This type of order is known as *good 'til cancel* or *GTC*.

MARKET ORDERS

A market order will guarantee that the investor's order is executed as soon as the order is presented to the market. A market order to either buy or sell guarantees the execution but not the price at which the order will be executed. When a market order is presented for execution, the market for the security may be very different from the market that was displayed when the order was entered. As a result, the investor does not know the exact price at which the order will be executed.

BUY LIMIT ORDERS

A buy limit order sets the maximum price that the investor will pay for the security. The order may never be executed at a price higher than the investor's limit price. Although a buy limit order guarantees that the investor will not pay over a certain price, it does not guarantee that the order will be executed. If the stock continues to trade higher away from the investor's limit price, the investor will not purchase the stock and may miss a chance to realize a profit.

SELL LIMIT ORDERS

A sell limit order sets the minimum price that the investor will accept for the security. The order may never be executed at a price lower than the investor's limit price. Although a sell limit order guarantees that the investor will not receive less than a certain price, it does not guarantee that the order will be executed. If the stock continues to trade lower away from the investor's limit price, the investor will not sell the stock and may miss a chance to realize a profit or may realize a loss as a result.

 FOCUSPOINT

Remember that even if investors see the stock trading at their limit price it does not mean that their order was executed, because there may have been stock ahead of them at that limit price.

STOP ORDERS/STOP LOSS ORDERS

A stop order or stop loss order can be used by investors to limit or guard against a loss or to protect a profit. A stop order will be placed away from the market in case the stock starts to move against the investor. A stop order is not a "live" order; it has to be elected. A stop order is elected and becomes a live order when the stock trades at or through the stop price. The stop price is also known as the trigger price. Once the stock has traded at or through the stop price, the order becomes a market order to either buy or sell the stock, depending on the type of order that was placed.

BUY STOP ORDERS

A buy stop order is placed above the market and is used to protect against a loss or to protect a profit on a short sale of stock. A buy stop order could also be used by a technical analyst to get long the stock after the stock breaks through resistance.

EXAMPLE An investor has sold 100 shares of ABC short at $40 per share. ABC has declined to $30 per share. The investor is concerned that if ABC goes past $32 it may return to $40. To protect his profit, the investor enters an order to buy 100 ABC at 32 stop. If ABC trades at or through $32, the order will become a market order to buy 100 shares, and the investor will cover the short at the next available price.

SELL STOP ORDERS

A sell stop order is placed below the market and is used to protect against a loss or to protect a profit on the purchase of a stock. A sell stop order could also be used by a technical analyst to get short the stock after the stock breaks through support.

Pretest

DEFINITION OF TERMS

1. Which of the following is NOT considered to be a person under the Uniform Securities Act (USA)?

   a. A joint stock company

   b. A trust

   c. A 17-year-old honor student

   d. A government agency

2. Which of the following is NOT considered a sale of a security?

   a. A gift of assessable stock

   b. A contract to convey ownership for value

   c. A pledge of securities as collateral for a margin loan

   d. A bonus of securities

3. The minimum financial requirement for an individual to be considered a qualified purchaser is:

   a. $1,000,000.

   b. $2,500,000.

   c. $5,000,000 individually or $10,000,000 jointly with a spouse.

   d. $5,000,000 individually or jointly with a spouse.

4. As it pertains to the USA, which of the following are considered institutional investors?

    I. A bank

    II. An insurance company

    III. An employee benefit plan with $800,000 in assets

    IV. A trust

    a. I and II

    b. I and IV

    c. I, II, and IV

    d. I, II, III, and IV

5. All of the following are considered securities, EXCEPT:

    a. whiskey warehouse receipts.

    b. a trust indenture.

    c. a commodity future option.

    d. interest in a marketing scheme.

6. A parent gives 1,500 shares of assessable stock to his child. Under the USA this is:

    a. subject to approval of the state securities administrator.

    b. considered an offer of securities.

    c. subject to a transfer tax.

    d. considered a sale of securities.

7. Which of the following is considered an investment adviser?

    a. The publisher of a market report based on market internals

    b. A publisher of a financial newspaper

    c. An accountant

    d. A person paid a commission for executing a securities transaction

8. Which of the following is considered a qualified purchaser?

    a. An individual with $1,000,000 in investments held jointly with a spouse and with an annual income of $375,000

    b. A publicly held company with at least $5,000,000 in net assets

    c. A pension plan with $2,000,000 in assets

    d. A family-owned business with at least $5,000,000 in assets

9. XYZ common stock trades on a U.S. stock exchange. XYZ common stock is an example of a(n):

   a. blue-chip security.

   b. federally covered security.

   c. exempt security.

   d. security of an exempt issuer.

10. A security is represented by an interest in which of the following?

    I. Farmland or animals

    II. A cooperative

    III. A marketing scheme

    IV. A multilevel distributorship

    a. None of these

    b. I and II

    c. I, II, and III

    d. I, II, III, and IV

11. Under the USA, which of the following is an investment adviser?

    I. XYZ Advisers, Inc.

    II. Mr. Jones, the owner of XYZ Advisers, Inc.

    III. The publisher of a market letter based on economic trends

    IV. A partner for XYZ who solicits new clients for XYZ advisers

    a. I only

    b. I and III

    c. I, II, and IV

    d. I, II, III, and IV

12. Which of the following is NOT one of the Howey test criteria for determining whether an investment is a security?

    a. Third-party management

    b. Investment of money

    c. A common enterprise

    d. The promise of a profit

13. A broker is a(n):

    a. registered representative.

    b. duly licensed agent.

    c. issuer of collateralized securities.

    d. person who executes transactions for the accounts of others.

14. An offer of securities is considered to have been made in which of the following circumstances?

    a. A sales presentation for a fixed annuity

    b. Delivering a market report

    c. Mailing a form letter

    d. Delivering a prospectus

15. The Uniform Securities Act defines an issuer as which of the following?

    a. A broker dealer

    b. A bank

    c. A corporation proposing the sale of common shares

    d. A savings and loan

16. Which of the following individuals is considered to be an agent?

    a. An individual who represents a bank as the issuer of securities

    b. An individual who represents a corporate issuer in the sale of large-denomination commercial paper

    c. An individual represents a Canadian province

    d. An individual represents an out-of-state broker dealer selling securities to residents

17. Which of the following is NOT a broker dealer?

    I. A firm with no office in the state that transacts business only with existing customers who do not reside within the state.

    II. A firm with no office in the state that transacts business only with broker dealers in state.

    III. A firm with an office in state that only transacts business with other broker dealers.

    IV. A firm with no office in the state that only transacts business with wealthy clients in state.

    a. I and II

    b. II and IV

    c. I, II, and IV

    d. I, II, III, and IV

18. Which of the following is NOT a federally covered security?

    a. A security issued by an investment company

    b. A security issued by a unit investment trust (UIT)

    c. Exchange-listed common shares

    d. A security listed on the Nasdaq OTC BB

19. A guarantee may be issued by which of the following?

    I. An insurance company

    II. The U.S. government

    III. A parent company

    IV. An investment adviser

    a. I and IV

    b. I and III

    c. I, II, and III

    d. I, II, III, and IV

20. An offer to sell has been made:

    a. when stock has been pledged as collateral for a loan at the bank.

    b. when a gift of securities to a charity results in tax credit for the donor.

    c. when a representative calls a client and recommends a security.

    d. when an account is transferred to the surviving party under joint tenants with rights of survivorship.

Securities Industry Rules and Regulations

INTRODUCTION

Federal and state securities laws, as well as industry regulations, have been enacted to ensure that all industry participants adhere to a high standard of just and equitable trade practices. In this chapter, we will review the rules and regulations that create the framework for securities industry regulation.

THE SECURITIES ACT OF 1933

The Securities Act of 1933 was the first major piece of securities industry regulation, which was brought about largely as a result of the stock market crash of 1929. Other laws were also enacted to help prevent another meltdown of the nation's financial system, such as the Securities Exchange Act of 1934, which will be discussed next.

The Securities Act of 1933 regulates the primary market. The primary market consists exclusively of transactions between issuers of securities and investors. In a primary market transaction, the issuer of the securities receives the proceeds from the sale of the securities. The Securities Act of 1933 requires nonexempt issuers, typically corporate issuers, to file a registration statement with the Securities and Exchange Commission (SEC). The SEC will review the registration statement for a minimum of 20 days. During this time, known as the cooling-off period, no sales of securities may take place. If the SEC requires additional information regarding the offering, the SEC may issue a deficiency letter or a stop order that will extend the cooling-off period beyond the original 20 days. The cooling-off period will continue until the SEC has received all of the information it has requested. The registration statement, formally known as an S1, is the issuer's full-disclosure document for the registration of the securities with the SEC.

THE PROSPECTUS

While the SEC is reviewing the securities' registration statement, registered representatives are very limited as to what they may do with regard to the new issue. During the cooling-off period, the only thing registered representatives may do is obtain indications on interest from clients by providing them with a preliminary prospectus, also known as a red herring. The term *red herring* originated from the fact that all preliminary prospectuses must have a statement printed in red ink on the front cover stating: "These securities have not yet become registered with the SEC and therefore may not be sold." The preliminary prospectus must be delivered in hard copy to all interested parties. An indication of interest is an investor's or broker dealer's statement that it may be interested in purchasing the securities being offered. The preliminary prospectus contains most of the same information that will be contained in the final prospectus, except for the offering price and the proceeds to the issuer. All information contained in a preliminary prospectus is subject to change or revision.

THE FINAL PROSPECTUS

All purchasers of new issues must be given a final prospectus before any sales may be allowed. The final prospectus serves as the issuer's full-disclosure document for the purchaser of the securities. If the issuer has filed a prospectus with the SEC and the prospectus can be viewed on the SEC's website, a prospectus will be deemed to have been provided to the investor through the access equals delivery rule. Once the issuer's registration statement becomes effective, the final prospectus must include:

- Type and description of the securities.
- Price of the security.
- Use of the proceeds.
- Underwriter's discount.
- Date of offering.
- Type and description of underwriting.
- Business history of issuer.
- Biographical data for company officers and directors.

- Information regarding large stockholders.
- Company financial data.
- Risks to purchaser.
- Legal matters concerning the company.
- SEC disclaimer.

SEC DISCLAIMER

The SEC reviews the issuer's registration statement and the prospectus but does not guarantee the accuracy or adequacy of the information. The SEC disclaimer must appear on the cover of all prospectuses. It states: "These securities have not been approved or disapproved by the SEC nor have any representations been made about the accuracy or the adequacy of the information."

MISREPRESENTATIONS

Financial relief for misrepresentations made under the Securities Act of 1933 is available for purchasers of any security that is sold under a prospectus that is found to contain false or misleading statements. Purchasers of the security may be entitled to seek financial relief from any or all of the following:

- The issuer.
- The underwriters.
- Officers and directors.
- All parties who signed the registration statement.
- Accountants and attorneys who helped prepare the registration statement.

Issuers may use forward-looking statements to provide details about its future prospects to purchasers. These forward-looking statements must be identified by key words such as expect, predict, estimate, anticipate, or potential. These words are used so that the reader clearly understands that the statements are management's projections.

THE SECURITIES EXCHANGE ACT OF 1934

The Securities Exchange Act of 1934 was the second major piece of legislation that resulted from the market crash of 1929. The Securities Exchange Act regulates the secondary market that consists of investor-to-investor transactions. All transactions between two investors that are executed on any of the exchanges or in the over-the-counter (OTC) market are secondary market transactions. In a secondary market transaction, the selling security holder receives the money, not the issuing corporation. The Securities Exchange Act of 1934 also regulates all individuals and firms that conduct business in the securities industry. The Securities Exchange Act of 1934:

- Created the SEC.
- Requires registration of broker dealers and agents.
- Regulates the exchanges and FINRA.
- Requires net capital for broker dealers.
- Regulates short sales.
- Regulates insider transactions.
- Requires public companies to solicit proxies.
- Requires segregation of customer and firm assets.
- Authorizes the Federal Reserve Board to regulate the extension of credit for securities purchases under Regulation T.
- Regulates the handling of client accounts.

THE SECURITIES AND EXCHANGE COMMISSION (SEC)

One of the biggest components of the Securities Exchange Act of 1934 was the creation of the SEC. The SEC is the ultimate securities industry authority and is a direct government body. Five commissioners are appointed to 5-year terms by the president, and each must be approved by the Senate. No more than three commissioners may be from any one political party. The SEC is not a self-regulatory organization (SRO) or a designated examining authority (DEA). An SRO is an organization that regulates its own members, such as the NYSE or FINRA. A DEA inspects a broker dealer's books and records and can also be the NYSE or FINRA. All broker dealers, exchanges, agents, and securities must register with the SEC. All exchanges are required to file a registration statement with the SEC that includes its articles of incorporation, bylaws, and constitution. All new rules and regulations adopted by the exchanges must be disclosed to the SEC as soon as they are enacted. Issuers of securities with more than 500 shareholders and with assets exceeding $5,000,000 must register with the SEC, file quarterly and annual reports, and solicit proxies from stockholders. A broker dealer that conducts business with the public must register with the SEC and maintain a certain level of financial solvency known as net capital. All broker dealers are required to forward a financial statement to all customers of the firm. Additionally, all employees of the broker dealer who are involved in securities sales, have access to cash and securities, or who supervise employees must be fingerprinted.

EXTENSION OF CREDIT

The Securities Act of 1934 gave the authority to the Federal Reserve Board (FRB) to regulate the extension of credit by broker dealers for the purchase of securities by their customers. The following is a list of the regulations of the different lenders and the regulation that gave the Federal Reserve Board the authority to govern their activities:

- Regulation T: Broker dealers
- Regulation U: Banks
- Regulation G: All other financial institutions

PUBLIC UTILITIES HOLDING COMPANY ACT OF 1935

The Public Utilities Holding Company Act of 1935 regulates all companies that are in business to provide retail distribution of gas and electric power. Because the companies are regulated by this act, their securities are exempt from state registration requirements.

FINANCIAL INDUSTRY REGULATORY AUTHORITY (FINRA)

The Maloney Act of 1938 was an amendment to the Securities Exchange Act of 1934 that allowed the creation of the National Association of Securities Dealers (NASD). The NASD, now part of FINRA, is the SRO for the OTC market, and its purpose is to regulate the broker dealers that conduct business in the OTC market. FINRA has four major bylaws. They are:

1. The Rules of Fair Practice.
2. The Uniform Practice Code.
3. The Code of Procedure.
4. The Code of Arbitration.

THE TRUST INDENTURE ACT OF 1939

The Trust Indenture Act of 1939 requires that corporate bond issues in excess of $5,000,000 dollars that are to be repaid during a term in excess of 1 year issue a trust indenture for the issue. The trust indenture is a contract between the issuer and the trustee. The trustee acts on behalf of all of the bondholders and ensures that the issuer is in compliance with all of the promises and covenants made to the bondholders. The trustee is appointed by the corporation and is usually a bank or a trust company. The Trust Indenture Act of 1939 only applies to corporate issuers. Both federal and municipal issuers are exempt.

INVESTMENT ADVISERS ACT OF 1940

The Investment Advisers Act of 1940 regulates industry professionals who charge a fee for the advice they offer to clients. The Investment Advisers Act sets forth registration requirements for advisers as well as disclosure requirements relating to the adviser's:

- Recommendation methods.
- Types of securities recommended.
- Professional background and qualifications.
- Fees to be charged.
- Method for computing and charging fees.
- Types of clients.

INVESTMENT COMPANY ACT OF 1940

The Investment Company Act of 1940 regulates companies that are in business to invest or reinvest money for the benefit of their investors. The Investment Company Act sets forth registration requirements for the three types of investment companies. They are:

1. Management investment companies.
2. Unit investment trusts (UITs).
3. Face-amount companies (FACs).

RETAIL COMMUNICATIONS/COMMUNICATIONS WITH THE PUBLIC

Member firms will seek to increase their business and exposure through the use of both retail and institutional communications. Strict regulations are in place in order to ensure that all communications with the public adhere to industry guidelines. Some communications with the public are available to a general audience and include:

- Television/radio.
- Publicly accessible websites.
- Motion pictures.
- Newspapers/magazines.
- Telephone directory listings.
- Signs/billboards.
- Computer/Internet postings.
- Videotape displays.
- Other public media.
- Recorded telemarketing messages.

Other types of communications are offered to a targeted audience. These communications include:

- Market reports.
- Password-protected websites.
- Telemarketing scripts.
- Form letters or e-mails (sent to more than 25 people).
- Circulars.
- Research reports.
- Printed materials for seminars.
- Option worksheets.
- Performance reports.
- Prepared scripts for TV or radio.
- Reprints of ads or sales literature.

FINRA RULE 2210 COMMUNICATIONS WITH THE PUBLIC

FINRA Rule 2210 replaces the advertising and sales literature rules previously used to regulate member communications with the public. FINRA Rule 2210 streamlines member communication rules and reduces the number of communication categories from six to three. The three categories of member communication are:

1. Retail Communication.
2. Institutional Communication.
3. Correspondence.

RETAIL COMMUNICATION

Retail communication is defined as any written communication distributed or made available to 25 or more retail investors in a 30-day period. The communication may be distributed in hard copy or in electronic formats. The definition of a *retail investor* is any investor that does not meet the definition of an institutional investor. Retail communications now contain all components of advertising and sales literature. All retail communications must be approved by a registered principal prior to first use. The publication of a post in a chat room or other online forum will not require the prior approval of a principal so long as such post does not promote the business of the member firm and does not provide investment advice. Additionally, generic advertising will also be exempt from the prior approval requirements. All retail communication must be maintained by the member for 3 years. If the member firm is a new member firm that has been in existence for less than 12 months based on the firm's approval date in the central registration depository (CRD), the member must file all retail communications with FINRA 10 days prior to its first use unless the communication has been previously filed and contains no material changes or has been filed by another member, such as an investment company or ETF sponsor. Member firms that have been established for more than 12 months may file retail communications with FINRA 10 days after the communication is first used. Retail communications regarding investment companies, ETF sponsors, and variable annuities must be filed 10 days prior to first use if the communication contains nonstandardized performance rankings. Should FINRA determine that a member firm is making false or misleading statements in its retail communications with the public, FINRA may require the member to file all of its retail communications with the public with the association 10 days prior to its first use.

TAKENOTE!

Research reports concerning only securities listed on a national securities exchange are excluded from Rule 2210's filing requirements. Additionally, a free writing prospectus is exempt from filing with the SEC and not subject to Rule 2210's filing or content standards.

INSTITUTIONAL COMMUNICATIONS

Intuitional communication is defined as any written communication distributed or made available exclusively to institutional investors. The communication may be distributed in hard copy or in electronic formats. Institutional communications do not have to be approved by a principal prior to first use so long as the member has established policies and procedures regarding the use of institutional communications and has trained its employees on the proper use of institutional communication. Institutional communication is also exempt from FINRA's filing requirement, but like retail communications, it must be maintained by a member for 3 years. If the member believes that the institutional communication or any part thereof may be seen by even a single retail investor, the communication must be handled as retail communication and is subject to the approval and filing requirements of a retail communication. An institutional investor is a person or firm that trades securities for his or her own account or for the accounts of others. Institutional investors are generally limited to large financial companies. Because of their size and sophistication, fewer protective laws cover institutional investors. It is important to note that there is no minimum size for an institutional account. Institutional investors include:

- Broker dealers.
- Investment advisers.
- Investment companies.
- Insurance companies.
- Banks.
- Trusts.
- Savings and loans.
- Government agencies.

- Employment benefit plans with more than 100 participants.
- Any non-natural person with more than $50,000,000 in assets.

CORRESPONDENCE

Correspondence consists of electronic and written communications between the member and up to 25 retail investors in a 30-day period. With the increase in acceptance of e-mail as business communication, it would be impractical for a member to review all correspondence between the member and a customer. The member instead may set up procedures to review a sample of all correspondence, both electronic and hard copy. If the member reviews only a sample of the correspondence, the member must train its associated people on the firm's procedures relating to correspondence and must document the training and ensure that the procedures are followed. Even though the member is not required to review all correspondence, the member must still retain all correspondence. The member should, where practical, review all incoming hard copy correspondence. Letters received by the firm could contain cash, checks, securities, or complaints.

BLIND RECRUITING ADS

A blind recruiting ad is an ad placed by the member firm for the specific purpose of finding job applicants. Blind recruiting ads are the only form of advertising that does not require the member's name to appear in the ad. The ads may not distort the opportunities or salaries of the advertised position. All other ads are required to disclose the name of the member firm, as well as the relationship of the member to any other entities that appear in the ad.

GENERIC ADVERTISING

Generic advertising is generally designed to promote firm awareness and to advertise the products and services generally offered through the firm. Generic ads will generally include:

- Securities products offered (i.e., stocks, bonds, mutual funds).
- Contact name, number, and address.
- Types of accounts offered (i.e., individual, IRA, 401K).

TOMBSTONE ADS

A tombstone ad is an announcement of a new security offering coming to market. Tombstone ads may be run while the securities are still in registration with the SEC and may only include:

- A description of the securities.
- A description of the business.
- A description of the transaction.
- Required disclaimers.
- Time and place of any stockholder meetings regarding the sale of the securities.

Tombstone ads must include the following:

- A statement that the securities registration has not yet become effective
- A statement that responding to the ad does not obligate the prospect
- A statement as to where a prospectus may be obtained
- A statement that the ad does not constitute an offer to sell the securities and that an offer may only be made by the prospectus

All retail communications is required to be approved by a principal of the firm prior to its first use. A general security principal (Series 24) may approve most retail communications. Any retail communications relating to options must be approved by a registered option principal or the compliance registered options principal. Research reports must be approved by a supervisory analyst.

TESTIMONIALS

From time to time, broker dealers will use testimonials made by people of national or local recognition in an effort to generate new business for the firm. If the individual giving the testimonial is quoting past performance, relating to the firm's recommendations, it must be accompanied by a disclaimer that past performance is not indicative of future performance. It must be disclosed if the individual giving the testimony was compensated in any way. Should the individual's testimony imply that the person making the testimony is an expert, a statement regarding the person's qualifications as an expert must also be contained in the ad or sales literature. Research prepared by outside parties must disclose the name of the preparer.

 TAKENOTE!

Investment advisers are prohibited from using testimonials or statements regarding a client's experience with the adviser as part of any advertisement or sales literature.

FREE SERVICES

If a member firm advertises free services to customers or to people who respond to an ad, the services must actually be free to everyone and with no strings attached.

FREE LUNCH SEMINARS

The practice of providing so-called free lunch seminars presents several unique compliance concerns. Firms that sponsor seminars that are marketed to investors as educational workshops often provide attendees with a "free lunch" as a way to help market the seminar and state that "no investment products will be offered or sold" at the seminar. However, firms who sponsor these seminars clearly intend to establish a business relationship with the attendees. The firms may try to get the attendees to open an account either at the seminar or during a follow-up solicitation to offer investment products. Firms who sponsor free lunch seminars must ensure that strict compliance procedures are followed by the agents who lead the seminars. Without strict compliance to conduct and disclosures rules, The North American Securities Administrators Association/ NASAA considers free lunch seminars a prohibited practice. Of particular concern are seminars that are marketed to seniors.

MISLEADING COMMUNICATIONS

The following are some examples of misleading statements, which are not allowed to appear in communications with the public:

- Excessive hedge clauses
- Implying an endorsement by FINRA, the NYSE, or the SEC
- Printing the FINRA logo in type that is larger than the type of the member's name

- Implying that the member has larger research facilities than it actually has
- Implying that an individual has higher qualifications than he or she actually has

SECURITIES INVESTOR PROTECTION CORPORATION ACT OF 1970 (SIPC)

The Securities Investor Protection Corporation (SIPC) is a government-sponsored corporation that provides protection to customers in the event of a broker dealer's failure. All broker dealers that are registered with the SEC are required to be SIPC members. All broker dealers are required to pay annual dues to SIPC's insurance fund to cover losses due to broker dealer failure. If a broker dealer fails to pay its SIPC assessment, it may not transact business until it is paid.

NET CAPITAL REQUIREMENT

All broker dealers are required to maintain a certain level of net capital in order to ensure that they are financially solvent. A broker dealer's capital requirement is contingent upon the type of business that the broker dealer conducts. The larger and more complex the firm's business, the greater the firm's net capital requirement. If a firm falls below its net capital requirement, it is deemed to be insolvent, and SIPC will petition in court to have a trustee appointed to liquidate the firm and protect the customers. The trustee must be a disinterested party. Once the trustee is appointed, the firm may not conduct business or try to conceal any assets.

CUSTOMER COVERAGE

SIPC protects customers of a brokerage firm in much the same way that the FDIC protects customers of banks. SIPC covers customer losses that result from broker dealer failure, not for market losses. SIPC covers customers for up to $500,000 per separate customer. Of the $500,000, up to $250,000 may be in cash. Most broker dealers carry additional private insurance to cover larger accounts, but SIPC is the industry-funded insurance and is required by all broker dealers. The following are examples of separate customers:

Customer	Securities Market Value	Cash	SIPC Coverage
Mr. Jones	$320,000	$75,000	All
Mr. & Mrs. Jones	$290,000	$90,000	All
Mrs. Jones	$397,000	$82,000	All

All of the accounts shown would be considered separate customers, and SIPC would cover the entire value of all of the accounts. If an account has in excess of $250,000 in cash, the individual would not be covered for any amount exceeding $250,000 in cash and would become a general creditor for the rest. SIPC does not consider a margin account and cash account as separate customers and the customer would be covered for the maximum of $500,000. SIPC does not offer coverage for commodities contracts, and all member firms must display the SIPC sign in the lobby of the firm.

FIDELITY BOND

All SIPC members are required to obtain a fidelity bond to protect customers in the event of employee dishonesty. Some things that a fidelity bond will insure against are check forgery and fraudulent trading. The minimum amount of the fidelity bond is $25,000; however, large firms are often required to carry a higher amount.

THE SECURITIES ACTS AMENDMENTS OF 1975

The Securities Acts Amendments of 1975 gave the authority to the Municipal Securities Rulemaking Board (MSRB) to regulate the issuance and trading of municipal bonds. The MSRB has no enforcement division. Its rules are enforced by other regulators.

THE INSIDER TRADING AND SECURITIES FRAUD ENFORCEMENT ACT OF 1988

The Insider Trading and Securities Fraud Enforcement Act of 1988 established guidelines and controls for the use and dissemination of nonpublic material information. Nonpublic information is information that is not known by people outside of the company. Material information is information regarding a situation or development that will materially affect the company in the present or future. It is not intended solely for insiders to have this type of information, but it is also required for them to do their jobs effectively. It is, however, unlawful for an insider to use this information to profit from a forthcoming move in the stock price. An insider is defined as any officer, director, 10% stockholder, or anyone who is in possession of nonpublic material information, as well as the spouse of any such person. Additionally, it is unlawful for the insider to divulge any of this information to any outside party. Trading on inside information has always been a violation of the Securities

Exchange Act of 1934, but the Insider Trading Act prescribed penalties for violators, which include:

- A fine of 300% of the amount of the gain or 300% of the amount of the loss avoided for the person who acts on the information.
- A civil or criminal fine for the person who divulges the information.
- Insider traders may be sued by the affected parties.
- Criminal prosecutions that may result in a fine of up to $1,000,000 and 20 years in prison.

Information becomes public information once it has been disseminated over public media. The SEC will pay a reward of up to 10% to informants who turn in individuals who trade on inside information. In addition to the insiders already listed, the following are also considered insiders:

- Accountants
- Attorneys
- Investment bankers

FIREWALL

Broker dealers who act as underwriters and investment bankers for corporate clients must have access to information regarding the company in order to advise the company properly. The broker dealer must ensure that no inside information is passed between its investment banking department and its retail trading departments. The broker dealer is required to physically separate these divisions by a firewall. The broker dealer must maintain written supervisory procedures to adequately guard against the wrongful use or dissemination of inside information.

THE TELEPHONE CONSUMER PROTECTION ACT OF 1991

The Telephone Consumer Protection Act of 1991 regulates how telemarketing calls are made by businesses. Telemarketing calls that are designed to have consumers invest in or purchase goods, services, or property must adhere to the strict guidelines of the act. All firms must:

- Call only between the hours of 8 a.m. and 9 p.m.
- Maintain a Do-Not-Call list. Individuals placed on the Do-Not-Call list may not be contacted by anyone at the firm for 5 years.

- Give the prospect the firm's name, address, and phone number when soliciting.
- Follow adequate policies and procedures to maintain a Do-Not-Call list.
- Train representatives on calling policies and use of the Do-Not-Call list.
- Ensure that any fax solicitations have the firm's name, address, and phone number.

EXEMPTION FROM THE TELEPHONE CONSUMER PROTECTION ACT OF 1991

The following are exempt from the Telephone Consumer Protection Act of 1991:

- Calls to existing customers
- Calls to a delinquent debtor
- Calls from a religious or nonprofit organization

Calls may be made prior to 8 a.m. or after 9 p.m. to places of business. The time regulation only relates to contacting noncustomers at home.

NATIONAL SECURITIES MARKET IMPROVEMENT ACT OF 1996

The National Securities Market Improvement Act of 1996, also known as the Coordination Act, eliminated the duplication of effort among state and federal regulators. Some of the key points of the act include:

- Federal law overrides state law.
- Registration requirements for investment advisers.
- Capital requirements.
- Increased industry competition by eliminating collusive behavior.

The act ensured that no action by any state or political subdivision could impose laws or requirements upon any broker dealer that differed from or are in addition to those of the Securities Exchange Act of 1934 relating to:

- Capital requirements.
- Recordkeeping.
- Financial reporting.

- Margin.
- Custody.

THE UNIFORM SECURITIES ACT

In the early half of the twentieth century, state securities regulators developed their state's rules and regulations for transacting securities business within their state. The result was regulations that varied widely from state to state. The Uniform Securities Act (USA) laid out model legislation for all states in an effort to make each state's rules and regulations more uniform and easier to address. The USA, also known as The Act, sets minimum qualification standards for each state securities administrator. The state securities administrator is the top securities regulator within the state. The state securities administrator may be the attorney general of that state or an individual appointed specifically to that post. The USA also:

- Prohibits the state securities administrator from using the post for personal benefit or from disclosing information.
- Gives the state securities administrator authority to enforce the rules of the USA within that state.
- Gives the administrator the ability to set certain registration requirements for broker dealers, agents, and investment advisers.
- Permits state administrators to set fee and testing requirements within the state.
- Administrators may suspend or revoke the state registration of a broker dealer, agent, investment adviser, a security, or a security's exemption from registration.
- The USA also sets civil and criminal penalties for violators.

The state-based laws set forth by the USA are also known as blue-sky laws.

THE PATRIOT ACT

The Patriot Act, as incorporated in The Bank Secrecy Act, requires broker dealers to have written policies and procedures designed to detect suspicious activity. The firm must designate a principal to ensure compliance with the firm's policies and to train firm personnel. The firm is required to file a Suspicious Activity Report for any transaction of more than $5,000 that appears questionable. The firm must file the report within 30 days of identifying any suspicious activity. Anti-money-laundering rules require that all firms implement a customer identification program to ensure that the firm knows the true identity of their customers. All customers who open an account with the firm, as well as individuals with trading authority, are subject to this rule. The firm must ensure that its customers do not appear on any list of known or suspected terrorists. A firm's anti-money-laundering program must be approved by senior management. All records relating to the SAR filing including a copy of the SAR report must be maintained by the firm for 5 years. The money laundering process begins with the placement of the funds. This is when the money is deposited in an account with the broker dealer. The second step of the laundering process is known as layering. The layering process will consist of multiple deposits in amounts less than $10,000. The funds will often be drawn from different financial institutions; this is also known as structuring. The launderers will then purchase and sell securities in the account. The integration of the proceeds back into the banking system completes the process. At this point, the launderers may use the money to purchase goods and services if they appear to have come from legitimate sources. Firms must also identify the customers who open the account and must make sure that they are not conducting business with anyone on the OFAC list. This list is maintained by the Treasury Department Office of Foreign Assets Control. It consists of known and suspected terrorists, criminals, and members of pariah nations. Individuals and entities who appear on this list are known as Specially Designated Nationals and Blocked Persons. Conducting business with anyone on this list is strictly prohibited. Registered representatives who aid the laundering of money are subject to prosecution and face up to 20 years in prison and a $500,000 fine per transaction. The representative does not even have to be involved in the scheme or know about it to be prosecuted. FinCEN is a bureau of the U.S. Department of the Treasury. FinCEN's mission is to safeguard the financial system and guard against money laundering and promote national security. FinCEN collects, receives, and maintains financial transactions data, and analyzes and disseminates that data for law enforcement purposes and for building global cooperation with counterpart organizations in other countries and with international bodies. FinCEN will e-mail a list of individuals and entities to a designated principal every few weeks. The principal is required to check the list against the firm's customer list. If a match is found, the firm must notify FinCEN within 14 calendar days.

REGULATION S-P

Regulation S-P requires that the firm maintain adequate procedures to protect the financial information of its customers. Firms must guard against unauthorized access to customer financial information and must employ policies to ensure its safety. Special concerns arise over the ability of a person to "hack" into a firm's customer database by gaining unauthorized access. Firms must develop and maintain specific safeguards for their computer systems and Wi-Fi access.

Regulation S-P was derived from the privacy rules of the Gramm-Leach-Bliley Act. A firm must deliver:

- An initial privacy notice to customers when the account is opened.
- An annual privacy notice to all customers.

The annual privacy notice may be delivered electronically via the firm's website, as long as the customer has agreed to receive it electronically in writing and it is clearly displayed. The privacy notice must describe the type of information that is collected and the type of nonaffiliated parties with whom it may be shared. Regulation S-P also states that a firm may not disclose non-public personal information to nonaffiliated companies for clients who have opted out of the list. The method by which a client may opt out may not be unreasonable. It is considered unreasonable to require a customer to write a letter to opt out. Reasonable methods are e-mails or a toll-free number. The rule also differentiates between who is a customer and who is a consumer. A customer is anyone who has an ongoing relationship with the firm (i.e., has an account). A consumer is someone who is providing information to the firm and is considering becoming a customer or who has purchased a product from the firms and has no other contact with the firm. The firm must give the privacy notice to consumers prior to sharing any nonpublic information with a nonaffiliated company.

 TAKENOTE!

A client of a brokerage firm may not opt out of the sharing of information with an affiliated company.

Regulation S-AM prohibits broker dealers from soliciting business based upon information received from affiliated third parties unless the potential marketing had been clearly disclosed to the potential customer, and the potential customer was provided an opportunity to opt out and did not opt out.

IDENTITY THEFT

The fraudulent practice of identity theft may be used by criminals in an attempt to obtain access to the assets or credit of another person. The Federal Trade Commission (FTC) requires banks and broker dealers to establish and maintain written identity theft prevention programs. A broker dealer's written supervisory procedures manual must reference its identity theft program. The program must be designed to detect red flags relating to the known suspicious activity employed during an attempt at identity theft. The identity theft prevention program should be designed to allow the firm to respond quickly to any attempted identity theft to mitigate any potential damage.

FINRA RULES ON FINANCIAL EXPLOITATION OF SENIORS

While many people are living active and productive lives well into their eighties and beyond, FINRA has enacted rules designed to protect the financial interests of seniors who are 65 or older. FINRA is particularly concerned about clients being taken advantage of by unscrupulous or otherwise self-serving people. Registered representatives should have a clear understanding of the financial needs, resources, and behavior of their clients. This is specifically important when dealing with older clients who may require the assets to meet their current financial needs, and who, can fall victim to bad actors. Registered representatives should be particularly concerned with any requests to withdraw money from an account that is outside the normal actions of the client.

EXAMPLE   Sally is a retired school administrator who is 83 years old and is living on her assets. Sally and her late husband had planned well for their retirement. She has the proceeds from her husband's life insurance policy and a significant savings and retirement account, as well as her social security. Sally has been a client of your firm for 10 years and generally moves $1,800 to $2,000 per month from her brokerage account to her checking account. Twice per year she travels and moves $5,000 to her checking account to pay her travel expenses.

One day Sally calls up and says she needs $35,000 wired to an out-of-state bank account. When the agent inquires what this is for, Sally says her friend has told her of an investment opportunity in real estate that she would like to take advantage of. When the agent inquiries about the opportunity, the details Sally provides do not sound right to the agent.

ANALYSIS   This is a serious red flag, and in this situation the agent has a significant conflict. On the one hand, the agent is required to do as the client requests. On the other, the agent feels a duty to protect the client and senses that their client may be the victim of senior exploitation. Even discussing the matter with a principal of the firm is not enough to determine if the client is being taken advantage of.

FINRA's rules allow broker dealers to withhold distributions to senior clients for 15 business days in cases of suspected financial exploitation. During this time the broker dealer should investigate the client's request and obtain as much information regarding the receiving party as they can. To further protect seniors, broker dealers should obtain the name and contact information of a "trusted contact" for senior clients. The firm in very limited circumstances may contact the trusted contact to inquire about requests to withdraw money when financial exploitation is suspected. The firm may also contact the person to inquire as to the welfare of the client and to inquire as to the identity of any individual who may hold power of attorney or who may be named as executor of the client's will. If the end of 15 business days the firm has gathered information relating to the request that indicates that this is a case of financial exploitation, it may withhold the funds for another 10 business days. The firm should share their findings with the center for elder abuse as well as with law enforcement.

REGULATION BEST INTEREST

Regulation Best Interest (Reg BI) was adopted by the SEC in June of 2019 as an amendment to the Securities Exchange Act of 1934. All broker dealers, investment advisers, and agents are subject to standards of conduct that require the firm and its agents to act in the best interest of retail customers. Regulation BI covers all recommendations to effect securities transactions as well as all recommendations regarding account establishment. That is to say, when recommending that a client open a joint, transfer on death, trust, or fee-based account, the type of account established must be in the client's best interest. In June of 2020, as part of Regulation BI, all broker dealers and investment advisers will be required to provide retail clients with a client relationship summary (CRS) and will be required to post the CRS on their publicly available website. The CRS may be provided in hardcopy or electronically. If the CRS is provided in hardcopy, the CRS may not be more than two pages long and the CRS must be the first page among any documents sent in the same package. The following rules are in place relating to the CRS:

- The CRS must be written in plain English using everyday terms.
- The CRS should be written using "active voice" with a strong, direct, and clear meaning.
- The CRS must follow the standard format and order as detailed by the SEC.
- The CRS should be written as if speaking to the retail investor directly.
- The CRS must be factual and avoid boilerplate, vague, or exaggerated language.
- The CRS may not include disclosures other than those required under Regulation BI.
- Electronic CRSs should use graphs and charts, specifically dual column charts to compare services.
- Electronic CRSs may use videos and popups and must provide access to any referenced information via hyperlink or other means.
- Electronic CRSs may be delivered via email provided that the email contains a direct link to the CRS.

Some of the required disclosures are referred to as "conversation starters." These conversation starters should be in bold or in other text to ensure that they are more noticeable than other disclosures. These conversation starters include questions such as:

1. Who is my primary contact and does he or she represent a broker dealer or an investment adviser?
2. Who can I speak to about how the person is treating me?
3. Given my financial situation, should I choose a brokerage service? Why or why not?
4. Given my financial situation, should I choose an investment advisory service? Why or why not?
5. How will you choose investments to recommend to me?

6. What is your relevant experience, including licenses, education, and qualifications? What do these qualifications mean?

7. What fees will I pay?

8. How will these fees affect my investments? If I give you $10,000, how much will go toward fees and expenses and how much will be invested for me?

9. What are your legal obligations to me when providing recommendations (broker dealer)?

10. What are your legal obligations to me when acting as my investment adviser?

11. How else does your firm make money?

12. How do your financial professionals make money?

13. What conflicts of interest do you have?

14. Does the firm or its financial professionals have legal or disciplinary history?

Both broker dealers and investment advisers are required to adhere to the standards of conduct under Regulation BI. As such, both must disclose that they must put the interests of the client ahead of theirs when making a recommendation and that the way the firm makes money for providing the services causes a conflict of interest. These conflicts include recommending proprietary products, receiving payments from third parties, principal trading, or revenue sharing.

Online broker dealers who only provide access to trading, as well as investment advisers who only offer automated services and who do not offer access to specific registered individuals must disclose this fact in the CRS and must provide a section on their website that answers questions relating to the conversation starters. If a broker dealer or investment adviser provides both online services and access to registered personnel, a registered person must be made available to discuss the conversation starters.

Broker dealers are required to provide the CRS to customers before or upon the earlier of recommending the type of account to establish or an investment strategy or upon opening an account or placing an order. Investment advisers must provide the CRS to clients prior to or at the time the contract is entered into even if the contract is oral. The CRS is now known as ADV part 3. For entities who are registered as both a broker dealer and as an investment adviser, the CRS must be delivered upon the earliest requirement for either registration. Any changes required to be made to the CRS must be completed within 30 days and an updated CRS clearly reflecting the changes must be sent to existing customers within 60 days. All broker dealers and investment advisers are required to file the CRS along with any changes with the SEC. Broker dealers will file through the Central Registration Depository (CRD) system and investment advisers will file through the Investment Adviser Registration Database (IARD). The relationship summary must be provided to a client upon request within 30 days.

Pretest

SECURITIES INDUSTRY RULES AND REGULATIONS

1. The Securities Exchange Act of 1934 regulates which market?
   a. Third
   b. Fourth
   c. Primary
   d. Secondary

2. In the securities industry, which of the following is the ultimate industry authority with regards to conduct?
   a. NYSE
   b. SRO
   c. SEC
   d. FINRA

3. A testimonial by a compensated expert, citing the results he realized following a FINRA member's recommendations, must include which of the following?

    I. A statement detailing the expert's credentials

    II. A statement that past performance is not a guarantee of future performance

    III. A statement that the individual is a compensated spokesperson

    IV. The name of the principal who approved the ad

    a. I, II, and III

    b. II and IV

    c. I and II

    d. I, II, III, and IV

4. Which of the following acts gave the NASD the authority to regulate the OTC market?

    a. The NASD Act of 1929

    b. The Securities Act of 1933

    c. The Securities Act of 1934

    d. The Maloney Act of 1938

5. FINRA considers which of the following to be retail communications?

    I. Videotape displays

    II. Listing of services in local yellow pages

    III. Circulars

    IV. Telemarketing scripts

    a. II and III

    b. I and II

    c. I, II, III, and IV

    d. I and III

6. Your brokerage firm has placed an ad in the local newspaper advertising its new line of services being offered to investors. The firm must maintain the ad for how long?

   a. 24 months

   b. 36 months

   c. 12 months

   d. 18 months

7. According to Rule 135, as it relates to generic advertising, which of the following is FALSE?

   a. The ad may contain information about the services a company offers.

   b. The ad may describe the nature of the investment company's business.

   c. The ad may contain information about exchange privileges.

   d. The ad may contain information about the performance of past recommendations.

8. A syndicate has published a tombstone ad prior to an issue becoming effective. Which of the following must appear in the tombstone?

   I. A statement that the registration has not yet become effective

   II. A statement that the tombstone ad is not an offer to sell the securities

   III. Contact information

   IV. A "no commitment" statement

   a. III and IV

   b. II and III,

   c. I and II

   d. I, II, III, and IV

Economic Fundamentals

INTRODUCTION

Economics, put simply, is the study of shortages: supply versus demand. As the demand for a product or service rises, the price of those products or services will tend to rise. Alternatively, if the provider of those goods or services tries to flood the market with those goods or services, the price will tend to decline as the supply outpaces the demand. The supply and demand model works for all goods and services including stocks, bonds, real estate, and money. Series 66 candidates will see a fair number of questions on economics.

GROSS DOMESTIC PRODUCT

A country's gross domestic product (GDP) measures the overall health of a nation's economy. The GDP is defined as the value of all goods and services produced in a country including consumption, investments, government spending, and exports minus imports during a given year.

Economists chart the health of the economy by measuring the country's GDP and by monitoring supply and demand models, along with the nation's business cycle. A country's economy is always in flux. Periods of increasing output are always followed by periods of falling output. The business cycle has four distinct stages:

1. Expansion
2. Peak

3. Contraction
4. Trough

EXPANSION

During an expansionary phase, an economy will see an increase in overall business activity and output. Corporate sales, manufacturing output, wages, and savings will all increase while the economy is expanding or growing. An economy cannot continue to grow indefinitely and GDP will top out at the peak of the business cycle. An economic expansion is characterized by:

- Increasing GDP.
- Rising consumer demand.
- Rising stock market.
- Rising production.
- Rising real estate prices.

PEAK

As the economy tops out, the GDP reaches its maximum output for this cycle as wages, manufacturing, and savings all peak.

CONTRACTION

During a contraction, GDP falls, along with productivity, wages, and savings. Unemployment begins to rise, the stock market begins to fall, and corporate profits decline as inventories rise.

TROUGH

The economy bottoms out in the trough as GDP hits its lowest level for the cycle. As GDP bottoms out, unemployment reaches its highest level, wages bottom out, and savings bottom out. The economy is now poised to enter a new expansionary phase and start the cycle all over again.

RECESSION

A recession is defined as a period of declining GDP, which lasts at least 6 months or 2 quarters. Recessions may vary in degree of severity and in duration. Extended recessions may last up to 18 months and may be accompanied by steep downturns in economic output. In the most severe recessions, falling prices erode businesses' pricing power, margins, and profits as deflation takes hold. Recessions are generally triggered by an overall decrease in spending by businesses and consumers. As businesses and consumers pull back spending, overall demand falls. Businesses and consumers will often reduce spending as a cautionary measure in response to an economic event or shock, such as a financial crisis, or the busting of a bubble in an inflated asset class, such as real estate or the stock market.

DEPRESSION

A depression is characterized by a decline in GDP, which lasts at least 18 months or 6 consecutive quarters. GDP often falls by 10% or more during a depression. A depression is the most severe type of recession and is accompanied by extremely high levels of unemployment and frozen credit markets. The steep fall in demand is more likely to lead to deflation during a depression.

ECONOMIC INDICATORS

There are various economic activities that one can look at to try to identify where the economy is in the business cycle. An individual can also use these economic indicators as a way to try and predict the direction of the economy in the future. The three types of economic indicators are:

1. Leading indicators
2. Coincident indicators
3. Lagging indicators

LEADING INDICATORS

Leading indicators are business conditions that change prior to a change in the overall economy. These indicators can be used as a gauge for the future direction of the economy. Leading indicators include:

- Building permits.
- Stock market prices.
- Money supply (M2).
- New orders for consumer goods.
- Average weekly initial claims in unemployment.
- Changes in raw material prices.
- Changes in consumer or business borrowing.
- Average work week for manufacturing.
- Changes in inventories of durable goods.

COINCIDENT INDICATORS

Changes in the economy cause an immediate change in the activity level of coincident indicators. As the business cycle changes, the level of activity in coincident indicators can confirm where the economy is. Coincident indicators include:

- GDP.
- Industrial production.
- Personal income.
- Employment.
- Average number of hours worked.
- Manufacturing and trade sales.
- Nonagricultural employment.

LAGGING INDICATORS

Lagging indicators will only change after the state of the economy has changed direction. Lagging indicators can be used to confirm the new direction of the economy. Lagging indicators include:

- Average duration of unemployment.
- Corporate profits.

- Labor costs.
- Consumer debt levels.
- Commercial and industrial loans.
- Business loans.

SCHOOLS OF ECONOMIC THOUGHT

The study of economics is a social science with many different schools of thought. Economics has been referred to as the dismal science as it is largely focused on the study of shortages. Economists all generally believe that low inflation and low unemployment are signs of a healthy economy. However, the different schools of economic thought believe that economic prosperity can be restored or maintained through very different approaches.

CLASSICAL ECONOMICS

The classical economic theory, also known as supply side economics, believes that lower taxes and less government regulation will stimulate growth and increase demand through higher employment. Less regulation of business creates lower barriers to entry for employers and allows employers to produce goods at lower prices and to create more jobs. As a result of the lower prices, lower taxes, and higher employment, aggregate demand in the economy will increase positively impacting the nation's gross domestic product.

KEYNESIAN ECONOMICS

John Maynard Keynes first published his theories on economics in 1936 during the Great Depression. The Keynesian economic model believes that a mixed economy based on private and public sector efforts will produce desired economic conditions. Keynesians believe that the decisions made in the private sector can lead to supply and demand imbalances, and that an active policy response from the public sector in the form of government spending (fiscal policy) and adjustments to the money supply (monetary policy) is required.

THE MONETARISTS

Economists who subscribe to monetary economics believe that the supply of money in the economy can influence the direction of the economy and prices as a whole. During times of low demand and high unemployment the economy can be stimulated by increasing the money supply. As more money enters the system interest rates fall increasing demand. As more money enters the system the value of the currency tends to decline, and during times of expansionary monetary policy, inflation may increase. Milton Friedman, the founder of the monetarist movement, believed that the main focus of central banks should be on price stability.

ECONOMIC POLICY

The government has two tools that it can use to try to influence the direction of the economy. Monetary policy, which is controlled by the Federal Reserve Board, determines the nation's money supply, while fiscal policy is controlled by the president and Congress and determines government spending and taxation.

TOOLS OF THE FEDERAL RESERVE BOARD

The Federal Reserve Board will try to steer the economy through the business cycle by adjusting the level of money supply and interest rates. The Fed may:

- Change the reserve requirement for member banks.
- Change the discount rate charged to member banks.
- Set target rates for federal fund loans.
- Buy and sell U.S. government securities through open-market operations.
- Change the amount of money in circulation.
- Use moral suasion.

INTEREST RATES

Interest rates, put simply, are the cost of money. Overall interest rates are determined by the supply and demand for money, along with any upward price movement in the cost of goods and services, known as inflation. There are several key interest rates upon which all other rates depend:

- Discount rate
- Federal funds rate
- Broker call loan rate
- Prime rate

DISCOUNT RATE

The discount rate is the interest rate that the Federal Reserve Bank charges on loans to member banks. A bank may borrow money directly from the Federal Reserve by going to the discount window, and the bank will be charged the discount rate. The bank is then free to lend out this money at a higher rate and earn a profit, or it may use these funds to meet a reserve requirement shortfall. Although a bank may borrow money directly from the Federal Reserve, this is discouraged, and the discount rate has become largely symbolic.

FEDERAL FUNDS RATE

The federal funds rate is the rate that member banks charge each other for overnight loans. The federal funds rate is widely watched as an indicator for the direction of short-term interest rates.

BROKER CALL LOAN RATE

The broker call loan rate is the interest rate that banks charge on loans to broker dealers to finance their customers' margin purchases. Many broker dealers will extend credit to their customers to purchase securities on margin. The broker dealers will obtain the money to lend to their customers from the bank, and the loan is callable or payable on demand by the broker dealer.

PRIME RATE

The prime rate is the rate that banks charge their largest and most creditworthy corporate customers on loans. The prime rate has lost a lot of its significance in recent years because mortgage lenders are now basing their rates on other rates, such as the 10-year Treasury note. The prime rate is, however, very important for consumer spending, because most credit card interest rates are based on prime plus a margin.

RESERVE REQUIREMENT

Member banks must keep a percentage of their depositors' assets in an account with the Federal Reserve. This is known as the reserve requirement. The reserve requirement is intended to ensure that all banks maintain a certain level of liquidity. Banks are in business to earn a profit by lending money. As the bank accepts accounts from depositors, it pays them interest on their money. The bank, in turn, takes the depositors' money and loans it out at higher rates, earning the difference. If the Fed wanted to stimulate the economy, it might reduce the reserve requirement for the banks, which would allow the banks to lend more. By making more money available to borrowers, interest rates will fall and, therefore, demand will increase, helping to stimulate the economy. If the Fed wanted to slow down the economy, it might increase the reserve requirement. The increased requirement would make less money available to borrowers. Interest rates would rise as a result and the demand for goods and services would slow down. Changing the reserve requirement is the least-used Fed tool.

CHANGING THE DISCOUNT RATE

The Federal Reserve Board may change the discount rate in an effort to guide the economy through the business cycle. Remember, the discount rate is the rate that the Fed charges member banks on loans. This rate is highly symbolic, but as the Fed changes the discount rate, all other interest rates change with it. If the Fed wanted to stimulate the economy, it would reduce the discount rate. As the discount rate falls, all other interest rates fall with it, making the cost of money lower. The lower interest rate should encourage borrowing and demand to help stimulate the economy. If the Fed wanted to slow the economy down, it would increase the discount rate. As the discount rate increases, all other rates go up with it, raising the cost of borrowing. As the cost of borrowing increases, demand and the economy slow down.

FEDERAL OPEN MARKET COMMITTEE

The Federal Open Market Committee (FOMC) is the Fed's most flexible tool. The FOMC will buy and sell U.S. government securities in the secondary market through open market operations in order to control the money supply. If the Fed wants to stimulate the economy and reduce rates, it will buy government securities. When the Fed buys the securities, money is instantly sent into the banking system. As the money flows into the banks, more money is available to lend. Because there is more money available, interest rates will go down and borrowing and demand should increase to stimulate the economy. If the Fed wants to slow the economy down, it will sell U.S. government securities. When the Fed sells the securities, money flows from the banks and into the Fed, thus reducing the money supply. Because there is less money available to be loaned out, interest rates will increase, slowing borrowing and demand. This will have a cooling effect on the economy. The FOMC also issues statements that can "jawbone" investors to take certain actions and sets a benchmark for what it believes the fed funds rate should be. However, the marketplace is the ultimate factor in setting the fed funds rate.

MONEY SUPPLY

Prior to determining an appropriate economic policy, economists must have an idea of the amount of money that is in circulation, along with the amount of other types of assets that will provide access to cash. Economists gauge the money supply using three measures. They are:

1. M1
2. M2
3. M3

M1

M1 is the largest and most liquid measure of the nation's money supply and it includes:

- Cash
- Demand deposits (Checking accounts)

M2

Includes all the measures in M1 plus:

- Money market instruments
- Time deposits of less than $100,000
- Negotiable CDs exceeding $100,000
- Overnight repurchase agreements

M3

Includes all of the measures in M1 and M2 plus:

- Time deposits greater than $100,000
- Repurchase agreements with maturities greater than 1 day

DISINTERMEDIATION

Disintermediation occurs when people take their money out of low yielding accounts offered by financial intermediaries or banks and invest money in higher yielding investments.

MORAL SUASION

The Federal Reserve Board often will use moral suasion as a way to influence the economy. The Fed is very powerful and very closely watched. By simply implying or expressing their views on the economy, they can slightly influence the economy.

Monetarists believe that a well-managed money supply, with an increasing bias, will produce price stability and will promote the overall economic health of the economy. Milton Friedman is believed to be the founder of the monetarist movement.

FISCAL POLICY

Fiscal policy is controlled by the president and Congress and determines how they manage the budget and government expenditures to help steer the economy through the business cycle. Fiscal policy may change the levels of:

- Federal spending
- Federal taxation
- Creation or use of federal budget deficits or surpluses

Fiscal policy assumes that the government can influence the economy by adjusting its level of spending and taxation. If the government wanted to stimulate the economy, it may increase spending. The assumption here is that as the government spends more, it will increase aggregate demand and, therefore, productivity. Additionally, if the government wanted to stimulate the economy, it may reduce the level of taxation. As the government reduces taxes, it leaves a larger portion of earnings for the consumers and businesses to spend. This should also have a positive impact on aggregate demand. Alternatively, if the government wanted to slow down the economy, it may reduce spending to lower the level of aggregate demand or raise taxes to reduce demand by taking money out of the hands of the consumers. John Maynard Keynes believed that it was the duty of the government to be involved with controlling the direction of the economy and the nation's overall economic health.

As both the Federal Reserve Board and the government monitor the overall health of the U.S. economy, they look at various indicators, some of which are:

- Consumer price index
- Inflation/deflation
- Real GDP

CONSUMER PRICE INDEX (CPI)

The consumer price index is made up of a basket of goods and services that consumers most often use in their daily lives. The consumer price index is used to measure the rate of change in overall prices. A CPI that is rising would indicate that prices are going up and that inflation is present. A falling CPI would indicate that prices are falling and deflation is present.

INFLATION/DEFLATION

Inflation is the persistent increase in prices, while deflation is the persistent decrease in prices. Both economic conditions can harm a country's economy. Inflation will eat away at the purchasing power of the dollar and results in higher prices for goods and services. Deflation will erode corporate profits as weak demand in the marketplace drives prices for goods and services lower.

REAL GDP

Real GDP is adjusted for the effects of inflation or deflation over time. GDP is measured in constant dollars so that the gain or loss of the dollar's purchasing power will not show as a change in the overall productivity of the economy.

Both monetary policy and fiscal policy have a major effect on the stock market as a whole.

The following are bullish for the stock market:

- Falling interest rates
- Increasing money supply
- Increase in government spending
- Falling taxes

The following are bearish for the stock market:

- Increasing taxes
- Increasing interest rates
- Falling government spending
- Falling money supply

INTERNATIONAL MONETARY CONSIDERATIONS

The world has become a global marketplace. Each country's economy is affected to some degree by the economies of other countries. Currency values relative to other currencies will impact a country's international trade and the balance of payments. The amount of another country's currency that may be received for a country's domestic currency is known as the exchange rate. The balance of payments measures the net inflow (surplus) or outflow (deficit) of money. The largest component of the balance of payments is the balance of trade. As the exchange rates fluctuate, one country's goods may become more expensive, while another country's goods become less expensive. A weak currency benefits exporters, while a strong currency benefits importers.

LONDON INTERBANK OFFERED RATE (LIBOR)

LIBOR is the most widely used measure of short-term interest rates around the world. The LIBOR rate is the market-driven interest rate charged by and between financial institutions, similar to the fed funds rate in the United States. LIBOR loans range from 1 day to 1 year and the rate is calculated by the British Banker's Association in a variety of currencies including euros, U.S. dollars, and yen.

YIELD CURVE ANALYSIS

Economists and investors may analyze both the cost of borrowed funds given various maturities and the general health of the economy by looking at the shape of the yield curve. With a normal, ascending, positive, or upward sloping yield curve, the level of interest rates increase as the term of the maturity increases. Simply put, lenders are going to demand higher interest rates on longer-term loans. The longer the lenders have to wait to be repaid and the longer their money is at risk, the higher the level of compensation (interest) required to make the loan. Higher interest rates also compensate the lenders for the time value of money. The dollars received in 10, 20, or 30 years will be worth less than the value of the dollars loaned to borrowers today. An upward sloping curve is present during times of economic prosperity and depicts the expectation of increased interest rates in the future. The yield curve will also graphically demonstrate investors' expectations about inflation. The higher the expectations are for inflation, the higher the level of corresponding interest rates are for the period of high inflation. Occasionally, the yield curve may become inverted, negative, or downward sloping during times when demand for short-term funds are running much higher than the demand for longer-term loans. This may also occur in times when the Federal Reserve Board has increased short-term rates to combat an economy that is growing too quickly and threatening long-term price stability. With an inverted yield curve, interest rates on short-term loans far exceed the interest rates on longer-term loans. An inverted yield curve tends to normalize quickly and is often a precursor to a recession. The yield curve may also flatten out when the interest rates for both short-term and long-term loans are approximately equal to one another.

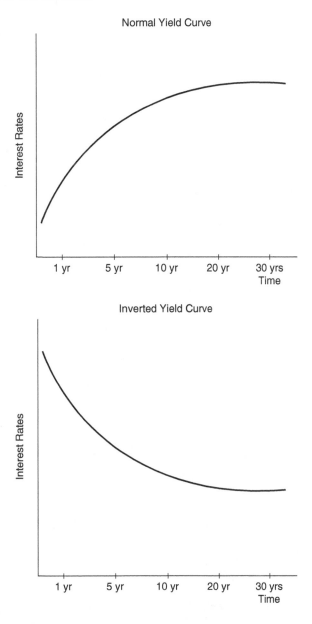

Pretest

ECONOMIC FUNDAMENTALS

1. During an inflationary period, the price of which one of the following will fall the most?
   a. Preferred stock
   b. Treasury bills
   c. Treasury bonds
   d. Common stock

2. All of the following are bullish for the stock market, EXCEPT:
   a. Falling taxes
   b. Increasing government spending
   c. Increasing money supply
   d. Increasing interest rates

3. Economic theories believe all of the following to be true, EXCEPT:
   a. As supply rises, price tends to fall.
   b. As supply rises, prices tend to rise.
   c. A moderately increasing money supply promotes price stability.
   d. As demand rises, price tends to rise.

4. Which one of the following interest rates is controlled by the Federal Reserve Board?

    a. Prime rate

    b. Federal funds rate

    c. Broker call loan rate

    d. Discount rate

5. All of the following indicate a downturn in the business cycle, EXCEPT:

    a. Rising inventories

    b. High consumer debt

    c. Falling inventories

    d. Falling stock prices

6. A bank with a shortfall meeting their reserve requirement could borrow money from another bank and pay the:

    a. Federal funds rate

    b. Broker call loan rate

    c. Prime rate

    d. Discount rate

7. The government has two tools it can use to try to influence the direction of the economy; they are:

    a. Monetary policy and fiscal policy

    b. Prime rate policy and fiscal policy

    c. Monetary policy and prime rate policy

    d. Fiscal policy and money market policy

8. Fiscal policy is controlled by:

    I. President

    II. FOMC

    III. Congress

    IV. FRB

    a. I and IV

    b. I and II

    c. II and IV

    d. I and III

9. The Federal Reserve Board sets all of the following EXCEPT:

    a. Monetary policy

    b. Reserve requirement

    c. Governmental spending

    d. Discount rate

10. A decline in the GDP must last at least how long to be considered a recession?

    a. Two quarters

    b. One quarter

    c. Six quarters

    d. Four quarters

Customer Recommendations, Professional Conduct, and Taxation

INTRODUCTION

All recommendations to customers must be suitable based upon the customer's investment objectives, financial profile, and attitude towards investing. Advisers usually make verbal recommendations to customers. Advisers will review their customers' investment objectives with them and offer facts to support the basis for their particular recommendations, as well as an explanation as to how the recommendations will help a customer meet his or her specific objectives. Any predictions about the performance of an investment should be stated strictly as an opinion or belief, not as a fact. If the firm uses reports that cite past performance of the firm's previous recommendations, the report must contain:

- The prices and dates when the recommendations were made.
- General market conditions.
- The recommendations in all similar securities for 12 months.
- A statement disclosing that the firm is a market maker (if applicable).
- A statement regarding whether the firm or its officers or directors own any of the securities being recommended or options or warrants for the same security.
- If the firm managed or co-managed an underwriting of any of the issuer's securities in the last 3 years.

- A statement regarding the availability of supporting documentation for the recommendations.

  When making a recommendation, an adviser may not:

- Guarantee or promise a profit or promise no loss.
- Make false, misleading, or fraudulent statements.
- Make unfair comparisons to dissimilar products.

PROFESSIONAL CONDUCT BY INVESTMENT ADVISERS

The fiduciary duty of an investment adviser goes beyond that of a broker dealer. The investment adviser is required to develop a client profile when opening the client's account and must update it regularly as the client's needs change. Investment advisers have a fiduciary duty to provide only suitable advice to clients. Violations of state and federal laws may result in fines, expulsion from the state or industry, or a jail term. Investment advisers are expected to adhere to all of the rules and regulations set forth in the Investment Advisers Act of 1940, as well as all state and federal laws.

THE UNIFORM PRUDENT INVESTORS ACT OF 1994

The Uniform Prudent Investors Act of 1994 (UPIA) sets the basic standards by which all investment professionals acting in a fiduciary capacity must abide. The UPIA updates the requirements and definitions of prudent standards in light of the application of modern portfolio theory and the advancement in the understanding of the behavior of capital markets. The UPIA laid out five fundamental changes in the approach to prudent investing for investment professionals acting in a fiduciary capacity. Those changes are:

1. The main consideration of a fiduciary is the management and trade off between risk and reward.
2. The standard of prudence for each investment will be viewed in relationship to the overall portfolio rather than as a stand-alone investment.
3. The rules regarding diversification have become part of the definition of prudent investing.
4. The restrictions from investing in various types of investments have been removed, and the trustee may invest in anything that is appropriate in

light of the objectives of the trust and in line with other requirements of prudent investing.

5. The rules against delegating the duties of the trustee have been removed and the trustee may now delegate investment functions subject to safeguards.

FAIR DEALINGS WITH CLIENTS

All investment advisers are required to act in good faith in all of their dealings with customers and are required to uphold just and equitable trade practices. An investment adviser may not employ or engage in:

- Churning.
- Manipulative and deceptive devices.
- Unauthorized trading.
- Fraudulent acts.
- Blanket recommendations.
- Selling dividends.
- Misrepresentations.
- Omitting material facts.
- Making guarantees.
- Recommending speculative securities without knowing whether the customer can afford the risk.
- Short-term trading in mutual funds.
- Switching fund families.

CHURNING

Many advisers are compensated when a customer makes a transaction based on their recommendation. Churning is the practice of making transactions that are excessive in size or frequency, with the intention of generating higher commissions. When determining if an account has been churned, regulators will look at the frequency of the transactions, the size of the transactions, and the amount of commission earned by the representative. Customer profitability is not an issue when determining if an account has been churned.

In addition to churning where the agent or firm executes too many transactions to increase revenue, a practice known as reverse churning is also a violation. Reverse churning is the practice of placing inactive accounts or accounts that do not trade frequently into fee-based programs that charge an annual fee based on the assets in the account. This fee covers all advice and execution charges. Since these inactive accounts do not trade frequently, it will cause the total fees charged to the account to increase and makes a fee-based account unsuitable for inactive accounts and for accounts that simply buy and hold securities for a long period of time. These accounts will generally be charged an annual fee in the range of 1–2% of the total value of the assets in lieu of commissions when orders are executed.

MANIPULATIVE AND DECEPTIVE DEVICES

It is a violation for an adviser to engage in or employ any artifice or scheme that is designed to gain an unfair advantage over another party. Some examples of manipulative or deceptive devices are:

- Capping.
- Pegging.
- Front running.
- Trading ahead.
- Painting the tape/matched purchases/matched sales.

> **Capping:** A manipulative act designed to keep a stock price from rising or to keep the price down.
>
> **Pegging:** A manipulative act designed to keep a stock price up or to keep the price from falling.
>
> **Front running:** The entering of an order for the account of an agent or firm prior to the entering of a large customer order. The firm or agent is using the customer's order to profit on the order it has entered for its own account.
>
> **Trading ahead:** The entering of an order for a security based on the prior knowledge of a soon to be released research report.
>
> **Painting the tape:** A manipulative act by two or more parties designed to create false activity in the security without any beneficial change in ownership. The increased activity is used to attract new buyers.

CUSTOMER COMPLAINTS

All written complaints received from a customer or from an individual acting on behalf of the customer must be reported promptly to the principal of the firm. The firm must maintain a separate customer complaint folder even if it has not received any written customer complaints. If the firm's file contains complaints, the file must state what action was taken by the firm, if any, and it must disclose the location of the file containing any correspondence relating to the complaint. When a written complaint is received by mail or e-mail, the customer who has issued the complaint must be notified that the complaint has been received. If a customer files a complaint and subsequently withdraws the complaint, the firm is still requested to maintain the correspondence relating to the complaint in the firm's complaint file.

UNAUTHORIZED TRADING

An unauthorized transaction is one that is made for the benefit of a customer's account at a time when the customer has no knowledge of the trade and the adviser does not have discretionary power over the account.

FRAUD

Fraud is defined as any act that is employed to obtain an unfair advantage over another party. Fraudulent acts include:

- False statements.
- Deliberate omissions of material facts.
- Concealment of material facts.
- Manipulative and deceptive practices.
- Forgery.
- Material omission.
- Lying.

BLANKET RECOMMENDATIONS

It is inappropriate for an adviser to make blanket recommendations in any security, especially low-priced speculative securities. No matter what type of investment is involved, a blanket recommendation to a large group of people will always be wrong for some investors. Different investors have different objectives, and the same recommendation will not be suitable for every investor.

EXAMPLE

Mr. Jones, an agent with XYZ brokers, has a large customer base that ranges from young investors who are just starting to save to institutions and retirees. Mr. Jones has been doing a significant amount of research on WSIA Industries, a mining and materials company. Mr. Jones strongly believes that WSIA is significantly undervalued based on its assets and earning potential. Mr. Jones recommends WSIA to all his clients. In the next 6 months the share price of WSIA increases significantly as new production dramatically increases sales, just as Mr. Jones's research suggested. The clients then sell WSIA at Mr. Jones's suggestion and realize a significant profit.

ANALYSIS

Even though the clients who purchased WSIA based on Mr. Jones's recommendation made a significant profit, Mr. Jones has still committed a violation because he recommended it to all of his clients. Mr. Jones's clients have a wide variety of investment objectives, and the risk or income potential associated with an investment in WSIA would not be suitable for every client. Even if an investment is profitable for the client it does not mean it was suitable for the client. Blanket recommendations are never suitable.

 TAKE**NOTE!**

An investment adviser who has discretion over client accounts may in certain circumstances be found to have made unsuitable blanket recommendations if the adviser purchases a significant amount of an illiquid security for a large number of client accounts. This action could also be deemed to be market manipulation.

SELLING DIVIDENDS

Selling dividends is a violation that occurs when advisers use a pending dividend payment as the sole basis of their recommendation to purchase a stock or mutual fund. Additionally, using the pending dividend as a means to create urgency on the part of the investor to purchase the stock is a prime example of this type of violation. If the investor purchased the shares just prior to the ex dividend date simply to receive the dividend, the investor in many cases would end up worse off. The dividend in this case would actually be a return of the money that the investor used to purchase the stock, and then the investor would have a tax liability upon receipt of the dividend.

MISREPRESENTATIONS

An adviser may not knowingly make any misrepresentations regarding:

- A client's account status.
- The representative.
- The firm.

- An investment.
- Fees to be charged.

OMITTING MATERIAL FACTS

A representative may not omit any material fact, either good or bad, when recommending a security. A material fact is one that an investor would need to know in order to make a well-informed investment decision. The adviser may, however, omit an immaterial fact.

GUARANTEES

No representative, broker dealer, or investment adviser may make any guarantees of any kind. A profit may not be guaranteed, and a promise of no loss may not be made.

RECOMMENDING MUTUAL FUNDS

An adviser recommending a mutual fund should ensure that the mutual fund's investment objective meets the customer's investment objective. If the mutual fund company or broker dealer distributes advertising or sales literature regarding the mutual fund, the following should be disclosed:

- The highest sales charge charged by the fund
- The fund's current yield based on dividends only
- A graph of the performance of the fund versus a broad-based index
- The performance of the fund for 10 years or the life of the fund, whichever is less
- No implication that a mutual fund is safer than other investments
- The sources of graphs and charts

PERIODIC PAYMENT PLANS

When recommending or advertising a periodic payment plan, the following must be disclosed:

- A statement that a profit is not guaranteed.
- A statement that investors are not protected from a loss.
- A statement that the plan involves continuous investments, regardless of market conditions.

DISCLOSURE OF CLIENT INFORMATION

Investment advisers may not disclose any information regarding clients to a third party without the client's expressed consent or without a court order. If the client is an issuer of securities and the broker dealer is an underwriter, transfer agent, or paying agent for the issuer, then the broker dealer is precluded from using the information it obtains, regarding the issuer's security holders for its own benefit.

BORROWING AND LENDING MONEY

Borrowing and lending of money between registered persons and customers is strictly regulated. If the broker dealer allows borrowing and lending between representatives and customers, the firm must have policies in place that will allow for the loans to be made. Loans may be made between an agent or a customer if the customer is a bank or other lending institution, where there is a personal or outside business relationship and that relationship is the basis for the loan, or between two agents registered with the same firm.

DEVELOPING THE CLIENT PROFILE

Recommendations to an advisory client must be suitable based on the client's investment objective and client profile. The adviser should obtain enough information about the customer to ensure that the recommendations are suitable based on a review of the client's:

- Investment objectives.
- Financial status.
- Income.
- Investment holdings.
- Retirement needs.
- College and other major expenses.
- Tax bracket.
- Attitude toward investing.

The more you know about a client's financial position, the better you will be able help the client meet his or her objectives. You should always ask questions like:

- How long have you been making these types of investments?
- Do you have any major expenses coming up?

- How long do you usually hold investments?
- How much risk do you normally take?
- What tax bracket are you in?
- How much money do you have invested in the market?
- Have you done any retirement planning?
- How old are you?
- Are you married?
- Do you have any children?
- How long have you been employed at your current job?

Advisers, who help people invest to meet a specific objective, must make sure that their recommendations meet that client's objective. Should a person have a primary and a secondary objective, an adviser must make sure that the recommendation meets the investor's primary objective first and the secondary objective second. When developing the client's profile, advisers should also calculate the client's:

- Assets.
- Liabilities.
- Net worth.
- Monthly discretionary cash flow or income.

TYPES OF ADVISORY CLIENTS

When an adviser meets with a potential new client, the adviser must determine the legal structure under which the client operates. Clients may hold investments in their own name or in any of the following entities:

- A sole proprietorship
- A C corporation
- An S corporation
- A partnership
- A limited partnership
- A family limited partnership
- A trust

Sole proprietorships: are easily established to allow a person to conduct business under a trade name. For all intents and purposes the sole proprietorship is an extension of the proprietor. All taxes are reported on the individual's return and there is no asset protection.

Corporations: A corporation is its own legal entity and has a perpetual life independent from its owners. How the corporation is taxed depends upon how the corporation is organized. C corporations are taxed at the corporate rate independent from the owners' tax rates. An S corporation allows the income to flow through to the owners and to be taxed as ordinary income. No more than 75 people can own an S corporation, and the S corporation must be organized as a domestic corporation.

Partnerships: A partnership is an association of two or more people who are either in business together or who hold assets in a partnership. The partnership agreement will detail each partner's ownership interest and authority to act on behalf of the partnership.

Limited partnership: A limited partnership consists of at least one general partner and one or more limited partners. It is the duty of the general partner to manage the partnership in accordance with the partnership's objectives. The limited partners put up the investment capital required but may not exercise management or control over the partnership.

Family limited partnership: A family limited partnership is often used for estate planning. Parents may place significant assets into a family limited partnership as a way to transfer their ownership. Usually the parents will act as the general partners and will transfer limited partnership interests to their children. As the interests are transferred to the children the parents may become subject to gift taxes. However, the gift taxes will usually be lower than they would have suffered without the partnership.

Limited partnerships, LLCs, and S corporations provide asset protection and avoid double taxation by distributing income and losses to the owners or members.

The ultimate selection of the business structure largely depends on the needs of the person and the type of business that is being conducted. Specific consideration should be given to the tax implications, ease of establishment, and asset protection. LLCs have become popular choices for smaller businesses as they allow for the flow through of taxes, are easily established, and provide the asset protection of a corporation. A C corporation would be the most suited for a business that needed to raise a substantial amount of capital or was projected to be very profitable.

INVESTMENT OBJECTIVES

All investors want to make or preserve money. However, these objectives can be achieved in different ways. Some of the different investment objectives are:

- Income.
- Growth.
- Preservation of capital.
- Tax benefits.
- Liquidity.
- Speculation.

INCOME

Many investors are looking to have their investments generate additional income to help meet their monthly expenses. Some investments that will help to meet that objective are:

- Corporate bonds.
- Municipal bonds.
- Government bonds.
- Preferred stocks.
- Money market funds.
- Bond funds.

GROWTH

Investors who are seeking capital appreciation over time want their money to grow in value and are not seeking any current income. The only investments that will achieve this goal are:

- Common stocks.
- Common stock funds.

PRESERVATION OF CAPITAL

People who have preservation of capital as an investment objective are very conservative investors and are more concerned with keeping the money they have saved. For these investors, high-quality debt will be an appropriate recommendation. Investment choices that will achieve this include:

- Money market funds.
- Government bonds.
- Municipal bonds.
- High grade corporate bonds.

TAX BENEFITS

For investors seeking tax advantages, the only two possible recommendations are:

1. Municipal bonds
2. Municipal bond funds

LIQUIDITY

Investors who need immediate access to their money need to own liquid investments that will not fluctuate wildly in value in case they need to use the money. The following is a list from the most liquid to the least liquid:

- Money market funds
- Stocks/bonds/ mutual funds
- Annuities
- Collateralized mortgage obligations
- Direct participation programs
- Real estate

SPECULATION

A customer investing in a speculative manner is willing to take a high degree of risk in order to earn a high rate of return. Some of the more speculative investments are:

- Penny stocks.
- Small cap stocks.
- Some growth stocks.
- Junk bonds.

RISK VS. REWARD

Risk is the reciprocal of reward. An investor must be offered a higher rate of return for each unit of additional risk the investor is willing to assume. Many types of risks are involved when investing money, including:

- Capital risk.
- Market risk.
- Nonsystematic risk.
- Legislative risk.
- Timing risk.
- Credit risk.
- Reinvestment risk.
- Call risk.
- Liquidity risk.

CAPITAL RISK

Capital risk is the risk that an investor may lose all or part of the capital that has been invested. Investors who purchase securities are not assured of the return of their invested principal.

MARKET RISK

Market risk is also known as a systematic risk; it is the risk that is inherent in any investment in the markets. For example, you could own stock in the greatest company in the world and you could still lose money because the value of your stock is going down, simply because the market as a whole is going down.

NONSYSTEMATIC RISK

Nonsystematic risk is the risk that pertains to one company or industry. For example, the problems that the tobacco industry faced a few years ago would not have affected a computer company.

LEGISLATIVE RISK

Legislative risk is the risk that the government will do something that adversely affects an investment. For example, beer manufacturers probably did not fare too well when the government enacted Prohibition.

TIMING RISK

Timing risk is simply the risk that an investor will buy and sell at the wrong time and will lose money as a result.

CREDIT RISK

Credit risk is the risk of default inherent in debt securities. An investor may lose all or part of an investment because the issuer has defaulted and cannot pay the interest or principal payments owed to the investor.

REINVESTMENT RISK

When interest rates decline and higher yielding bonds have been called or have matured, investors will not be able to receive the same return given the same amount of risk. This is called reinvestment risk, and the investor is forced to either accept the lower rate or take more risk to obtain the same rate.

INTEREST RATE RISK

Interest rate risk is the risk that the price of bonds will fall as interest rates increase. As interest rates rise, the value of existing bonds falls. This may subject the bondholder to a loss if he or she needs to sell the bond.

CALL RISK

Call risk is the risk that as interest rates decline, higher yielding bonds and preferred stocks will be called and investors will be forced to reinvest the proceeds at a lower rate of return or at a higher rate of risk to achieve the same return. Call risk only applies to preferred stocks and bonds with a call feature.

OPPORTUNITY RISK

Investors who hold long-term bonds until maturity must forgo the opportunities to invest that money in other potentially higher yielding investments.

LIQUIDITY RISK

Liquidity risk is the risk that an investor will not be able to liquidate an investment when needed or that the investor will not be able to liquidate the investment without adversely affecting its price.

ALPHA

A stock's or portfolio's alpha is its projected independent rate of return or the difference between an investment's expected (benchmark) return and its actual return. Portfolio managers whose portfolios have positive alphas are adding value through their asset selection.

BETA

A stock's beta is its projected rate of change relative to the market as a whole. If the market was up 10% for the year, a stock with a beta of 1.5 could reasonably be expected to be up 15%. A stock with a beta greater than 1.0 has a higher level of volatility than the market as a whole and is considered to be more risky than the overall market. A stock with a beta of less than 1.0 is less volatile than prices in the overall market and is considered to be less risky. An example of a low beta stock would be a utility stock. The price of utility stocks does not tend to move dramatically. A security's beta measures its nondiversifiable or systematic risk. For each incremental unit of risk an investor takes on, the investor must be compensated with additional expected returns. If the portfolio's actual return exceeds its expected return, the portfolio has generated excess returns. The Sharpe ratio can measure a portfolio's risk-adjusted return. If two portfolios both return 8%, but portfolio A contains dramatically more risk than portfolio B, then portfolio B is a much better investment choice. The Sharpe ratio tells investors how well they are being compensated for the investment risk they are assuming. The Sharpe ratio takes the portfolio's return (R) and subtracts the risk-free return (RFR) offered on short-term Treasury bills (usually 90 days) to determine the level of return that the investor earned over the risk-free return. The risk premium is then divided by the portfolio's standard deviation (SD):

Sharpe ratio = (R − RFR)/SD

Series 66 candidates will have to be able to identify the Sharpe ratio but most likely will not be required to calculate it. The degree to which a portfolio's performance is designed to mirror the return of a standard benchmark or index is measured by R-squared. If the portfolio has 100% of its assets tied to an index, such as in an index fund, the portfolio will have an R-squared value of 100, and the performance of the portfolio will mirror the performance of the index. The higher the R-squared value for the portfolio, the higher the degree of correlation to the index. R-squared values range from 0–100, with the lower values having lower correlation to the index. A portfolio with a higher R-squared value will have a more accurate beta coefficient, and as a result the volatility of the portfolio will be more predictable.

 TAKENOTE!

Beta measures systematic risk in the price volatility of a security relative to the market as whole. Standard deviation measures both systematic and unsystematic risk in the volatility of the return of a security versus its expected return.

CAPITAL ASSET PRICING MODEL (CAPM)

The capital asset pricing model (CAPM) operates under the assumption that investors are risk averse. Investors who take on risk through the purchase of an investment must be compensated for that risk through a higher expected rate of return known as the risk premium. A security's risk is measured by its beta. Therefore, securities with higher betas must offer investors a higher expected return in order for the investor to be compensated for taking on the additional risk associated with that investment. Proponents of CAPM have developed the capital market line or CML to evaluate and measure the expected returns of a diversified portfolio relative to the expected returns of the market and the expected risk-free return. The CML also measures the standard deviation of the portfolio relative to the standard deviation of the market. A further derivative measure known as the security market line or SML is used to measure the expected return of a single security based on its beta relative to the expectations of the market and risk-free rate of return. The CML is not based on alpha or beta, while the SML is partially computed based on the beta of the single security in question.

EFFICIENT MARKET THEORY

The efficient market theory believes that all of the available information is priced into the market at any given time and that it is impossible to beat the market by taking advantage of price or time inefficiencies. Proponents of the efficient market theory may follow the theory in the following ways:

Weak-form efficiency: States that the future price of a security cannot be predicted by studying the past price performance of the security. This form of the theory believes that technical analysis cannot produce excess returns.

Semi-strong form efficiency: States that the market price of a security adjusts too rapidly to newly available information to achieve an excess return by trading on that information.

Strong-form efficiency: States that the current price of a security reflects all information known and unknown to the public and that there is no opportunity to earn excess returns.

EXPECTED RETURN

Modern portfolio managers try to manage risk and evaluate investments by employing a variety of concepts under modern portfolio theory. Modern portfolio theory states that the expected rate of return for an investment is the sum of its weighted returns. An investment's weighted return is its possible return multiplied by the likelihood of that return being realized. The following table details the expected return for XYZ:

Opinion	Expected Return	Probability of Expected Return	Weighted Return
Outperform	20%	25%	5%
Market perform	10%	50%	5%
Underperform	5%	25%	1.25%
Expected return			11.25%

The following table details the expected return for ABC:

Opinion	Expected Return	Probability of Expected Return	Weighted Return
Outperform	40%	10%	4%
Market perform	20%	70%	14%
Underperform	(33.75%)	20%	(6.75%)
Expected return			11.25%

Notice that the expected rate of return for both XYZ and ABC is 11.25%. However, an investment in XYZ contains less risk than an investment in ABC because the distribution of potential returns is not as wide as the distribution of potential returns for ABC. An investor who is considering investing in either XYZ or ABC would consider the 11.25% expected return offered by XYZ to be more attractive than the same expected return offered by ABC. The distribution of an investment's varying expected returns is measured by the investment's standard deviation. The wider the distribution of an investment's expected returns, the greater its standard deviation. Investments with higher standard deviations contain more risk than investments with lower standard deviations. As an investment's results are plotted over time, there is a 95% chance that its actual return will be within two standard deviations of its expected return and a 67% chance that it will be within one standard deviation of its expected return. Portfolio managers will use computer simulations to examine the possibilities of various portfolio strategies. The Monte Carlo simulation is one such simulation used by portfolio managers.

TIME VALUE OF MONEY

As time progresses, inflation eats away at the value or the purchasing power of the dollar. That is to say that a dollar today is worth more than a dollar tomorrow. Investors can determine the future value of a sum invested if they know the interest rate, the time horizon, and the compounding schedule. The future value of a sum invested today can be determined by using the following formula:

$$FV = PV (1 + R)^T$$

Where:

FV = future value

PV = present value

R = interest rate

T = the number of compounding periods for which the money will be invested

EXAMPLE	FV = ?

PV = $1,000

R = 5%

T = 5 years compounded annually

$$FV = \$1,000 (1 + .05)^5$$

$$FV = \$1,000 (1.276)$$

$$FV = \$1,276$$

The future value of the investment will increase as the number of compounding periods increases. Let's look at what would happen to the same investment of $1,000 for 5 years at 5% if the interest was compounded semiannually. Everything would remain the same except that T would be 10 and the interest rate for each semiannual period would be half the annual rate. In this instance, we get:

$$FV = \$1,000 \ (1 + .025)^{10}$$

$$FV = \$1,000 \ (1.28)$$

$$FV = \$1,280$$

More compounding periods increase the investor's total return.

An investor can also determine the present value of a future payment by using the following formula:

$$PV = \frac{FV}{(1 + R)^T}$$

Investors can also use the present value formula to determine how much they would have to invest today to have a given sum of money in the future. For example, let's say that an investor wants to have $10,000 saved for his child's college tuition 5 years from now. If the investor knows that he can receive 6% on his money, he can determine how much he must invest today. The present value of $10,000, 5 years from now at a 6% rate is found as follows:

$$PV = \frac{\$10,000}{(1 + .06)^5}$$

$$PV = \frac{\$10,000}{1.338}$$

$$PV = \$7,473$$

The investor would have to invest $7,473 today at a 6% rate to have $10,000 in 5 years. Investors can also use the present value and future value to determine an investment's internal rate of return through a process called iteration.

NET PRESENT VALUE

An investor may calculate the net present value (NPV) of an income-producing investment by discounting the series of future payments produced by the investment into the current value of one lump sum. When calculating the current value of a future stream of dividend or interest payments, the investor will take into consideration the amount of time until the payments are received as well as the overall interest rate environment. Payments that are made further out on the time horizon are discounted more heavily than payments received sooner and are therefore less valuable. The interest rate environment in which the NPV is calculated has a large influence on the present value of a future payment. If a higher interest rate is used in the NPV calculation, it will cause a greater discount to be applied to the future payment. Higher interest rates will cause future payments to be less valuable, whereas lower rates will cause the future payments to be discounted less and to be more valuable. The formula for calculating an investment's NPV is as follows:

NPV = NPV of future cash flows − NPV of cash outflows

The cash outflow in the above calculation equals the amount of money required to be invested to purchase the investment. If the NPV calculation results in a positive number, the investment should be made.

INTERNAL RATE OF RETURN

The internal rate of return (IRR) is the annualized average return expected during the life or holding period of an investment. Like an NPV calculation, it is a discounted cash flow method used to determine the merits of an income-producing investment. The IRR is the rate that would make the discounted present value of future cash flows equal to the current market price of the investment.

WEIGHTED RETURNS

An investor who is evaluating the performance of a portfolio manager must take into consideration the impact that any contributions or withdrawals made by the investor will have on the overall performance of the account. In evaluating the performance of a manager who is overseeing an account where the investor will be making contributions and withdrawals, the investor should evaluate the performance by using the dollar-weighted return method. The dollar-weighted return method can be used to determine the IRR of the portfolio by taking into consideration the cash flows in and out of the account. If the investor will not be making additional contributions to or making withdrawals from the account, the investor may use the time-weighted return method to determine the IRR of the portfolio.

ADDITIONAL WAYS TO MEASURE RETURNS

In addition to the weighted returns discussed above to provide additional and comparable return data, investors may look at the total return, the holding period return, and the annualized return.

Total Return: To determine the total return of an investment, all dividend or interest cash flow must be taken into consideration. If the investment has increased in value, the sum of the cash flow is added to any capital appreciation. The addition of the cash flow will cause the total return to be higher. If the security has fallen in value, the total of the cash flow may partially or totally offset the loss of value of the security in question.

Holding Period Return: The holding period for a security may be very long or very short depending on the investor. Some investors hold securities for years while others may only hold securities for a few days or less. The total return from any cash flow plus or minus any capital appreciation or depreciation realized during the time the investment was held equals the holding period return.

Annualized Return: Once the holding period return has been calculated it can then be used to determine the annualized rate of return. An investment's annualized rate of return will allow investors to compare the investment's return against the performance of relevant benchmarks. If a security was held for less than 1 year, its results would have to be multiplied to determine an annualized rate of return. If the holding period was more than 1 year, the results would have to be divided to determine the annualized rate of return. Examples of total return, holding period return, and annualized return appear as follows:

EXAMPLE

SIA common stock appreciated 8% over an 18-month period and paid a 2% cash dividend over the 18 months.

The total return in the this case would be 10%, found by adding the 2% in cash flow to the 8% appreciation.

The holding period return would be 10% over the 18 months during which the investment was held.

The annualized return would be 6.66%, found by dividing the 10% return by 1.5 as 18 months equals 1.5 years.

10 / 1.5 = 6.66

MODERN PORTFOLIO THEORY

As money management developed over the last century, analysts began to shift their focus from the returns available from individual investments to the returns available from an entire portfolio. This approach became known as modern portfolio theory. Modern portfolio theory is based on the concept that investors are risk averse. Through diversification of investments and asset classes, portfolios can be constructed with higher levels of expected return for each unit of risk assumed. Asset classes are divided into three main categories: stocks, bonds, and cash and cash equivalents. Portfolio managers, through modern portfolio theory, can construct portfolios based on various allocations over the three main asset classes whose return will be the greatest given each unit of risk. This level of optimal performance is known as the efficient frontier. Any portfolio whose returns are expected to be less than optimal are said to be operating behind the efficient frontier. Optimal portfolio performance will be achieved by constructing a portfolio whose securities' prices move independently of one another or whose prices move inversely to one another. Allocating a client's assets over various asset classes to achieve a given investment objective is known as strategic asset allocation. As the investment results of the different asset classes vary over time, the assets may have to be rebalanced. Asset rebalancing can be divided into two categories: systematic rebalancing and active rebalancing. Systematic rebalancing is designed to keep the original asset allocation model in place. For example, if a client's portfolio is designed to be 70%, 25%, and 5% in stocks, bonds, and cash, respectively, as the percentages shift, the portfolio manager would rebalance the assets to maintain the original percentages. Systematic rebalancing can be done at regular intervals, such as quarterly, or whenever the asset allocation shifts by a certain percentage, such as by 5% or more. Active rebalancing assumes that a portfolio manager can effectively shift the asset allocation to take advantage of shifts in the performance of the various asset classes. If an investor has the same original portfolio allocation of 70/25/5 and the portfolio manager thinks that the bond market will outperform all other investments, the portfolio manager may use tactical rebalancing to rebalance the portfolio as 40/55/5. Alternatively, investors may elect to employ a buy-and-hold strategy and let the allocations go where they may. This buy-and-hold strategy would reduce transaction costs and tax consequences.

PREDICTING PORTFOLIO INCOME

Investors, especially in retirement, want to know how long their money will last given the fact that they need to draw down on their savings to support their lifestyle. On the exam you may be required to estimate the amount of time it will take to exhaust the principal in an investment account given a certain interest rate and a fixed withdrawal. Since students do not receive financial calculators, the number of years must be approximated by calculating the interest based on the declining balance and working the numbers out over time.

EXAMPLE

An investor who has saved $200,000 and is about to retire next year places the money in an account with a fixed interest rate of 4%. The investor wants to take out $20,000 at the beginning of each year starting at retire- ment. Given the principal, interest rate, and withdrawal rate, how long will the money last? The answer is approximately 14 years. At the end of 14 years the account will have slightly over $60 remaining.

Year	Withdrawal	Beginning Balance	Interest/Growth	Ending Balance
1	0	$200,000	$8,000	$208,000
2	$20,000	$188,000	$7,520	$195,520
3	$20,000	$175,250	$7,010	$182,260
4	$20,000	$162,260	$6,490	$168,750
5	$20,000	$148,750	$5,950	$154,700
6	$20,000	$134,700	$5,388	$140,088
7	$20,000	$120,088	$4,803	$124,891
8	$20,000	$104,891	$4,195	$109,086
9	$20,000	$89,086	$3,563	$92,649
10	$20,000	$72,649	$2,905	$75,554
11	$20,000	$55,554	$2,222	$57,776
12	$20,000	$37,776	$1,511	$39,287
13	$20,000	$19,287	$771	$20,058
14	$20,000	$58	$2.32	$60.32

PERPETUAL INCOME ACCOUNTS

An investor may wish to establish a fixed income for themselves, their spouse, a child, or a grandchild with the objective of providing the income forever. An account may be established to provide perpetual income or income in perpetuity based on some simple calculations. If the investor knows the desired income level to be provided and the interest rate the account will generate, the lump sum needed to fund the account may be calculated. To determine the lump sum needed, divide the annual income benefit by the annual interest rate.

EXAMPLE   If an investor wanted to generate a monthly income of $2,000 in perpetuity, the annual income benefit would be $24,000. If the investor was placing the money in an account with a fixed rate of 6%, the investor would have to place $400,000 in the account, found as follows:

$$\$24,000 \, / \, .06 = \$400,000$$

THE RULE OF 72

The Rule of 72 will tell an investor how many years it will take for the principal of an account to double in value. The rule of 72 assumes that the interest or earnings of the account are compounded. An investor who knows the interest rate that will be earned can simply divide 72 by that number to determine how long it will take the principal to double.

EXAMPLE   An investor who has $10,000 invested at an annual rate of 8% would like to know when the value of the account will reach $20,000. The answer is found by simply dividing 72 by the interest rate of 8%, as follows:

$$72 \, / \, 8 = 9 \text{ years}$$

The rule of 72 can also be used to calculate the rate of return on an investment given an initial value and a current value over time. If an investor placed $10,000 in an account 12 years ago and the value of that account has grown to $40,000, the value has doubled twice. The compound rate of return can be found by dividing 72 by the amount of time it took for the account to double once. Since the account doubled twice in 12 years, it therefore doubled once in 6 years.

$$72 \, / \, 6 = 12\%$$

FUNDAMENTAL ANALYSIS

Fundamental analysts examine the company's financial statements and financial ratios to ascertain the company's overall financial performance. The analyst will use the following to determine a value for the company's stock:

- The balance sheet
- The income statement
- Financial ratios

- Liquidity ratios
- Valuation ratios

THE BALANCE SHEET

The balance sheet will show an investor everything that the corporation owns, or its assets, and everything that the corporation owes, or its liabilities, at the time the balance sheet was prepared. A balance sheet is a snapshot of the company's financial health on the day it was created. The difference between the corporation's assets and its liabilities is its net worth. The corporation's net worth is the shareholders' equity. Remember that the shareholders own the corporation. The basic balance sheet equation is:

assets – liabilities = net worth

The balance sheet equation may also be presented as:

assets = liabilities + shareholder's equity

The two columns on the balance sheet contain the company's assets on the left and its liabilities and shareholders' equity on the right. The total dollar amount of both sides must be equal, or balance. The entries on a balance sheet look as follows:

Assets	Liabilities
Current assets	Current liabilities
Fixed assets	Long-term liabilities
Other assets	Equity/net worth
	Preferred stock par value
	Common stock par value
	Additional paid in surplus
	Treasury stock
	Retained earnings

The assets are listed in order of liquidity. Current assets include cash and assets that can be converted into cash within 12 months. Current assets include:

- Money market instruments.
- Marketable securities.

- Accounts receivable net of any delinquent accounts.
- Inventory, including work in progress.
- Prepaid expenses.

Fixed assets are assets that have a long, useful life and are used by the company in the operation of its business. Fixed assets include:

- Plant and equipment.
- Property and real estate.

Other assets are intangible assets that belong to the company. Other assets include:

- Goodwill.
- Trademarks.
- Patents.
- Contract rights.

The liabilities of the corporation are listed in the order in which they become due. Current liabilities are obligations that must be paid within 12 months. Current liabilities include:

- Wages payable, including salaries and commissions owed to employees.
- Accounts payable to vendors and suppliers.
- Current portion of long-term debt; that is, any portion of the company's long-term debt due within 12 months.
- Taxes due within 12 months.
- Short-term notes due within 12 months.

Long-term liabilities are debts that will become due after 12 months. Long-term liabilities include:

- Bonds.
- Mortgages.
- Notes.

TAKENOTE!

The corporation's debt, which comes due in 5 years or more, is known as funded debt.

Stockholders' equity is the net worth of the company. Stockholders' equity is broken up into the following categories:

Capital stock at par: The aggregate par for both common and preferred stock.

Additional paid in surplus: Any sum paid over par by investors when the shares were issued by the company.

Retained earnings: Profits that have been kept by the corporation, sometimes called earned surplus.

CAPITALIZATION

The term *capitalization* refers to the sources and makeup of the company's financial picture. The following are used to determine the company's capitalization:

- Long-term debt
- Equity accounts, including par value of common and preferred and paid in and earned surplus

A company that borrows a large portion of its capital though the issuance of bonds is said to be highly leveraged. Raising money through the sale of common stock is considered to be a more conservative method for a corporation to raise money because it does not require the corporation to pay the money back. When a company borrows funds, it is trying to use that borrowed capital to increase its return on equity.

A fundamental analyst may look at the balance sheet to determine the following financial information:

- Net worth
- Working capital

- Current ratio
- Quick assets
- Acid-test ratio/quick ratio
- Cash assets ratio
- Debt-to-equity ratio
- Common stock ratio
- Preferred stock ratio
- Bond ratio

Measure	Formula	Purpose
Book value per share	(assets – liabilities – intangibles – par value of preferred)/number of outstanding common shares	To determine the value of the company's common stock
Working capital	current assets – current liabilities	To determine the company's liquidity
Current ratio	current assets/current liabilities	The relationship between current assets and liabilities
Quick assets	current assets – inventory	To determine highly liquid assets
Acid-test ratio/quick ratio	quick assets/current liabilities	To determine the company's liquidity
Cash assets ratio	cash & equivalents/current Liabilities	The most stringent liquidity measure
Debt-to-equity ratio	total long-term debt/total shareholders' equity	To examine the company's capital structure
Common stock ratio	common shareholders' equity/total capitalization	To examine the company's capital structure
Preferred stock ratio	preferred stock/total capitalization	To examine the company's capital structure
Bond ratio	total long-term debt/total capitalization	To examine the company's capital structure

TAX STRUCTURE

Taxes may be progressive or regressive. A progressive tax levies a larger tax on higher income earners. Examples of progressive taxes are:

- Income taxes.
- Estate taxes.

Regressive taxes level the same tax rate on everyone, regardless of their income. As a result, a larger portion of the lower income earner's earnings will go toward the tax. Examples of regressive taxes are:

- Sales taxes.
- Property taxes.
- Gasoline taxes.
- Excise taxes.

INVESTMENT TAXATION

Investors must be aware of the impact that federal and state taxes will have on their investment results. A taxable event will occur in most cases when an investor:

- Sells a security at a profit.
- Sells a security at a loss.
- Receives interest or dividend income.

CALCULATING GAINS AND LOSSES

When investors sell their shares, in most cases they will have a capital gain or loss. In order to determine if there is a gain or loss, investors must first calculate their cost basis, or cost base. The cost base, in most cases, is equal to the price the investor paid for the shares, plus any commissions or fees paid in connection with the purchase. An investor's holding period begins the day after the purchase date and ends on the day of sale. Once an investor knows the cost base, calculating any gain or loss becomes easy. A capital gain is realized when the investor sells the shares at a price that is greater than the cost base.

EXAMPLE   An investor who purchased a stock at $10 per share 3 years ago and receives $14 per share when the shares are sold has a $4 capital gain. This is found by subtracting the cost base from the sales proceeds: $14 − $10 = $4. If the investor had 1,000 shares, the capital gain would be $4,000.

An investor's cost base is always returned to the investor tax free. A capital loss is realized when investors sell shares at a price that is less than their cost base. If the investor in the previous example were to have sold the shares at $8 instead of $14, the investor would have a $2 capital loss, or a total capital loss of $2,000 for the entire position. Again, this is found by subtracting the cost base from the sales proceeds: $8 − $10 = −$2.

Capital gains and losses are further classified as short- or long-term capital gains or losses. Any gain or loss on an investment held for less than 1 year is classified as a short-term gain or loss. A short-term capital gain will be taxed as ordinary income. Long-term capital gains on assets held for more than 1 year will be taxed at a maximum rate of 15% for ordinary income earners and at a a rate of 20% for high income earners.

COST BASE OF MULTIPLE PURCHASES

Investors who have been accumulating shares through multiple purchases must determine their cost base at the time of sale through one of the following methods:

- FIFO (first in, first out)
- Share identification
- Average cost

FIFO

If the investor does not identify which shares are being sold at the time of sale, the IRS will assume that the first shares that were purchased are the first shares that are sold under the FIFO method. In many cases, this will result in the largest capital gain and, as a result, the investor will have the largest tax liability under this method.

SHARE IDENTIFICATION

An investor may, at the time of the sale, specify which shares are being sold. By keeping a record of the purchase prices and the dates that the shares were purchased, the investor may elect to sell the shares that create the most favorable tax consequences.

AVERAGE COST

An investor may decide to sell shares based on the average cost. The average cost can be determined by using the following formula:

$$\text{average cost} = \frac{\text{total dollars invested}}{\text{total \# of shares purchased}}$$

Once an investor has elected to use the average cost method to calculate gains and losses, the method used to calculate future gains and losses may not be changed without IRS approval.

DEDUCTING CAPITAL LOSSES

An investor may use capital losses to offset capital gains dollar for dollar in the year in which they are realized. A net capital loss may be used to reduce the investor's taxable ordinary income by up to $3,000 in the year in which it is realized. Any net capital losses that exceed $3,000 may be carried forward into future years and may be deducted at a rate of $3,000 from ordinary income every year until the loss is used up. If the investor has a capital gain in subsequent years, the investor may use the entire amount of the net capital loss remaining to offset the gain up to the amount of the gain.

WASH SALES

Investors may not sell a security at a loss and shortly after repurchase the security, or a security that is substantially the same, to reestablish the position if they intend to claim the loss for tax purposes and deduct the loss from their ordinary income. This is known as a wash sale, and the IRS will disallow the loss. In order to claim the loss, the investor has to have held the securities for 30 days and must wait at least 30 days before repurchasing the same securities or securities that are substantially the same. The total number of days in the wash sale rule is 61.

Securities that are substantially the same include call options, rights, warrants, and convertibles.

TAXATION OF INTEREST INCOME

Interest earned by investors may or may not be subject to taxes. The following table illustrates the tax consequences of various interest payments received by investors:

Resident	Investment	Taxation
New Jersey	Corporate bond	All taxes
New Jersey	CMO	All taxes
New Jersey	GNMA	All taxes
New Jersey	T bond	Federal taxes only
New Jersey	New York muni bond	New Jersey taxes only
New Jersey	New Jersey muni bond	No taxes
New Jersey	Puerto Rico/Guam muni bond	No taxes

 TAKENOTE!

Investors may deduct margin interest only to the extent of their investment income. Investors may not deduct margin expenses from municipal bonds.

INHERITED AND GIFTED SECURITIES

If an investor dies and leaves securities to another person, that person's cost base for those securities is the fair market value of the securities on the day the decedent died. The cost base of the original investor does not transfer to the person who inherited the securities. Any capital gain on the sale of inherited securities will be considered long term. If during the course of an investor's life, the investor gives securities to another person, the recipient will have two cost bases. The recipient's cost base for determining a capital gain will be the giver's cost base; the recipient's cost base for determining a capital loss will be the giver's cost base or the fair market value of the securities on the day the gift was made, whichever is less.

DONATING SECURITIES TO CHARITY

An investor who donates securities to a charity will receive a tax deduction equal to the value of the securities. If the investor has an unrealized gain and has held the securities for more than 12 months, the investor will not owe any taxes on the appreciation. If the securities were held less than 12 months, the investor will be responsible for taxes on the appreciation. The recipient's cost base will be equal to the value of the securities on the day it received the gift.

TRUSTS

Trusts may be revocable or irrevocable. With a revocable trust, the individual who established the trust and contributes assets to the trust, known as the grantor or settlor, may, as the name suggests, revoke the trust and take the assets back. The income generated by a revocable trust is generally taxed as income to the grantor. If the trust is irrevocable, the grantor may not revoke the trust and take the assets back. With an irrevocable trust, the trust usually pays the taxes as its own entity or the beneficiaries of the trust are taxed on the income they receive. If the trust is established as a simple trust, all income generated by the trust must be distributed to the beneficiaries in the year the income is earned. If the trust is established as a complex trust the trust may retain some or all of the income earned and the trust will pay taxes on the income that is not distributed to the beneficiaries. The grantor of an irrevocable trust is generally not taxed on the income generated by the trust unless the assets in the trust are held for the benefit of the grantor, the grantor's spouse, or if the grantor has an interest in the income of the trust of greater than 5%. A trust may also be established to hold or to distribute assets after a person's death under the terms of their Will. Trusts that are established under the terms of a Will are known as Testamentary trusts. All assets placed into a Testamentary trust are subject to both estate taxes and probate.

TOTTEN TRUST

A Totten trust is effectively a pay-on-death account opened by a grantor or settler at a bank. This type of trust is incredibly easy to open. To establish a Totten trust, the grantor simply goes to the bank and fills out paperwork naming the beneficiaries to receive the funds in the event of the grantor's death. The grantor may easily change the beneficiaries by simply filling out new paperwork at the bank. The funds will pass directly to the beneficiaries and will not go through probate.

GIFT TAXES

When gifts are made to family members or others individuals, the donor does not receive any tax deduction. The donor's cost base will transfer to the recipient for tax purposes. Individuals may give gifts of up to $15,000 per person per year without incurring any tax liability. If a gift in excess of $15,000 is given to an individual, the donor owes the gift tax. Gifts to charity are always tax free, as is paying someone's educational expenses or medical expenses.

 TAKE**NOTE!**

A husband and wife may give up to $30,000 per year per person. The IRS considers half of the gift to be coming from each spouse. The annual gift limit has been indexed for inflation since 1999.

ESTATE TAXES

The value of an estate that may be left to heirs (nonspouse) without subjecting the beneficiaries to estate taxes has been constantly changing. There is an unlimited marital deduction or unified credit that allows surviving spouses to inherit the entire estate tax free. An individual's gross estate includes all of the assets owned at the time of death, including assets placed in any revocable trusts. Assets placed in an irrevocable trust are excluded from the individual's estate. Certain items will be added to the individual's gross estate, including:

- Assets transferred within 3 years of death.
- Annuity payouts payable to the estate or heirs.
- Life insurance.

The following are deducted from the value of the estate:

- Debts owed by the individual or estate
- Funeral expenses
- Charitable gifts made after death

Assets that are left to relatives more remote than children, for example, grandchildren, may be subject to a special tax if the amount exceeds $1,000,000. This is known as generation skipping.

WITHHOLDING TAX

All broker dealers are required to withhold 31% of all sales proceeds if the investor has not provided a Social Security number or a tax identification number. Similarly, 31% of all distributions from a mutual fund will also be withheld without a Social Security number or a tax identification number.

CORPORATE DIVIDEND EXCLUSION

Corporations that invest in the shares of other corporations will pay taxes only on 30% of the dividends it receives from those investments; 70% of the dividends are tax free to the corporation.

ALTERNATIVE MINIMUM TAX (AMT)

Certain items that receive beneficial tax treatment must be added back into the taxable income for some high-income earners. These items include:

- Interest on some industrial revenue bonds.
- Some stock options.
- Accelerated depreciation.
- Personal property tax on investments that do not generate income.
- Certain tax deductions passed through from direct participation programs.

TAXES ON FOREIGN SECURITIES

U.S. investors who own securities issued in a foreign country will owe U.S. taxes on any gains or income realized. In the event that the foreign country withholds taxes, the investor may file for a credit with the IRS at tax time. Most foreign governments that withhold taxes will withhold 15%.

Pretest

CUSTOMER RECOMMENDATIONS, PROFESSIONAL CONDUCT, AND TAXATION

1. Creating false activity in a security to attract a new purchaser is a fraudulent practice known as:

   a. trading ahead.

   b. painting the tape.

   c. active concealment.

   d. front running.

2. Which of the following could be subject to an investor's AMT?

   a. A limited partnership

   b. An open-end mutual fund

   c. A convertible preferred stock owned by a wealthy investor

   d. An industrial revenue bond

3. An investor has a conservative attitude towards investing and is seeking to invest $50,000 into an interest-bearing instrument that will provide current income and safety. Which of the following would be the most appropriate recommendation?

   a. Treasury bill

   b. Ginnie Mae pass-through certificate

   c. Treasury strip

   d. Bankers' acceptance

4. A client has phoned in concerned about what will happen to his investment in a waste management company if new EPA laws are enacted requiring disposal companies to reduce pollution. What type of risk is he concerned with?

   a. Call risk

   b. Environmental risk

   c. Investment risk

   d. Legislative risk

5. A customer has a large position in GJH, a thinly traded stock whose share price has remained flat for some time. The customer contacts the agent and wants to sell his entire position. The customer is most subject to which of the following types of risk?

   a. Liquidity risk

   b. Credit risk

   c. Conversion risk

   d. Execution risk

6. An investor who is most concerned with changes in interest rates would be least likely to purchase which of the following?

   a. Long-term warrants

   b. Long-term corporate bonds

   c. Long-term equity

   d. Call options

7. An investor is looking for a risk-free investment. Which of the following would be the best recommendation?

   a. Series HH government savings bonds

   b. 90-day T bill

   c. Convertible preferred stock

   d. Bankers' acceptances

8. Which of the following is true regarding the purchase of a stock just prior to the ex date?

    a. If the investor buys shares just prior to the ex date, he will have part of his investment money returned as the dividend.

    b. After the investor's money is returned, he will still be liable for taxes on the dividend amount.

    c. A registered representative may not use the pending dividend payment as the sole basis for recommending the stock purchase.

    d. All of the above.

9. A new investor is in the 15% tax bracket and is seeking some additional current income. Which of the following would you recommend?

    a. Growth fund

    b. Government bond fund

    c. Municipal bond fund

    d. Corporate bond fund

10. An investor gets advanced notice of a research report being issued and enters an order to purchase the security that is the subject of the research report. This is known as:

    a. front running.

    b. trading ahead.

    c. insider trading.

    d. advance trading.

11. An investor who is seeking some current income would most likely invest in which of the following?

    a. Commercial paper

    b. Treasury bond

    c. Income bond

    d. Bankers' acceptance

12. You have recommended a collateralized mortgage obligation (CMO) to a sophisticated investor. Which of the following would the investor be most concerned with?

    a. Default risk

    b. Foreclosure risk

    c. Interest rate risk

    d. Prepayment risk

13. Mr. and Mrs. Jones, a couple in their early forties, enjoy watching their son play baseball on the weekends. He is planning to go to college 11 years from September, and they are looking to start saving for their college cost expenses. What would you recommend?

    a. Educational IRA

    b. Growth fund

    c. Treasury STRIP

    d. Custodial account

14. Which of the following is NOT a violation?

    a. Recommending a security because of its future price appreciation

    b. Recommending a mutual fund based on a pending dividend to an investor seeking income

    c. Implying that FINRA has approved the firm

    d. Showing a client the past performance of a mutual fund for the last 3 years since its inception

15. An investor who may lose part or all of his investment is subject to:

    a. capital risk.

    b. market risk.

    c. reinvestment risk.

    d. credit risk.

16. A couple in their early thirties are seeking an investment for the $40,000 they have saved. They are planning on purchasing a new home in the next 2 years. Which of the following would be the best recommendation?

    a. Preferred stock

    b. Common stock and common stock funds

    c. Money market funds

    d. Municipal bonds

Variable Annuities, Retirement Plans, and Life Insurance

INTRODUCTION

This chapter will cover a variety of important topics relating to annuity products and retirement plans. Many investors choose to purchase annuities to help plan for retirement. Over the years a wide range of annuity products have been developed to meet different investment objectives and risk profiles. This section will cover both variable and fixed annuities products as well as a number of types of retirement plans.

A full understanding of annuities and retirement plans will be needed in order to successfully complete the exam.

ANNUITIES

An annuity is a contract between an individual and an insurance company. Once the contract is entered into, the individual becomes known as the annuitant. The three basic types of annuities are designed to meet different objectives. The three types of annuities are:

1. Fixed annuity
2. Variable annuity
3. Combination annuity

Although all three types allow the investor's money to grow tax-deferred, the type of investments made and how the money is invested varies according to the type of annuity.

FIXED ANNUITY

A fixed annuity offers investors a guaranteed rate of return regardless of whether the investment portfolio can produce the guaranteed rate. If the performance of the portfolio falls below the rate that was guaranteed, the insurance company owes investors the difference. Because the purchaser of a fixed annuity does not have any investment risk, a fixed annuity is considered an insurance product, not a security. Representatives who sell fixed annuity contracts must have an insurance license. Because fixed annuities offer investors a guaranteed return, the money invested by the insurance company will be used to purchase conservative investments such as mortgages and real estate, investments whose historical performance is predictable enough so that a guaranteed rate can be offered to investors. All of the money invested into fixed annuity contracts is held in the insurance company's general account. Because the rate that the insurance guarantees is not very high, the annuitant may suffer a loss of purchasing power due to inflation risk.

VARIABLE ANNUITY

An investor seeking to achieve a higher rate of return may elect to purchase a variable annuity. Variable annuities seek to obtain a higher rate of return by investing in stocks, bonds, or mutual fund shares. These securities traditionally offer higher rates of return than more conservative investments. A variable annuity does not offer the investor a guaranteed rate of return and the investor may lose all or part of their principal. Because the annuitant bears the investment risk associated with a variable annuity, the contract is considered both a security and an insurance product. Representatives who sell variable annuities must have both their securities license and their insurance license. The money and securities contained in a variable annuity contract are held in the insurance company's separate account. The separate account is named as such because the variable annuity's portfolio must be kept separate from the insurance company's general funds. The insurance company must have a net worth of $1,000,000 or the separate account must have a net worth of $1,000,000 in order for the separate account to begin operating. Once the separate account begins operations, it may invest in one of two ways.

1. Directly
2. Indirectly

DIRECT INVESTMENT

If the money in the separate account is invested directly into individual stocks and bonds, the separate account must have an investment adviser to actively manage the portfolio. If the money in the separate account is actively managed and invested directly, then the separate account is considered an open-end investment company under the Investment Company Act of 1940 and must register as such.

INDIRECT INVESTMENT

If the separate account uses the money in the portfolio to purchase mutual fund shares, it is investing in the equity and debt markets indirectly, and an investment adviser is not required to actively manage the portfolio. If the separate account purchases mutual fund shares directly, then the separate account is considered a unit investment trust (UIT) under the Investment Company Act of 1940 and must register as such.

COMBINATION ANNUITY

For investors who feel that a fixed annuity is too conservative and that a variable annuity is too risky, a combination annuity offers the annuitant features of both a fixed and variable contract. A combination annuity has a fixed portion that offers a guaranteed rate and a variable portion that tries to achieve a higher rate of return. Most combination annuities will allow the investor to move money between the fixed and variable portions of the contract. The money invested in the fixed portion of the contract is invested in the insurance company's general account and used to purchase conservative investments such as mortgages and real estate. The money invested in the variable side of the contract is invested in the insurance company's separate account and used to purchase stocks, bonds, or mutual fund shares. Representatives who sell combination annuities must have both their securities license and their insurance license.

BONUS ANNUITY

An insurance company that issues variable annuity contracts may offer incentives to investors who purchase their annuities. Such incentives are often referred to as bonuses. One type of bonus is known as premium enhancement. Under a premium enhancement option, the insurance company will make an additional contribution to the annuitant's account based on the premium paid by the annuitant. For example, if the annuitant is contributing $1,000 per month, the insurance company may offer to contribute an additional 5%, or $50 per month, to the account.

Another type of bonus offered to annuitants is the ability to withdraw the greater of the account's earnings or up to 15% of the total premiums paid without a penalty. Although the annuitant will not have to pay a penalty to the insurance company, there may be income taxes and a 10% penalty tax owed to the IRS. Bonus annuities often have higher expenses and longer surrender periods than other annuities, and these additional costs and surrender periods need to be clearly disclosed to prospective purchasers. In order to offer bonus annuities the bonus received must outweigh the increased costs and fees associated with the contract. Fixed annuity contracts may not offer bonuses to purchasers.

EQUITY-INDEXED ANNUITIES

Equity-indexed annuities offer investors a return that varies according to the performance of a set index, such as the S&P 500. Equity-indexed annuities will credit additional interest to the investor's account based on the contract's participation rate. If a contract sets the participation rate at 70% of the return for the S&P 500 index, and the index returns 5%, the investor's account will be credited for 70% of the return, or 3.5%. The participation rate may also be shown as a spread rate. If the contract had a spread rate of 3% and the index returned 10%, the investor's contract would be credited 7%. Equity indexed annuities may also set a floor rate and a cap rate for the contract. The floor rate is the minimum interest rate that will be credited to the investor's account. The floor rate may be zero or it may be a positive number depending on the specific contract. The contract's cap rate is the maximum rate that will be credited to the contract. If the return of the index exceeds the cap rate, the investor's account will only be credited up to the cap rate. If the S&P 500 index returns 11% and the cap rate set in the contract is 9%, the investor's account will only be credited 9%.

Feature	Fixed Annuity	Variable Annuity
Payment received	Guaranteed/fixed	May vary in amount
Return	Guaranteed minimum	No guarantee/return may vary in amount
Investment risk	Assumed by insurance company	Assumed by investor
Portfolio	Real estate, mortgages, and fixed-income securities	Stocks, bonds, or mutual fund shares
Portfolio held in	General account	Separate account
Inflation	Subject to inflation risk	Resistant to inflation
Representative registration	Insurance license	Insurance and securities license

RECOMMENDING VARIABLE ANNUITIES

There are a number of factors that will determine if a variable annuity is a suitable recommendation for an investor. Variable annuities are meant to be used as supplements to other retirement accounts such as IRAs and corporate retirement plans. Variable annuities should not be recommended to investors who are trying to save for a large purchase or expense such as college tuition or a second home. Variable annuity products are more appropriate for an investor who is looking to create an income stream. A deferred annuity contract would be appropriate for someone seeking retirement income at some point in the future. An immediate annuity contract would be more appropriate for someone seeking to generate current income and who is perhaps already retired. Many annuity contracts have complex features and cost structures that may be difficult for both the representative and investor to understand. The benefits of the contract should outweigh the additional costs of the contract to ensure the contract is suitable for the investor. Illustrations regarding performance of the contract may use a maximum growth rate of 12% and all annuity applications must be approved or denied by a principal based on suitability within 7 business days of receipt. A Series 24 or Series 26 principal may approve or deny a variable annuity application presented by either a Series 6 or Series 7 registered representative. 1035 exchanges allow investors to move from one annuity contract to another without incurring tax consequences. 1035 exchanges can be a red flag and a cause for concern over abusive sales practices. Because most annuity contracts have surrender charges that may be substantial, 1035 exchanges may result in the investor being worse off and may constitute churning. FINRA is concerned about firms who employ compensation structures for representatives that may incentivize the sale of annuities over other investment products with lower costs and may be more appropriate for investors. Firms should guard against incentivizing agents to sell annuity products over other investments. Members should ensure proper product training for registered representatives and principals for annuities and they must have adequate supervision to monitor sales practices and to test their product knowledge. The focus should be on detecting problematic and abusive sales practices. L share annuity contracts are designed with shorter surrender periods, but have higher costs to investors. The sale of L share annuity contracts can be a red flag for compliance personnel and may constitute abusive sales practices.

ANNUITY PURCHASE OPTIONS

An investor may purchase an annuity contract in one of three ways:

1. Single-payment deferred annuity
2. Single-payment immediate annuity
3. Periodic-payment deferred annuity

SINGLE-PAYMENT DEFERRED ANNUITY

With a single-payment deferred annuity, the investor funds the contract completely with one payment and defers receiving payments from the contract until some point in the future, usually after retirement. Money being invested in a single-payment deferred annuity is used to purchase accumulation units. The number and value of the accumulation units varies as the distributions are reinvested and the value of the separate account's portfolio changes.

SINGLE-PAYMENT IMMEDIATE ANNUITY

With a single-payment immediate annuity, the investor funds the contract completely with one payment and begins receiving payments from the contract immediately, normally within 60 days. The money that is invested in a single-payment immediate annuity is used to purchase annuity units. The number of annuity units remains fixed and the value changes as the value of the securities in the separate account's portfolio fluctuates.

PERIODIC-PAYMENT DEFERRED ANNUITY

With a periodic-payment annuity, the investor purchases the annuity by making regularly scheduled payments into the contract. This is known as the accumulation stage. During the accumulation stage, the terms are flexible and, if the investor misses a payment, there is no penalty. The money invested in a periodic-payment deferred annuity is used to purchase accumulation units. The number and value of the accumulation units fluctuate with the securities in the separate portfolio.

ACCUMULATION UNITS

An accumulation unit represents the investor's proportionate ownership in the separate account's portfolio during the accumulation or deferred stage of the contract. The value of the accumulation unit will fluctuate as the value of the securities in the separate account's portfolio changes. As the investor makes contributions to the account or as distributions are reinvested, the number of accumulation units will vary. An investor will only own accumulation units during the accumulation stage, when money is being paid into the contract or when receipt of payments is being deferred by the investor, such as with a single-payment deferred annuity.

 TAKENOTE!

Most annuities allow the investor to designate a beneficiary who will receive the greater of the value of the account or the total premiums paid if the investor dies during the accumulation stage.

ANNUITY UNITS

When an investor changes from the pay-in or deferred stage of the contract to the payout phase, the investor is said to have annuitized the contract. At this point, the investor trades in his or her accumulation units for annuity units. The number of annuity units is fixed and represents the investor's proportional ownership of the separate accounts portfolio during the payout phase. The number of annuity units that the investor receives when the contract is annuitized is based on the payout option selected, the annuitant's age and sex, the value of the account, and the assumed interest rate.

ANNUITY PAYOUT OPTIONS

Annuity contracts are not subject to the contribution limits or the required minimum distributions of qualified plans. An investor in an annuity has the choice of taking a lump sum distribution or receiving scheduled payments from the contract. If the investor decides to annuitize the contract and receive scheduled payments, once the payout option is selected it may not be changed. The following is a list of typical payout options in order from the largest monthly payment to the smallest:

- Life only/straight life
- Life with period certain
- Joint with last survivor

LIFE ONLY/STRAIGHT LIFE

This payout option will give the annuitant the largest periodic payment from the contract, and the investor will receive payments from the contract for the rest of his or her life. When the investor dies, however, no additional benefits are paid to the investor's estate. If an investor has accumulated a large sum of money in the contract and dies unexpectedly shortly after annuitizing the contract, the insurance company keeps the money in its account.

LIFE WITH PERIOD CERTAIN

A life with period certain payout option will pay out from the contract to the investor or to the investor's estate for the life of the annuitant or for the period certain, whichever is longer. If an investor selects a 10-year period certain when the contract is annuitized and the investor lives for 20 years more, payments will cease upon the annuitant's death. However, if the same investor died only 2 years after annuitizing the contract, payments would go to the investor's estate for another 8 years.

JOINT WITH LAST SURVIVOR

When an investor selects a joint with last survivor option, the annuity is jointly owned by more than one party and payments will continue until the last owner of the contract dies. For example, if a husband and wife are receiving payments from an annuity under a joint with last survivor option and the husband dies, payments will continue to the wife for the rest of her life. The payments received by the wife could be at the same rate as when the husband was alive or at a reduced rate, depending on the contract. The monthly payments will initially be based on the life expectancy of the youngest annuitant.

FACTORS AFFECTING THE SIZE OF THE ANNUITY PAYMENT

All of the following determine the size of the annuity payment:

- Account value
- Payout option selected
- Age
- Sex
- Account performance vs. the assumed interest rate (AIR)

THE ASSUMED INTEREST RATE (AIR)

When an investor annuitizes a contract, the accumulation units are traded for annuity units. Once the contract has been annuitized, the insurance company sets a benchmark for the separate account's performance, known as the assumed interest rate (AIR). The AIR is not a guaranteed rate of return; it is only used to adjust the value of the annuity units up or down based on the actual performance of the separate account. The AIR is an earnings target that the insurance company sets for the separate account. The separate account must meet this earnings target in order to keep the annuitant's payments at the same level. As the value of the annuity unit changes, so does the amount of the payment that is received by the investor. If the separate account outperforms the AIR, an investor would expect his or her payments to increase. If the separate account's performance falls below the AIR, the investor can expect his or her payments to decrease. The separate account's performance is always measured against the AIR, never against the previous month's performance. An investor's annuity payment is based on the number of annuity units owned by the investor multiplied by the value of the annuity unit. When the performance of the separate account equals the AIR, the value of the annuity unit will remain unchanged, and so will the investor's payment. Selecting an AIR that is realistic is important. If the AIR is too high and the separate account's return cannot equal the assumed rate, the value of the annuity unit will continue to fall, and so will the investor's payment. The opposite is true if the AIR is set too low. As the separate account outperforms the AIR, the value of the annuity unit will continue to rise, and so will the investor's payment. The AIR is only relevant during the payout phase of the contract when the investor is receiving payments and owns annuity units. The AIR does not concern itself with accumulation units during the accumulation stage or when benefits are being deferred.

TAXATION

Contributions made to an annuity are made with after-tax dollars. The money the investor deposits becomes the investor's cost basis and is allowed to grow tax-deferred. When the investor withdraws money from the contract, only the growth is taxed. The investor's cost base is returned tax-free. All money in excess of the investor's cost base is taxed as ordinary income. Both lump sum and random withdrawals are done on a last in, first out (LIFO) basis. The growth portion of the contract is always considered to be the last money that was deposited and is taxed at the ordinary income rate of the annuitant. If the annuitant is under the age of 59-1/2 and takes a lump sum or random withdrawal, the withdrawal will be subject to a 10% penalty tax, as well as ordinary income taxes. An investor who needs to access the money in a variable annuity contract may be allowed to borrow from the contract, and so long as interest is charged on the loan and the loan is repaid by the investor, the investor will not be subject to taxes.

SALES CHARGES

There is no maximum sales charge for an annuity contract. The sales charge that is assessed must be reasonable in relation to the total payments over the life of the contract. Most annuity contracts have back-end sales charges or surrender charges similar to a contingent deferred sales charge.

VARIABLE ANNUITY VS. MUTUAL FUND

Feature	Variable Annuity	Mutual Fund
Maximum sales charge	No maximum	8.5%
Investment adviser	Yes	Yes
Custodian bank	Yes	Yes
Transfer agent	Yes	Yes
Voting	Yes	Yes
Management	Board of managers	Board of directors
Taxation of growth and reinvestments	Tax-deferred	Currently taxed
Lifetime income	Yes	No
Costs and fees	Higher	Lower

RETIREMENT PLANS

For most people, saving for retirement has become an important investment objective for at least part of their portfolio. Investors may participate in retirement plans that have been established by their employers, as well as those they have established for themselves. Both corporate and individual plans may be qualified or nonqualified, and it is important for an investor to understand the difference before deciding to participate. The following is a comparison of the key features of both types of plans:

Feature	Qualified	Nonqualified
Contributions	Pre-tax	After-tax
Growth	Tax-deferred	Tax-deferred
Participation must be allowed	For everyone	The corporation may choose who gets to participate
IRS approval	Required	Not required
Withdrawals	100% taxed as ordinary income	Growth in excess of cost base is taxed as ordinary income

INDIVIDUAL PLANS

Individuals may set up a retirement plan that is qualified and allows contributions to the plan to be made with pre-tax dollars. Individuals may also purchase investment products, such as annuities, that allow their money to grow tax-deferred. The money used to purchase an annuity has already been taxed, making an annuity a nonqualified product.

INDIVIDUAL RETIREMENT ACCOUNTS (IRAs)

All individuals with earned income may establish an Individual Retirement Account (IRA). Contributions to traditional IRAs may or may not be tax deductible depending on the individual's level of adjusted gross income and whether the individual is eligible to participate in an employer-sponsored plan. Individuals who do not qualify to participate in an employer-sponsored plan may deduct their IRA contributions regardless of their income level. The level of adjusted gross income that allows an investor to deduct IRA contributions has been increasing since 1998. These tax law changes occur too frequently to make them a practical test question. Our review of IRAs will focus on the four main types:

1. Traditional
2. Roth
3. SEP
4. Educational

TRADITIONAL IRA

Currently, a traditional IRA allows an individual to contribute a maximum of 100% of earned income, or $6,000 per year or up to $12,000 per couple. If only one spouse works, the working spouse may contribute $6,000 to an IRA for him- or herself and $6,000 to a separate IRA for his or her spouse under the nonworking spousal option. Investors over age 50 may contribute up to $7,000 of earned income to an IRA. Regardless of whether the IRA contribution was made with pre- or after-tax dollars, the money is allowed to grow tax-deferred. All withdrawals from an IRA are taxed as ordinary income regardless of how the growth was generated in the account. Withdrawals from an IRA prior to age 59-1/2 are subject to a 10% penalty tax as well as ordinary income taxes. The 10% penalty will be waived for first-time homebuyers; for educational expenses; for the taxpayer's children, grandchildren, or spouse; if the account holder becomes disabled; or if the payments are part of a series of substantially equal payments. Withdrawals from an IRA must begin by April 1st of the year following the year in which the taxpayer reaches 70-1/2. (It is important to note that the Secure Act of 2020 increased the age from 70-1/2 to 72.) If an individual fails to make withdrawals that are sufficient in size and frequency, the individual will be subject to a 50% penalty on the insufficient amount. An individual who makes a contribution to an IRA that exceeds 100% of earned income or the annual limit, whichever is less, will be subject to a penalty of 6% per year on the excess amount for as long as the excess contribution remains in the account.

ROTH IRA

A Roth IRA is a nonqualified account. All deposits that are made to a Roth IRA are made with after-tax dollars. The same contribution limits apply for a Roth IRA. An individual may contribute the lesser of 100% of earned income, to a maximum of $6,000 per person or $12,000 per couple. Any contribution made to a Roth IRA reduces the amount that may be deposited in a traditional IRA and vice versa. All contributions deposited in a Roth IRA are allowed to grow tax-deferred, and all of the growth may be taken out of the account tax-free, provided that the individual has reached age 59-1/2 and the assets have been in the account for at least 5 years. A 10% penalty tax will be charged on any withdrawal of earnings prior to age 59-1/2 unless the owner is purchasing a home, has become disabled, or has died. There are no requirements for an individual to take distributions from a Roth IRA by a certain age.

TAKENOTE!

Individuals and couples who are eligible to open a Roth IRA may convert their traditional IRA to a Roth IRA. The investor will have to pay income taxes on the amount converted but will not be subject to the 10% penalty.

SIMPLIFIED EMPLOYEE PENSION IRA (SEP IRA)

A simplified employee pension (SEP) IRA is used by small corporations and self-employed individuals to plan for retirement. A SEP IRA is attractive to small employers because it allows them to set up a retirement plan for their employees rather quickly and inexpensively. The contribution limit for a SEP IRA far exceeds that of traditional IRAs. The contribution limit is the lesser of 25% of the employee's compensation or $57,000 per year. Should the employee wish to make their annual IRA contribution to their SEP IRA, they may do so, or they may make their standard contribution to a traditional or Roth IRA.

PARTICIPATION

All eligible employees must open an IRA to receive the employer's contribution to the SEP. If the employee does not open an IRA account, the employer must open one for them. The employee must be at least 21 years old, and have worked during three of the last 5 years for the employer, and have earned at least $550. All eligible employees must participate as well as the employer.

EMPLOYER CONTRIBUTIONS

The employer may contribute between 0 and 25% of the employee's total compensation to a maximum of $57,000. Contributions to all SEP IRAs, including the employer's SEP IRA, must be made at the same rate. An employee who is over 70-1/2 must also participate and receive a contribution. All eligible employees are immediately vested in the employer's contributions to the plan.

SEP IRA TAXATION

Employer's contributions to a SEP IRA are immediately tax-deductible by the employer. Contributions are not taxed at the employee's rate until the employee withdraws the funds. Employees may begin to withdraw money from the plan at age 59-1/2. All withdrawals are taxed as ordinary income and withdrawals prior to age 59-1/2 are subject to a 10% penalty tax. The employer may contribute up to 25% of the employee's income, up to $57,000.

EDUCATIONAL IRA

An educational IRA allows individuals to contribute up to $2,000 in after-tax dollars to an educational IRA for each student who is under 18 years of age. The money is allowed to grow tax-deferred and the growth may be withdrawn tax-free as long as the money is used for educational purposes. If all of the funds have not been used for educational purposes by the time the student reaches 30 years of age, the account must be rolled over to another family member who is under 30 years of age or distributed to the original student and subject to a 10% penalty tax as well as ordinary income taxes.

529 PLANS

Qualified tuition plans, more frequently referred to as 529 plans, may be set up either as a prepaid tuition plan or as a college savings plan. With the prepaid tuition plan, the plan locks in a current tuition rate at a specific school. The prepaid tuition plan can be set up as an installment plan or one where the contributor funds the plan with a lump sum deposit. Many states will guarantee the plans but may require either the contributor or the beneficiary to be a state resident. The plan covers only tuition and mandatory fees. A room and board option is available for some plans. A college cost-savings account may be opened by any adult and the donor does not have to be related to the child. The assets in the college savings plan can be used to cover all costs of qualified higher education including tuition, room and board, books, computers, and mandatory fees. These plans generally have no age limit when assets must be used. College savings accounts are not guaranteed by the state and the value of the account may decline in value depending on the investment results of the account. College savings accounts are not state specific and do not lock in a tuition rate. Contributions to a 529 plan are made with after-tax dollars and are allowed to grow tax deferred. The assets in the account remain under the control of the donor, even after the student reaches the age of maturity. The funds may be used to meet the student's educational needs and the growth may be withdrawn free of federal taxes. Most states also allow the assets to be withdrawn tax free. Any funds used for non-qualified education expenses will be subject to income tax and a 10% penalty tax. If funds remain or if the student does not attend or complete qualified higher education, the funds may be rolled over to another family member within 60 days without incurring taxes and penalties. There are no income limits for the donors and contribution limits vary from state to state. 529 plans have an impact on a student's ability to obtain need-based financial aid. However, because the 529 plans are treated as parental assets and not as assets of the student, the plans are assessed at the expected family contribution (EFC) rate of 5.64%. This will have a significantly lower impact than plans and assets that are considered to be assets of the student. Student assets will be assessed at a 20% contribution rate.

 TAKE**NOTE!**

For your exam, it is important to note that assets in a 529 savings plan may also be used to meet tuition payments for private K–12 schools.

LOCAL GOVERNMENT INVESTMENT POOLS (LGIPs)

Local government investment pools (LGIPs) allow states and local governments to manage their cash reserves and to receive money market rates on the funds. LGIPs may also be created to invest the proceeds of a bond offering if the proceeds of the offering are intended to be used to call in an existing bond issue. If the LGIP was created to prerefund an existing issue, additional restrictions will apply as to the type of investments that may be purchased by the pool. LGIPs that are created to manage cash reserves must only invest in securities on the state's legal or approved list. The legal list usually includes investments such as:

- Commercial paper rated in the two highest categories.
- U.S. government and agency debt.
- Bankers' acceptances.
- Repurchase agreement.
- Municipal debt issues within the state.
- Investment company securities.

- Certificates of deposit.
- Savings accounts.

Each state has an investment advisory board that works with the state treasury office to administer the pools. The main objective of these pools is safety of principal, with liquidity and interest income as secondary objectives. The pools require that the following be detailed in writing:

- Delegation of authority to make investments
- Annual investment activity reports
- Statement of safekeeping of securities

Municipal fund securities are not considered to be investment companies and are not required to register under the Investment Company Act of 1940. Additionally, prepaid tuition plans are not considered to be municipal fund securities. LGIP employees who market the plans directly to investors are exempt from MSRB rules; however, if the LGIP is marketed to investors by employees of a broker dealer, the broker dealer and all of its employees are subject to MSRB rules.

IRA CONTRIBUTIONS

Contributions to IRAs must be made by April 15th of the following calendar year, regardless of whether or not an extension has been filed by the taxpayer. Contributions may be made between January 1 and April 15 for the previous year, the current year, or both. All IRA contributions must be made in cash.

IRA ACCOUNTS

All IRA accounts are held in the name of the custodian for the benefit of the account holder. Traditional custodians include banks, broker dealers, and mutual fund companies.

IRA INVESTMENTS

Individuals who establish IRAs have a wide variety of investments to choose from when deciding how to invest the funds. Investors should always choose investments that fit their investment objectives. The following is a comparison of allowable and non-allowable investments:

Allowable	Non-Allowable
Stocks	Margin accounts
Bonds	Short sales
Mutual funds/ETFs/ETNs	Tangibles/collectibles/art
Annuities	Speculative option trading
UITs	Term life insurance
Limited partnerships	Rare coins
U.S. minted coins	Real estate

IT IS UNWISE TO PUT A MUNICIPAL BOND IN AN IRA

Municipal bonds or municipal bond funds should never be placed in an IRA because the advantage of those investments is that the interest income is free from federal taxes. Because their interest is free from federal taxes, the interest rate that is offered will be less than the rates offered by other alternatives. The advantage of an IRA is that money is allowed to grow tax-deferred; therefore, an individual would be better off with a higher yielding taxable bond of the same quality.

ROLLOVER VS. TRANSFER

An individual may want or need to move their IRA from one custodian to another. There are two ways this can be accomplished. An individual may rollover their IRA or they may transfer their IRA.

ROLLOVER

With an IRA rollover, the individual may take possession of the funds for a maximum of 60 calendar days prior to depositing the funds into another qualified account. An investor may only rollover their IRA once every 12 months. The investor has 60 days from the date of the distribution to deposit 100% of the funds into another qualified account or they must pay ordinary income taxes on the distribution and a 10% penalty tax if the investor is under 59-1/2.

TRANSFER

An investor may transfer their IRA directly from one custodian to another by simply signing an account transfer form. The investor never takes possession of the assets in the account and the investor may directly transfer their IRA as often as they like.

DEATH OF AN IRA OWNER

Should the owner of an IRA die, the account will become the property of the beneficiary named on the account by the owner. If the beneficiary is the spouse of the owner, special rules apply. The spouse may elect to roll over the IRA into his or her own IRA or retirement plan, such as a 401K. If this is elected, there will be no tax presently due on the money. However, the spouse is still subject to the required minimum distribution rule at age 70-1/2. The surviving spouse may also elect to cash in the IRA. The distributions will be subject to income tax but will not be subject to the 10% penalty tax. If the beneficiary is not the spouse, the money may not be rolled in to another IRA or retirement account. If the account owner died prior to age 70-1/2, when the required distributions need to be made, the money must all be distributed prior to the end of the fifth year, or the money may be distributed in equal installments based upon the beneficiary's life expectancy. If the account owner has died after the start of the required minimum distributions, the payment schedule of distributions will now be based on the life expectancy of the beneficiary.

KEOGH PLANS (HR-10)

A Keogh plan is a qualified retirement plan set up by self-employed individuals, sole proprietors, and unincorporated businesses. If the business is set up as a corporation, a Keogh may not be used.

CONTRIBUTIONS

Keoghs may only be funded with earned income during a period when the business shows a gross profit. If the business realizes a loss, no Keogh contributions are allowed. A self-employed person may contribute the lesser of 25% of their post-contribution income or $57,000. If the business has eligible employees, the employer must make a contribution for the employees at the same rate as their own contribution. Employee contributions are based on the employee's gross income and are limited to $57,000 per year. All money placed in a Keogh plan is allowed to grow tax-deferred and is taxed as ordinary income when distributions are made to retiring employees and plan participants. From time to time a self-employed person may make a non-qualified contribution to their Keogh plan; however, the total of the qualified and non-qualified contributions may not exceed the maximum contribution limit. Any excess contribution may be subject to a 10% penalty tax.

An eligible employee is defined as one who:

- Works full time (at least 1,000 hours per year).
- Is at least 21 years old.
- Has worked at least 1 year for the employer.

Employees who participate in a Keogh plan must be vested after 5 years. Withdrawals from a Keogh may begin when the participant reaches 59-1/2. Any premature withdrawals are subject to a 10% penalty tax. A Keogh, like an IRA, may be rolled over every 12 months. In the event of a participant's death, the assets will go to the individual's beneficiaries.

TAX-SHELTERED ANNUITIES/TAX-DEFERRED ACCOUNT

Tax-sheltered annuities (TSAs) and tax-deferred accounts (TDAs) are established as retirement plans for employees of nonprofit and public organizations such as:

- Public educational institutions (403B).
- Nonprofit organizations (IRC 501C3).
- Religious organizations.
- Nonprofit hospitals.

TSAs/TDAs are qualified plans and contributions are made with pre-tax dollars. The money in the plan is allowed to grow tax-deferred until it is withdrawn. TSAs/TDAs offer a variety of investment vehicles for participants to choose from, such as:

- Stocks.
- Bonds.
- Mutual funds.
- CDs.

PUBLIC EDUCATIONAL INSTITUTIONS (403B)

In order for a school to be considered a public school and qualify to establish a TSA/TDA for their employees, the school must be supported by the state, the local government, or a state agency. State supported schools are:

- Elementary schools.
- High schools.
- State colleges and universities.
- Medical schools.

Any individual who works for a public school, regardless of their position, may participate in the school's TSA or TDA.

NONPROFIT ORGANIZATIONS/TAX-EXEMPT ORGANIZATIONS (501C3)

Organizations that qualify under the Internal Revenue Code 501C3 as a nonprofit or tax-exempt entity may set up a TSA or TDA for their employees. Examples of nonprofit organizations are:

- Private hospitals.
- Charitable organizations.
- Trade schools.
- Private colleges.
- Parochial schools.
- Museums.
- Scientific foundations.
- Zoos.

All employees of organizations that qualify under the Internal Revenue Code 501C3 or 403B are eligible to participate as long as they are at least 21 years old and have worked full time for at least 1 year.

CONTRIBUTIONS

In order to participate in a TSA or TDA, employees must enter into a contract with their employer agreeing to make elective deferrals into the plan.

The salary reduction agreement will state the amount and frequency of the elective deferral to be contributed to the TSA. The agreement is binding on both parties and covers only 1 year of contributions. Each year a new salary reduction agreement must be signed to set forth the contributions for the new year. The employee's elective deferral is limited to a maximum of $19,500 per year. Employer contributions are limited to the lesser of 25% of the employee's earnings or $57,000.

TAX TREATMENT OF DISTRIBUTIONS

All distributions for TSAs/TDAs are taxed as ordinary income in the year in which the distribution is made. Distributions from a TSA/TDA prior to age 59-1/2 are subject to a 10% penalty tax as well as ordinary income taxes. Distributions from a TSA/TDA must begin by age 70-1/2 or be subject to an excess accumulation tax.

CORPORATE PLANS

A corporate retirement plan can be qualified or non-qualified. We will first review the non-qualified plans.

NON-QUALIFIED CORPORATE RETIREMENT PLANS

Non-qualified corporate plans are funded with after-tax dollars and the money is allowed to grow tax-deferred. If the corporation makes a contribution to the plan, they may not deduct the contribution from their corporate earnings until the plan participant receives the money. Distributions from a non-qualified plan that exceed the investor's cost base are taxed as ordinary income. All non-qualified plans must be in writing and the employer may discriminate as to who may participate.

PAYROLL DEDUCTIONS

The employee may set up a payroll deduction plan by having the employer make systematic deductions from the employee's paycheck. The money, which has been deducted from the employee's check, may be invested in a variety of ways. Mutual funds, annuities, and savings bonds are all usually available for the employee to choose from. Contributions to a payroll deduction plan are made with after-tax dollars.

DEFERRED COMPENSATION PLANS

A deferred compensation plan is a contract between an employee and an employer. Under the contract, the employee agrees to defer the receipt of money owed to the employee from the employer until after the employee retires. After retirement, the employee will traditionally be in a lower tax bracket and will be able to keep a larger percentage of the money. Deferred compensation plans are traditionally unfunded and, if the corporation goes out of business, the employee becomes a creditor of the corporation and may lose all of the money due under the contract. The employee may only claim the assets if they retire or become disabled; or, in the case of death, their beneficiaries may claim the money owed. Money due under a deferred compensation plan is paid out of the corporation's working funds when the employee or their estate claims the assets. Should the employee leave the corporation and go to work for a competing company, they may lose the money owed under a non-compete clause. Money owed to the employee under a deferred compensation agreement is traditionally not invested for the benefit of the employee, and as a result, does not increase in value over time. The only product that traditionally is placed in a deferred compensation plan is a term life policy. In the case of the employee's death, the term life policy will pay the employee's estate the money owed under the contract.

QUALIFIED PLANS

All qualified corporate plans must be in writing and set up as a trust. A trustee or plan administrator will be appointed for the benefit of all plan holders.

TYPES OF PLANS

There are two main types of qualified corporate plans: a defined benefit plan and a defined contribution plan.

DEFINED BENEFIT PLAN

A defined benefit plan is designed to offer the participant a retirement benefit that is known or "defined." Most defined benefit plans are set up to provide employees with a fixed percentage of their salary during their retirement such as 74% of their average earnings during their five highest paid years. Other defined benefit plans are structured to pay participants a fixed sum of money for life. Defined benefit plans require the services of an actuary to determine the employer's contribution to the plan based on the participant's life expectancy and benefits promised.

DEFINED CONTRIBUTION PLAN

With a defined contribution plan, only the amount of money that is deposited into the account is known, such as 6% of the employee's salary. Both the employee and the employer may contribute a percentage of the employee's earnings into the plan. The money is allowed to grow tax-deferred until the participant withdraws it at retirement. The ultimate benefit under a defined contribution plan is the result of the contributions into the plan as well as the investment results of the plan. The employee's maximum contribution to a defined contribution plan is $19,500 per year. Some types of defined contribution plans are:

- 401K
- Money purchase plan
- Profit sharing
- Thrift plans
- Stock bonus plans

All withdrawals from pension plans are taxed as ordinary income in the year in which the distribution is made.

EMPLOYEE STOCK OWNERSHIP PLANS/ESOP

ESOP plans are established by employers to provide a way for the employees to benefit from ownership of the company's stock. The plan allows the employer to take a tax deduction based on the market value of the stock.

PROFIT SHARING PLANS

Profit sharing plans let the employer reward the employees by letting them "share" in a percentage of the corporation's profits. Profit sharing plans are based on a preset formula and the money may be paid directly to the employee or placed in a retirement account. In order for a profit sharing plan to be qualified, the corporation must have substantial and recurring profits. The maximum contribution to a profit sharing plan is the lesser of 25% of the employee's compensation or $57,000.

401K THRIFT PLANS

401K and thrift plans allow the employee to contribute a fixed percentage of their salary to their retirement account, and have the employer match some or all of their contributions. The employer's contributions provide a current tax deduction to the employer and the employee is not taxed on the contributions until they are withdrawn.

ROLLING OVER A PENSION PLAN

An employee who leaves an employer may move their pension plan to another company's plan or to another qualified account. This may be accomplished by a direct transfer or by rolling over the plan. With a direct transfer, the assets in the plan go directly to another plan administrator and the employee never has physical possession of the assets. When the employee rolls over their pension plan, they take physical possession of the assets. The plan administrator is required to withhold 20% of the total amount to be distributed and the employee has 60 calendar days to deposit 100% of the assets into another qualified plan. The employee must file with the federal government at tax time to receive a return of the 20% of the assets that were withheld by the plan administrator.

EMPLOYEE RETIREMENT INCOME SECURITY ACT OF 1974 (ERISA)

This establishes legal and operational guidelines for private pension and employee benefit plans. Not all decisions directly involving a plan, even when made by a fiduciary, are subject to ERISA's fiduciary rules. These decisions are business judgment type decisions and are commonly called "settlor" functions. This caveat is sometimes referred to as the "business decision" exception to ERISA's fiduciary rules. Under this concept, even though the employer is the plan sponsor and administrator, it will not be considered as acting in a fiduciary capacity when creating, amending, or terminating a plan. Among the decisions that would be considered settlor functions are:

- Choosing the type of plan, or options in the plan.
- Amending a plan, including changing or eliminating plan options.

- Requiring employee contributions or changing the level of employee contributions.
- Terminating a plan, or part of a plan, including terminating or amending as part of a bankruptcy process.

ERISA also regulates all of the following:

- Pension plan participation
- Funding
- Vesting
- Communication
- Beneficiaries

PLAN PARTICIPATION

All plans governed by ERISA may not discriminate among who may participate in the plan. All employees must be allowed to participate if:

- They are at least 21 years old.
- They have worked at least 1 year full time (1,000 hours).

INVESTMENT POLICY STATEMENT

The investment policy statement governs the way the assets of the plan are invested. It sets guidelines for diversification and acceptable levels of risk. The investment adviser to the plan must design a portfolio in line with the plan's investment policy statement. Advisers who do not adhere to the investment policy statement may be held liable to plan participants for any losses.

FUNDING

Plan funding requirements set forth guidelines on how the money is deposited into the plan and how the employer and employee may contribute to the plan.

VESTING

Vesting refers to the process of how the employer's contribution becomes the property of the employee. An employer may be as generous as they like, but may not be more restrictive than either one of the following vesting schedules:

- Three- to 6-year gradual vesting schedule
- Three-year cliff: the employee is not vested at all until 3 years, when they become 100% vested

COMMUNICATION

All corporate plans must be in writing at inception and the employee must be given annual updates.

BENEFICIARIES

All plan participants must be allowed to select a beneficiary who may claim the assets in case of the plan participant's death.

ERISA 404C SAFE HARBOR

All individuals and entities acting in a fiduciary capacity must act solely in the interest of the plan participants. Investment advisers, trustees, and all individuals who exercise discretion over the plan, including those who select the administrative personnel or committee, are considered to be fiduciaries. ERISA Rule 404C provides an exemption from liability or a "safe harbor" for plan fiduciaries and protects them from liabilities that may arise from investment losses that result from the participant's own actions. This safe harbor is available so long as:

- The participant exercises control over the assets in their account.
- Participants have ample opportunity to enter orders for their account and to provide instructions regarding their account.
- A broad range of investment options is available for the participant to choose from and the options offer suitable investments for a variety of investment objectives and risk profiles.
- Information regarding the risks and objective of the investment options is readily available to plan participants.

THE DEPARTMENT OF LABOR FIDUCIARY RULES

The Department of Labor has been working to enact significant new legislation for financial professionals who service and maintain retirement accounts for clients. These new rules subject financial professionals to higher fiduciary standards. These standards require financial professionals to place the interest of the client ahead of the interest of the broker dealer or investment advisory firm. Professionals who service retirement accounts are still permitted to earn commissions and/or a fee based on the assets in the account and may still offer proprietary products to investors. However the rule requires that the client receive significant disclosures relating to the fees and costs associated with the servicing of the account. Simply charging the lowest fee will not ensure compliance with the fiduciary standard. Both the firm and the individual servicing the account must put the interests of the client ahead of their own. Broker dealers and advisory firms must establish written supervisory procedures and training programs designed to supervise and educate their personnel on the new requirements for retirement accounts. Many representatives will now be required to obtain the Series 65 or Series 66 license to comply with the new Department of Labor rules.

LIFE INSURANCE

Life insurance is a contract between an individual and an insurance company that is designed to provide financial compensation to the policyholder's beneficiaries in the event of the policyholder's death. There are several different types of life insurance policies, and it is important that the individual chooses a policy that best fits his or her needs. The types of life insurance covered on the Series 66 exam are:

- Whole life.
- Variable life.
- Universal life.
- Variable universal life.

WHOLE LIFE

A whole life insurance policy provides the insured with a guaranteed death benefit that is equal to the face amount of the policy as well as a guaranteed cash value that the policyholder may borrow against. The cash value of the policy is held in the insurance company's general account and is invested in conservative investments such as mortgages and real estate. The policy's cash value increases each year as the premiums are paid and invested. The death benefit and the premium payments are fixed by the insurance company at the time of issuance and remain constant for the life of the policy. The policyholder is covered from the date of issuance to the date of death, as long as the premiums are paid.

VARIABLE LIFE

A variable life insurance contract is both an insurance policy and a security because of the way the insurance company invests the cash reserves. A variable life policy is a fixed-premium plan that offers the contract holder a minimum death benefit. The holder of a variable life insurance policy may choose how the cash reserves are invested. A variable life policy typically offers stocks, bonds, mutual funds, and other portfolios as investment options. Although the performance of these investments may tend to outperform the performance of more conservative alternatives, the cash value of the policy is not guaranteed. The cash and securities held by the insurance company are invested in the insurance company's separate account and are kept segregated from the insurance company's general account. The separate account is required to register as either an open-end investment or as a UIT under The Investment Company Act of 1940. Representatives who sell these policies must have both a securities license and an insurance license. The insured is covered from the date of issuance to the date of death, as long as the premiums are paid.

UNIVERSAL LIFE

A universal life insurance policy, unlike whole and variable life policies, has no scheduled premium payments and a face amount that can be adjusted according to the policyholder's needs. A universal life policy allows the policyholder to decide when premiums are paid and to determine how large those payments will be. Should the insured determine that he or she needs to change the amount of the insurance, the face amount of the policy may be adjusted up or down. The policyholder has no scheduled premium payments, but the insured must make payments frequently enough to support the policy. The policy will stay in effect as long as there is enough cash value in the policy to support the payment of mortality and expense costs. The net premium payments are invested in the insurance company's general account, and a universal life policy is considered an insurance product. Universal life insurance policies have two interest rates associated with them: a contract rate, which sets a minimum interest rate that will be paid to the holder, and an annual rate that is set each year based on prevailing interest rates. Representatives who sell universal life insurance policies must have their insurance licenses.

VARIABLE UNIVERSAL LIFE/ UNIVERSAL VARIABLE LIFE

A variable universal life policy allows the policyholder the ability to determine when premiums are paid and to decide how large those payments are. The net premium is invested in the insurance company's separate account, and the policy's cash value and variable death benefit are determined by the investment experience of the separate account. A variable universal life insurance policy will remain in effect as long as there is enough cash value in the policy to support the cost of insurance. A variable universal life insurance policy may have a minimum guaranteed death benefit but does not have to. Representatives who sell variable universal life polices must have both insurance and securities licenses.

PREMIUMS AND DEATH BENEFITS

The premium and the minimum death benefit for a variable life policy are fixed at the time of the policy's issuance. The policyholder is covered from the date of issuance to the date of death, as long as the premiums are paid. The death benefit may vary in amount as a result of the investment performance of the separate account. As the performance of the separate account rises and falls, so does the policy's death benefit. However, the death benefit may never fall below the minimum guaranteed death benefit. As the policyholder makes premium payments, certain expenses are deducted from the gross premium, and the balance or the net premium is invested in the separate account. The expenses that are deducted from the gross premium are:

- Administrative fee.
- Sales load.
- State premium tax.

The administrative fee is a one-time fee to cover the costs of issuing the policy. The sales load pays commissions to compensate the representative who sold the policy, and the state premium tax goes to the state for policies sold within its borders. The net premium is invested in the insurance company's separate account, and the insurance company will make certain deductions from the separate account to cover the cost of the policy. Those costs are:

- Mortality risk fee.
- Investment management fee.
- Expense risk fee.

MORTALITY RISK FEE

The mortality risk to the insurance company is the risk that the individual may die unexpectedly after only making several premium payments. The insurance company deducts a fee from the separate account to cover this risk. The mortality risk fee is also known as the cost of insurance.

INVESTMENT MANAGEMENT FEE

Professional money managers must manage the portfolios in the variable insurance policy's separate account. These portfolio managers usually receive a fee based on the value of the separate account, and the insurance company will deduct a fee from the separate account to cover this expense.

EXPENSE RISK FEE

The insurance company must know the costs involved with the issuance of life insurance policies. The expense risk to the insurance company is that the costs of issuing policies may increase, making it unprofitable to issue policies. The insurance company will deduct a fee from the separate account to cover this expense.

ASSUMED INTEREST RATE

A variable life insurance policy has a minimum death benefit plus an additional death benefit, which may vary in amount according to the investment performance of the separate account. The performance of the separate account may increase or decrease the policy's death benefit, but the policy's death benefit may never fall below the minimum guaranteed death benefit. When a variable life insurance policy is issued, the insurance company sets an assumed interest rate (AIR) that is used to calculate the amount of the policy's variable death benefit.

If the separate account outperforms the AIR, the variable death benefit will increase. However, if the separate account underperforms the AIR for several months, the separate account will have to outperform the AIR by enough to offset any past poor performance before the death benefit may increase. Calculation of the variable death benefit must be made at least annually. The value of the separate account must be made daily, much like a mutual fund, and the policyholder's cash value must be calculated at least monthly. It is important to note that the AIR has nothing to do with the cash value of the policy; it only concerns itself with the variable death benefit. As long as the performance of the separate account is positive, the cash value will increase.

VARIABLE POLICY FEATURES

All variable life insurance policies must offer policyholders the following:

- 45-day free-look period
- Ability to borrow against cash value
- Contract exchange privileges
- Voting rights

45-DAY FREE LOOK

A variable life insurance policyholder must be given an opportunity to review the policy and may cancel the contract within the first 45 days, or 10 days from the receiving of the policy, whichever is longer. Any policyholder who cancels a contract under the free-look provision is entitled to receive a refund of all premiums paid.

LOANS

All variable life insurance policyholders must be allowed to borrow against their policy's cash value. At least 75% of the policy's cash value must be made available to the policyholder in the form of a loan. Interest must be charged on the loan; otherwise, it is taxed as a withdrawal. Should the separate account experience a drop in value while the loan is outstanding, causing the policyholder's cash value to fall into a negative balance, the policyholder has 31 days to repay enough of the loan to restore a positive cash value or the policy may be canceled. Should the death benefit become payable while a loan is outstanding, the death benefit will be reduced by the amount of the loan.

CONTRACT EXCHANGE

All variable life policyholders must be given the opportunity to exchange their variable life insurance policy for a whole life policy for at least 24 months, as required by federal law. The new whole life policy will have a death benefit that is equal to the minimum guaranteed death benefit of the variable life policy, and the contract's date of issuance will remain the same. The insurance company may not ask a policyholder who exchanges a variable life policy for a whole life policy to take another physical. When a policyholder exchanges one life insurance policy for another it is done without any tax consequences and is referred to as a 1035 exchange.

VOTING

Variable life policyholders must be given the right to vote on the major issues concerning the separate account, such as:

- Election of the investment adviser.
- Change in investment objectives.

Policyholders will receive one vote for every $100 in cash value and will receive fractional votes for fractional amounts of $100 of cash value.

SALES CHARGES

The maximum allowable sales charge for a variable life insurance policy is 9% of the total payments over the life of the policy. The life of the policy is considered the lesser of 20 years or the life expectancy of the insured. Policyholders who cancel their policies within the 45-day free-look period are entitled to a refund of all sales charges paid. Policyholders who cancel their policies within the first 2 years will be entitled to receive their cash value plus a partial refund of the sales charges assessed to date. A policyholder who cancels a contract within the first 2 years will receive a refund of all sales charges in excess of 30% of the first year's payments and a refund of all sales charges in excess of 10% of the second year's payments. If a policyholder cancels a contract after 2 years, he or she is only entitled to receive the cash value of the policy.

Characteristic	Whole	Variable	VUL/UVL
Premium	Fixed	Fixed	Flexible
Death benefit	Guaranteed	Guaranteed minimum	May have guaranteed minimum
Cash value	Guaranteed	Varies	Varies
Coverage	From date of issuance to date of death	From date of issuance to date of death	Policy remains in effect as long as there is enough cash value in the policy to support the cost of the policy
Cash value invested in	General account	Separate account	Separate account

LIFE SETTLEMENTS

There may be times when the owner of a life insurance policy elects to sell the interest in the policy to a third party in exchange for a lump sum payment during the insured's lifetime. The sale of the life insurance policy is known as a life settlement. The sale of a variable life insurance policy is considered to be the sale of a security and is regulated by both FINRA and the SEC. The buyer of the policy agrees to make all future premium payments and will be entitled to receive the payment of the death benefit upon the death of the insured. The market for life insurance policies is illiquid, and pricing of policies can vary greatly. FINRA requires any firm that assists in the selling of client policies obtain multiple bids for the policy to ensure that the client receives a fair price. The firm may not enter into any arrangement that would require the firm to sell all or substantially all of its client life insurance policies to any one buyer. FINRA requires agents assisting in the sale of life settlements, as well as the supervisors of the agents, to receive training relating to life settlements. FINRA further requires that the training be documented for each agent and supervisor.

TAX IMPLICATIONS OF LIFE INSURANCE

There are a number of tax implications that need to be understood by people who buy life insurance contracts. Generally, the premiums paid to the insurance company for the life insurance policy are not tax deductible for federal income tax purposes. However, should the death benefit become payable, the amount paid out to the beneficiary will be received tax free. Of critical importance when determining the tax implications of a life insurance policy is recognizing who the "owner" of the policy is. If the insured person is deemed to be the owner of the contract, the amount of the death benefit payable on the contract will be included in the value of the person's estate for estate tax purposes. The owner of the policy is the person who has the right to name a beneficiary, borrow from the policy, transfer ownership, and determine how dividends or cash value are invested. To ensure that the policy is not considered to be an asset of the estate when determining estate taxes, oftentimes people will establish the policy so that the policy is owned by their spouse or by an irrevocable life insurance trust (ILT). By establishing the ownership of the life insurance policy in an ILT, the death benefit will not impact the value of the insured's estate.

HEALTH SAVINGS ACCOUNTS

A tax advantaged health savings account may be established to help offset the potential impact of medical expenses incurred by individuals who maintain a high deductible health insurance plan. Many individuals select a health insurance plan with a high deductible to lower the monthly premium expenses. A high deductible health plan is often used to insure against catastrophic illness. Individuals covered by these plans may elect to establish a health savings account. The individual, their employer or both may make contributions to the health savings account. The contribution limit varies and is based on the person's age and the type of health insurance coverage. If a person is eligible on the first day of the last month of the year, the person may make a full contribution for that year. This is known as the "last month rule." Contributions to the health savings account may be made with pretax dollars. The money in the account grows tax free and can be used tax free for qualified medical expenses. The individual may use the money to pay the expense directly to the health care provider to reimburse themselves for payments they have made for qualified medical expenses incurred for themselves, their spouse or any dependent claimed on their tax return. Prescription drugs are considered to be qualified medical expenses. If the person requires a nonprescription drug to be covered the person still must get a prescription from their doctor. If money is used for non-qualified medical expenses the money will be subject to income taxes and could be subject to a 20% penalty tax. The money is allowed to accumulate over time and any unused amounts may be carried over to future years. If the owner of an HSA dies the account will pass to the owner's spouse and will be treated as the spouse's HSA. If the beneficiary is not the spouse the account will cease to be an HSA and the amount will be taxable to the beneficiary in the year in which the owner dies.

ABLE ACCOUNTS

An ABLE account, sometimes referred to as a 529 ABLE account, may be established as a tax-advantaged savings account to provide for the care of individuals with disabilities. The Achieving a Better Life Experience (ABLE) account regulations were passed in order to recognize the unique financial burdens inherent in caring for a disabled person. Individuals with disabilities may have only one ABLE account at a time and the individual with the disability is deemed to be both the account owner and the designated beneficiary. ABLE accounts may be transferred or rolled over into new ABLE accounts for the same beneficiary. Contributions to the account are made with after-tax dollars and are allowed to grow tax deferred. The contributions and the growth may be used tax free by the beneficiary for qualified care and quality-of-life expenses. Tax-free withdrawals may be made by the beneficiary to cover qualified expenses incurred or in anticipation of paying expenses to be incurred. Qualified expenses would include things such as:

- Medical care
- Wellness care
- Transportation
- Housing expenses (including mortgage, tax, rent, insurance and utilities)
- Transportation
- Assistive technology
- Education
- Job training

Withdrawals from an ABLE account for expenses that do not meet the definition of qualified expenses will be seen as part of the beneficiary's resources if retained past the month the distribution occurred. In order to qualify for an ABLE account, the individual must have been disabled by the time he or she reached their 26th birthday. The maximum annual contribution to an ABLE account is equal to the annual tax-free gift limit of $15,000 and is subject to change each year. Anyone may make contributions to an ABLE account and the account may be rolled over to another family member if that person meets the eligibility guidelines. The assets in the ABLE account will not impact the disabled person's eligibility for many assistance programs. When calculating eligibility for assistance, the first $100,000 in assets in the

ABLE account are excluded when estimating the amount of resources available. However, ABLE account balances that exceed $100,000 can cause the beneficiary of the account to be placed in a suspended status for receiving supplemental security income (SSI) until all resources in the ABLE and other accounts owned by the individual fall to $100,000 or lower. Upon the death of the beneficiary of an ABLE account, the remaining assets will be used to repay Medicaid for any payments made to the beneficiary.

Pretest

VARIABLE ANNUITIES, RETIREMENT PLANS, AND LIFE INSURANCE

1. A doctor makes the maximum contribution to his Keogh plan while earning $300,000 per year. How much can he contribute to an IRA?

   a. $57,000

   b. $2,000

   c. $25,000

   d. $6,000

2. An individual owns a variable annuity with an assumed interest rate of 5%. If the separate account earns 4%, the individual would expect:

   I. The monthly payment to go up

   II. The monthly payment to go down

   III. The value of the annuity unit to go up

   IV. The value of the annuity unit to go down

   a. II and IV

   b. I and III

   c. I and II

   d. II and III

3. A school principal has deposited $15,000 in a tax-deferred annuity through a payroll deduction plan. The account has grown in value to $22,000. The principal plans to retire and take a lump sum distribution. On what amount does he pay taxes?

   a. $22,000

   b. $15,000

   c. $7,000

   d. $0

4. The maximum amount that a couple may contribute to their IRAs at any one time is:

   a. 100% of the annual contribution limit

   b. 200% of the annual contribution limit

   c. 300% of the annual contribution limit

   d. 400% of the annual contribution limit

5. An investor has deposited $100,000 into a qualified retirement account over a 10-year period. The value of the account has grown to $175,000 and the investor plans to retire and take a lump sum withdrawal. The investor will pay:

   a. Capital gains tax on $75,000 only

   b. Ordinary income taxes on the $75,000 only

   c. Ordinary income taxes on the whole $175,000

   d. Ordinary income taxes on the $100,000 and capital gains on the $75,000

6. A 42-year-old investor wants to put $20,000 into a plan to help meet the educational expenses of his 12-year-old son. He wants to make a lump sum deposit. Which would you recommend?

   a. A 529 plan

   b. A Coverdell IRA

   c. A Roth IRA

   d. A growth mutual fund

7. A client who is 65 years old has invested $10,000 in a Roth IRA. It has now grown to $14,000. He plans to retire and take a lump sum distribution. He will pay taxes on:

   a. $0

   b. $14,000

   c. $4,000

   d. $10,000

8. A fixed annuity guarantees all of the following EXCEPT:

   a. Income for life

   b. Protection from inflation

   c. Rate of return

   d. Protection from investment risk

9. A self-employed individual may open an SEP IRA to plan for his retirement. The maximum contribution to the plan is:

   a. $3,000

   b. $6,000

   c. $12,000

   d. The lesser of 25% of the post-contribution income, up to $57,000

Registration of Broker Dealers, Investment Advisers, and Agents

INTRODUCTION

In this section we will examine the state registration process for broker dealers, investment advisers, and agents. An important part of this section will be to know when registration is required and when an exemption is offered to the subject in question.

REGISTRATION OF BROKER DEALERS

Prior to conducting business in any state, a broker dealer must be properly registered or exempt from registration in that state. The first test when deciding if the broker dealer must register is determining whether the firm has an office in the state. If the firm maintains an office within the state, it must register with that state. A broker dealer wishing to become registered in a state must first file an application with the state securities administrator. The broker dealer must also pay all filing fees and sign a consent to service of process. By signing the consent to service of process, the broker dealer appoints the administrator as its attorney in fact and allows the administrator to receive legal papers for the applicant. Any legal papers received by the administrator will have the same force and effect as if they were served on the broker dealer. All applications must also include:

- Type of organization (e.g., corporation, partnership).
- Address of business.

- Description of business to be conducted.
- Backgrounds and qualifications of officers and directors.
- Disclosure of any legal actions.
- Financial condition.

The firm's registration will become effective at noon 30 days after the initial application has been received or at noon 30 days after the administrator has received the last piece of required information. Registering a broker dealer in a state automatically requires that any officers and directors who act in a sales capacity register as agents. A broker dealer will not be deemed to have a place of business in a state where it does not maintain an office simply by virtue of the fact that the firm's website is accessible from that state so long as the following conditions are met:

- The firm's website clearly states that the firm may only conduct business in states where it is properly registered to do so.
- The firm's website only provides general information about the firm and does not provide specific investment advice.
- The firm may not respond to Internet inquiries with the intent to solicit business without first meeting the registration requirements in the state of the prospective customer.

 TAKE**NOTE!**

Broker dealers must always register with the SEC and with states where the firm conducts business with individual clients.

FINANCIAL REQUIREMENTS

A broker dealer must be able to meet the minimum capital requirements set forth by the state securities administrator. If the broker dealer is unable to meet this capital requirement, it must post a surety bond to ensure its solvency. Broker dealers that meet the Securities and Exchange Commission's (SEC) minimum net capital requirements are exempt from the Uniform Securities Act's capital and surety bond requirements. The Amount of the bond required by the administrator for broker dealers who have custody or discretion over client accounts is limited to the amount of capital required by the Securities

Exchange Act of 1934. No bond may be required of broker dealers whose capital exceeds the amount of the bond required by the administrator. The administrator may require that an officer or agent of the broker dealer take an exam that may be oral, written, or both.

 TAKENOTE!

No state or political subdivision may enact a requirement for registration that requires a broker dealer to meet a financial, record keeping, reporting, or custody requirement that goes beyond that required by the Securities Exchange Act of 1934.

AGENT REGISTRATION

It is unlawful for a broker dealer to employ any agent who is not duly registered under the Uniform Securities Act (USA). When determining if an agent must register, you must first look at whom the agent works for. If the agent works for a broker dealer, the agent must register. Agents must register in their state of residence even if their firm is located in another state.

EXAMPLE   An agent who lives in New Jersey and who commutes to an office in New York must register in both New Jersey and New York.

Agents must also register in the states where they sell securities or offer to sell securities as well as where they advertise. If the firm does not have an office in the state, it may or may not be required to register depending on whom it does business with. If a broker dealer does not have an office in the state and engages in securities transactions with the general public, then it must register. If a broker dealer with no office in the state conducts business exclusively with any of the following, it is not required to register in that state:

- Other broker dealers
- Issuers of securities
- Investment companies
- Insurance companies
- Banks

- Savings and loans
- Trust companies
- Pension plans with more than $1,000,000 in assets
- Other financial institutions
- Institutional buyers
- Existing customers with less than 30 days temporary residency in the state (on vacation or business trips)

The only exception is for officers and directors of a broker dealer who have no involvement with customers, securities transactions, or supervision. If the agent works for an exempt issuer, the agent is exempt from registration no matter what security is involved. Exempt issuers are:

- U.S. and municipal governments.
- Canadian federal and municipal governments.
- Foreign federal governments recognized by the United States.
- Banks, savings and loans, and trust companies.

Agents are also exempt from registering if they represent an issuer in the sale of an exempt security such as:

- Bankers' acceptances or time drafts with less than 270 days to maturity sold in denominations of $50,000 or more.
- Investment contracts relating to employee savings, stock purchases, pension plans, or other benefit plans as long as no commission is received for such sales.

Agents may also qualify for the *de minimis* exemption if they meet the following conditions:

- They are registered with FINRA.
- They are registered with at least one other state.
- They are not ineligible to register.
- Their broker dealer is registered in the state.

If the above conditions are met, an agent may conduct business with clients who are in the state in question for up to 30 days. If the client has moved to the state in question, the agent may conduct business with the client for up to 60 days while his or her registration is pending in that state.

HIRING NEW EMPLOYEES

A registered principal of a firm will be the individual who interviews and screens potential new employees. The principal will be required to make a thorough investigation into the candidate's professional and personal backgrounds. With few exceptions, other than clerical personnel, all new employees will be required to become registered as an associated person with the firm. The new employee will begin the registration process by filling out and submitting a Uniform Application for Securities Industry Registration, also known as Form U4. Form U4 is used to collect the applicant's personal and professional history, including:

- 10-year employment history
- 5-year resident history
- Legal name and any aliases used
- Any legal or regulatory actions

The principal of the firm is required to verify the employment information for the last 3 years and must attest to the character of the applicant by signing Form U4 prior to its submission to FINRA. All U4 forms will be sent to the Central Registration Depository (CRD) along with a fingerprint card for processing and recording. The employing firm must maintain written procedures to verify the accuracy of the information on the new hire's U4 form. A comprehensive review of the information must take place within 30 days of the form being submitted to FINRA. Fingerprint cards may be submitted in hard copy or electronically. The candidate's fingerprints will be submitted to the FBI for review. If after three good faith attempts to submit fingerprints the FBI determines that the fingerprints are ineligible or cannot be read the candidate will not be asked to submit a fourth set of fingerprints and the FBI will conduct a name check to search the candidate's history. Any applicant who has answered yes to any of the questions on the form regarding his or her background must give a detailed explanation in the DRP pages attached to the form. The applicant is not required to provide information regarding:

- Marital status
- Educational background
- Income or net worth

Information regarding the employee's finances is disclosed on Form U4 if the associated person has ever declared bankruptcy and if the employee has any unsatisfied judgements or liens. Any development that would cause an answer on the associated person's U4 to change requires that the member update the U4 within 30 days of when the member becomes informed of the event. In the case of an event that could cause the individual to become statutorily disqualified, such as a felony conviction or misdemeanor involving cash or securities, the member must update the associated person's U4 within 10 business days of learning of the event. Additionally, broker dealers are required to perform background checks on its employees every 5 years to ensure that no judgements, liens or disclosable events have gone unreported by the registered person. Registered persons who fail to disclose an unsatisfied judgements or liens are subject to significant regulatory action that could result in the person being barred from the industry in extreme cases.

RESIGNATION OF A REGISTERED REPRESENTATIVE

If a registered representative voluntarily resigns or has his or her association with a member firm terminated for any reason, the member must fill out and submit a Uniform Termination Notice for Securities Industry Registration, which is known as Form U5. The member must submit the form to FINRA within 30 days of the termination. The member firm is also required to give a copy of the form to the representative upon termination. The member must also state the reason for the termination, either voluntary or for cause. Voluntary terminations cover all terminations that were not the result of the agent being fired for violations of industry or company regulations, such as staff reductions. An associated person's registration is nontransferable. A representative may not simply move his or her registration from one firm to another. The employing firm that the representative is leaving must fill out and submit a Form U5 to FINRA, which terminates the representative's registration. The new employing firm must fill out and submit a new Form U4 to begin a new registration for the associated person with the new employer. The new employer is required to obtain a copy of the U5 form filed by the old employing member either from the employee or directly from FINRA within 60 days of submitting the new U4. The previous employer is not required to provide a copy to the new member firm. If the new employing member asks the associated person for a copy of the U5, the member has 2 business days to provide it. If the member requests a copy of the U5 from the agent who has not received a copy of his or her U5 from the old employer, the agent must promptly request it from the old employer and provide it to the new employer within 2 business days of receipt. Should an agent's previous employer discover facts that would alter the information on Form U5, the previous employer must file an amended Form U5 within 30 days and provide a copy to the former employee. A representative who leaves the industry for more than 24 months is required to requalify by exam. During a period of absence from the industry of 2 years or less, FINRA retains jurisdiction over the representative in cases involving customer complaints and violations.

 TAKENOTE!

A firm may not allow an inactive agent to "park" his or her license with the firm and may not maintain an inactive agent's license on the books simply to ensure that the agent does not have to requalify by exam. The one exception to the rule is for agents in the military who are called to active duty. While on active duty, the agent's registration and continuing education requirements will be "tolled" until he or she returns. While on active duty the agent may not conduct business but may receive commissions generated from his or her book of business. Once the agent returns from active duty he or she has 90 days to reenter the securities industry. If after 90 days the agent does not reenter the business, the 24-month window begins.

REGISTERING AGENTS

Most states require that agents successfully complete either the Series 63 or the Series 66 exam before they may conduct business within their state. In addition to successfully passing the Series 63 or Series 66, agents must also:

- Abide by and understand state securities laws and regulations.
- Recognize that the state may require additional certification regarding the state's securities laws.
- Understand that they may not conduct business until they are properly registered.

 TESTFOCUS!

- An agent does not become registered in a state simply by passing the exam. Agents become registered only when the state securities administrator notifies them that they have become registered.

- An agent may not be registered in any state without being employed by a broker dealer or issuer, and no broker dealer or issuer shall employ an agent that is not duly registered.

CHANGES IN AN AGENT'S EMPLOYMENT

When an agent changes firms, the agent, former employer, and new employer all must notify the state securities administrator. This is done in most cases quite easily through the Central Registration Depository (CRD) system for all firm and agent information. An agent's termination becomes effective 30 days after notifying the state unless the administrator is in the process of suspending or revoking the agent's registration. The administrator may still revoke an agent's registration for up to 1 year after the agent's registration has been terminated. If an agent is denied a registration as the result of information received on the U5 submitted by the agent's previous employer, the administrator will only notify the agent and the agent's new employer of the denial.

MERGERS AND ACQUISITIONS OF FIRMS

If a broker dealer from out of state is acquiring a broker dealer in state, the successor firm must file an application for registration within the state. The successor firm's registration will become effective upon completion of the transaction. The registration fees for the successor firm will be waived.

RENEWING REGISTRATIONS

All state registrations expire on December 31, and all broker dealers, investment advisers, and agents are required to file a renewal application and pay a renewal fee. The consent to service of process does not get re-filed with the renewal application. The consent to service of process remains in effect as long as the registration of the agent or firm is in effect with the state.

CANADIAN FIRMS AND AGENTS

Canadian firms and agents may engage in securities transactions with financial institutions and existing customers without registering under the USA as long as they do not maintain an office within the state. A Canadian broker dealer or agent who is a member in good standing with a Canadian securities regulator is allowed to register through a simplified registration process. The state registration will become effective 30 days after the application has been received with the consent to service process. The Canadian broker dealer must advise the state of any disciplinary action.

INVESTMENT ADVISER STATE REGISTRATION

It is unlawful for an investment adviser to conduct securities business without being duly registered or exempt from registration. State registration exemptions are provided for investment advisers who:

- Are federally registered.
- Manage portfolios for investment companies.
- Manage portfolios in excess of $110,000,000.
- Have no office in the state and conduct business exclusively with financial institutions.
- Have no office in the state and offer advice to no more than five clients in any 12-month period. This is known as the *de minimis* exemption.

If an investment adviser with no office in the state advertises to the public the ability to meet and offer investment advisory services with clients in a hotel or other temporary location, then the investment adviser is required to register with the state.

An investment adviser will not be deemed to have a place of business in a state where it does not maintain an office simply by virtue of the fact that the firm's website is accessible from that state so long as the following conditions are met:

- The firm's website clearly states that the firm may only conduct business in states where it is properly registered to do so.
- The firm's website only provides general information about the firm and does not provide specific investment advice.
- The firm may not respond to Internet inquiries with the intent to solicit business without first meeting the registration requirements in the state of the prospective customer.

THE NATIONAL SECURITIES MARKET IMPROVEMENT ACT OF 1996 (THE COORDINATION ACT)

The National Securities Markets Improvement Act of 1996 eliminated regulatory duplication of effort and established registration requirements for investment advisers. A federally covered investment adviser must register with the SEC and is any investment adviser:

- That manages at least $110,000,000.
- That manages investment company portfolios.
- That is not registered under state laws.

All federally registered investment advisers must pay state filing fees and notify the administrator in the states in which they conduct business. The state securities administrator may not audit a federally covered investment adviser unless that adviser's principal offices is located in that administrator's state. Investment advisers are required to register with the state if they manage less than $100,000,000. Once investment advisers reach $100,000,000 in assets under management (AUM), they become eligible for federal registration.

Investment advisers who manage between $100,000,000 and $110,000,000 may choose to register either with the state or with the SEC. Investment advisers who think that their asset base will exceed $110,000,000 should register with the SEC. Investment advisers who manage $110,000,000 or more must register with the SEC.

If a federally covered investment adviser's AUM falls below $90,000,000, the adviser must withdraw its federal registration by filing Form ADV-W and register with the appropriate states within 180 days. Like most regulations, there are rare exceptions to the rule of when an investment adviser may register with the SEC. The Dodd-Frank Wall Street Reform Act of 2010 increased the AUM for federal registration to its current levels and defined three categories of investment advisers:

1. Small adviser: Advisers with less than $25,000,000 AUM
2. Mid-size advisers: Advisers with $25,000,000–$100,000,000 AUM
3. Large advisers: Advisers with more than $100,000,000 AUM

Pension consultants must have at least $200,000,000 AUM to be eligible to become federally registered.

INVESTMENT ADVISER REPRESENTATIVE

All investment adviser representatives who maintain an office within the state must register within the state. An investment adviser representative is an individual who:

- Gives advice on the value of the securities.
- Gives advice on the advisability of buying or selling securities.
- Solicits new advisory clients.
- Is an officer, director, partner, or supervisor of the investment adviser.

An investment adviser may not employ any representative who is not properly registered. Clerical and administrative employees are not considered representatives and do not need to register. An investment adviser representative who has no place of business in the state and who offers to meet a client in a hotel or other place of convenience is not considered to have an office in the state so long as the representative does not advertise the office and only offers the ability to meet directly with clients.

TESTFOCUS!

Investment adviser representatives who represent federally covered investment advisers are only required to register in the state where they work even though they may have clients in other states, and the federally covered adviser is not required to register.

STATE INVESTMENT ADVISER REGISTRATION

An investment adviser must file the following with the state securities administrator before becoming registered:

- Application Form ADV
- Filing fees
- Consent to service of process

CAPITAL REQUIREMENTS

A state registered investment adviser must maintain a minimal level of financial solvency. For advisers with custody of a customers' cash and securities, the investment adviser must maintain minimum net capital of $35,000. Advisers who are unable to meet this requirement may post a surety bond. Deposits of cash and securities will alleviate the surety bond requirement. Advisers are considered to have custody if they have their customers' cash and securities held at their firm or if they have full discretion over their customers' accounts. Full discretion allows the adviser to withdraw cash and securities from the customer's account without consulting the customer. Advisers who have only limited discretionary authority over customers' accounts need to maintain a minimum of $10,000 in net capital. Advisers with limited discretionary authority may only buy and sell securities for the customer's benefit without consulting the customer. They may not withdraw or deposit cash or securities without the customer's consent. If a state registered investment adviser meets the capital requirements in its home state, it will be deemed to have met the capital requirements in any other state in which the adviser wishes to register, even if the other states have higher net capital or bonding requirements. Should a state registered adviser's net capital fall below the minimum requirement, the adviser must notify the state administrator by the close of the next business day of the adviser's net worth. The adviser must then file a financial disclosure report with the administrator by the end of the next business day. If the adviser has fallen below the net worth requirement, the adviser will be required to post a bond to cover the capital deficiency. The amount of the bond will be rounded up to the nearest $5,000. Investment advisers with custody of funds must maintain a positive net worth at all times. Investment adviser representatives are not required to maintain a minimum level of liquidity.

EXAMS

The state securities administrator may require investment adviser representatives as well as the officers and directors of the firm to take an exam, which may be oral, written, or both. All registrations become effective at noon 30 days after the application has been filed. The administrator may require that an announcement of the investment adviser's intended registration be published in the newspaper.

Requirement	Broker Dealer	Investment Adviser	Agents
Net capital	Yes	Yes	No
Surety bond	Yes	Yes	Yes
Exams	Yes	Yes	Yes
Fees	Yes	Yes	Yes

ADVERTISING AND SALES LITERATURE

All advertising and sales literature for an investment adviser must be filed with the state securities administrator. The administrator may require prior approval of:

- Form letters.
- Prospectuses.
- Pamphlets.

The following records must be kept for a minimum of 3 years for broker dealers and 5 years for investment advisers unless the state securities administrator requires a different period of time:

- Advertising and sales literature
- Account statements
- Order tickets/order memorandum

All investment advisers must keep accurate records relating to the following:

- Cash receipts and disbursements.
- Income and expense ledgers.
- Order tickets, including customer's name.
- Adviser's name, including executing broker and discretionary information.
- Ledgers and confirmations for all customers for whom the adviser has custody.
- Financial statements and trial balance.
- All written recommendations to customers.
- Copies of advertisements, circulars, and articles sent to more than 10 people. (NASAA requires copies of records sent to two or more people to be maintained.)
- Copies of calculations sent to more than 10 people. (NASAA requires copies of records sent to two or more people to be maintained.)

All books and records must be kept for 5 years readily accessible and for 2 years at the adviser's office. Records may be kept on a computer or microfiche as long as the data may be viewed and printed.

BROCHURE DELIVERY

An investment adviser is required to provide all prospective clients with a brochure or with Form ADV Part 2 at least 48 hours prior to the signing of the contract or at least at the time of the signing of the contract if the client is given a 5-day grace period to withdraw without penalty. The brochure or Form ADV Part 2 will state:

- How and when fees are charged.
- The types of securities the adviser does business in.
- How recommendations are made.
- The type of clients the adviser has.
- The qualifications of officers and directors.

 TAKENOTE!

A balance sheet must be given to clients if the adviser has custody of client funds or requires prepayment of advisory fees of more than $500 more than 6 months in advance.

The NASAA Model Rule regarding direct fee deductions from client accounts, by advisers who use a qualified custodian, requires advisers who automatically deduct fees to have written authorization from each client to deduct the fees directly from client accounts. An invoice must be sent to the clients detailing the fee as well as the formula for determining the fee. If the fee is based on the value of the account, the value of the account at the time the fee is charged must be provided. The statements for client accounts will be sent by the qualified custodian, not from the investment adviser. NASAA considers a qualified custodian to be any of the following three entities:

1. A banking institution covered by FDIC insurance
2. A registered broker dealer in the business of holding or carrying customer funds and securities
3. A foreign financial institution in the business of providing such services that segregates customer assets from its own

THE ROLE OF THE INVESTMENT ADVISER

An investment adviser charges a fee for his or her services for advising clients as to the value of securities or for making recommendations as to which securities should be purchased or sold. Unlike a broker dealer, the investment adviser has a contractual relationship with his or her clients and must always adhere to the highest standards of professional conduct.

ADDITIONAL COMPENSATION FOR AN INVESTMENT ADVISER

In addition to the fees charged by an investment adviser, an investment adviser may also:

- Receive commissions for executing a customer's transaction through certain broker dealers.
- Act as a principal in a customer's transaction.

The above sources of additional revenue must be disclosed to the client in writing prior to the investment adviser executing such transactions.

AGENCY CROSS TRANSACTIONS

An agency cross transaction is one in which the investment adviser represents both the purchasing and selling security holder either as an investment adviser or as a broker dealer. If the investment adviser is going to execute an agency cross transaction, the adviser must get the client's authorization in writing. The authorization may be pulled at any time verbally, and the adviser may not have solicited both sides of the trade. The investment adviser still maintains a duty to obtain the best execution for both clients and may not execute the cross at a price that favors one client over the other. The adviser must send notice to its clients annually detailing the number of all agency cross transactions completed by the adviser.

DISCLOSURES BY AN INVESTMENT ADVISER

An investment adviser must update its Form ADV annually within 90 days of the fiscal year end. Additionally, the investment adviser must provide each client with an updated brochure annually within 120 days of the adviser's fiscal year end. The brochure must be provided free of charge and must provide a summary of material changes to the advisory firm, including:

- Conflicts of interest.
- Sources of recommendations.
- Location of customers' funds for advisers with custody.
- Any legal actions taken against the adviser.
- Material facts.
- Soft-dollar arrangements.

If the change to the investment adviser's business is material, it must be disclosed promptly. Of critical importance is to know what changes to the investment advisory firm are deemed material and when those changes must be disclosed. Most investment advisory firms other than small sole proprietorships are organized either as corporations or as partnerships. A material change to the ownership or control of the adviser is considered to be material and must be disclosed promptly. If the adviser is a corporation and one of the firm's major stockholders sells, pledges, or assigns its block of controlling voting shares, this would be seen as both material and as an assignment of the contract and must be disclosed promptly. If the nature of the transfer is deemed to be an assignment, the client would also have to give consent to continue the relationship. A person is deemed to control the investment adviser if he or she owns 25% or more of the adviser's outstanding stock, has contributed 25% or more of the adviser's capital, or is entitled to receive 25% or more of the adviser's assets upon dissolution. However, disclosure is not required if an officer of the corporation leaves. If the advisory firm is organized as a partnership and a major partner dies or departs from the partnership, this would be considered material and as an assignment. Therefore, the material change must be disclosed promptly, and the client must give consent to continue the advisory relationship. However, if the partnership adds or removes minority partners, these events would not be deemed material.

An investment adviser may not:

- Borrow from a customer.
- Commingle customers' funds with the adviser's funds.
- Accept an order from a party not named on the account of the customer.
- Churn customer accounts.

- Make unsuitable recommendations.
- Charge unreasonable fees.

An investment adviser with custody of a customer's funds must:

- Segregate all customer funds and securities.
- Give the customer a written notice of the location of the funds.
- Establish a separate bank account for the customer's funds.
- Provide quarterly statements showing all transactions and the account status.
- Go through an annual surprise audit.

 TAKENOTE!

The state securities administrator may or may not allow advisers to have custody of clients' funds. If custody is allowed, the adviser must notify the state that it has custody and adhere to all requirements relating to custody of client funds.

INVESTMENT ADVISER CONTRACTS

All investment adviser contracts must be in writing and must contain disclosures of:

- Length.
- Services to be provided.
- Fees to be charged and how they are assessed.
- The amount of any prepaid fees to be returned upon cancellation of the contract.
- A statement prohibiting the investment adviser from assigning the contract without the customer's consent.
- A notification of any changes in the adviser's management.
- Limits on the adviser's discretionary authority over the customer's account, if any.

 **TAKENOTE!**

If an investment adviser uses an outside solicitor to refer business, such as an accounting firm, the client must get both the advisory's brochure and the solicitor's disclosure document or brochure. The resume or professional background of the solicitor is not required to be included in the solicitor's brochure only the compensation to be received by the solicitor and the relationship with the adviser is required.

ADDITIONAL ROLES OF INVESTMENT ADVISERS

As the business services offered by various professionals have expanded, so has the definition of who must register as an investment adviser. Sports and entertainment representatives now often advise their clients on how or with whom to invest their earnings. As a result, the representative is considered an investment adviser, even if investment advice is only a small part of the services they perform. Individuals who advise pension funds on the merits of portfolio managers or who act as pension consultants must also register as investment advisers.

PRIVATE INVESTMENT COMPANIES/HEDGE FUNDS

Private investment companies and 3c7 funds may charge performance-based compensation to clients provided that the clients have a minimum of $1,000,000 of assets under the adviser's management or have a net worth of $2,000,000. Corporations with $25 million in assets and individuals with at least $5 million in investments may also participate.

FULCRUM FEES

Advisers who manage accounts for investment companies or accounts with a value greater than $1 million, if those accounts are not for trusts or retirement plans, may charge fulcrum fees. A fulcrum fee provides the adviser with additional compensation for outperforming a broad-based index such as the S&P 500 and less compensation for underperforming the index. The amount of the additional compensation received for outperforming the index must be equal to the amount of compensation that would be lost for underperformance. The index used as the basis to determine the adviser's performance must contain similar securities and risks.

WRAP ACCOUNTS

A wrap account is an account that charges one fee for both the advice received as well as the cost of the transaction. All clients who open wrap accounts must be given the wrap account brochure that will provide all of the information that is found on Form ADV Part 2.

SOFT DOLLARS

Brokerage firms will oftentimes provide investment advisers with services to assist them in their business that go beyond execution and research. These services are provided in exchange for commission business and are known as soft dollars. The services received should normally be research related. However, in some instances the services received are used for other purposes and benefit the adviser. In order for the soft-dollar arrangement to be included in the safe harbor provisions, investment advisers must ensure that the services received are for the benefit of the client and pay careful attention to the disclosure requirements relating to all soft dollars arrangements. If an adviser receives soft-dollar compensation from a broker dealer to whom the adviser directs customer transactions (known as directed transactions), the adviser must disclose any arrangements to clients. The fees charged to execute the transactions should be fair and reasonable, in line with what is available in the marketplace as well as with the value of the services offered to the adviser and its clients. The execution fees are not required to be the lowest in the marketplace, and simply using a broker dealer whose services are more expensive will not constitute a breach of the adviser's fiduciary duty. If the adviser directs transactions to a broker dealer in exchange for services that benefit the adviser, the adviser must then disclose all facts relating to the arrangement and receive the client's written consent to enter into the arrangement. This holds true even if such an arrangement does not increase the costs to the client. If the adviser selects broker dealers to execute client orders based on the research or other services provided, it must be disclosed on Form ADV.

The SEC has divided soft-dollar consideration into the following categories:

- Goods/services
- Accounting fees

- Association membership fees
- Cable and Internet
- Commission rebates
- Computer hardware
- Computer software
- Conferences/seminars
- Consulting services
- Courier/postage/express mail
- Custodial fees
- Electronic databases
- Employee salary/benefits
- Execution assistance
- Industry publications
- Legal fees
- Management fees
- Miscellaneous expenses
- Office equipment/supplies
- Online quotation and news services
- Portfolio management software
- Rent
- Research/analysis reports
- Telephone expenses
- Travel expenses
- Tuition/training costs
- Utilities expenses

 TAKENOTE!

Only the items that can be deemed truly beneficial for the client are within the safe harbor. Valuation software and other research-related items are within the safe harbor, while paying for a laptop or rent for the adviser would not be within the safe harbor.

Pretest

REGISTRATION OF BROKER DEALERS, INVESTMENT ADVISERS, AND AGENTS

1. An individual representing which of the following is always required to register?

    a. A government agency

    b. A nonexempt issuer

    c. An issuer in the sale of commercial paper

    d. A broker dealer

2. A broker dealer is exempt from the $35,000 surety bond requirement if the broker dealer:

    a. does not maintain an office in the state.

    b. deals only with existing customers.

    c. meets the SEC's net capital requirement.

    d. has customer funds segregated from its own funds.

3. An investment adviser may conduct business with how many people and still qualify for the *de minimis* exemption at the state level?

    a. Fewer than 12 in 6 months

    b. Fewer than 10 in 12 months

    c. Fewer than 5 in 12 months

    d. Fewer than 8 in 12 months

4. A small New Jersey broker dealer with five partners who all manage client portfolios registers as a broker dealer in Connecticut. Which of the following is true?

   a. Only the partners with clients in Connecticut must register as agents in the state.

   b. Only one of the partners is required to register as a supervisor for all of the firm's activities in Connecticut.

   c. There is no requirement for the partners of a broker dealer to register in a state where the firm has no office.

   d. All of the partners must register.

5. You work for a newly formed investment adviser that has just received $107,000,000 to manage. The firm should register:

   a. with the SEC only.

   b. with the state only.

   c. with either the SEC or the state, depending on the prospects for receiving additional funds.

   d. None of the above. The adviser does not have to register if it has no office in the state.

6. All of the following must be disclosed to a new investment advisory client, EXCEPT:

   a. the type of clients served.

   b. the basis for recommendations.

   c. the advisory fees.

   d. the investment adviser representative's compensation.

7. Agents are exempt from registration if they represent which of the following?

   I. A municipality

   II. A Canadian corporation

   III. A broker dealer

   IV. The government of Brazil

   a. I and IV

   b. I and II

   c. I, II, and IV

   d. I, II, III, and IV

8. Which of the following must register as an investment adviser with the SEC?

    a. Publisher of financial newspapers

    b. Company representative who is paid a salary for explaining the employer's benefit plan to employees

    c. An accountant who advises clients on the advantages of municipal bonds

    d. A pension consultant who advises clients with $214,000,000 in assets

9. Which of the following must notify the state securities administrator when an agent changes firms?

    a. The old broker dealer

    b. The agent

    c. The new broker dealer

    d. All of the above

10. Which of the following is true regarding a broker dealer?

    a. A broker dealer may not also be registered as an investment adviser.

    b. A broker dealer may not be an individual.

    c. A broker dealer may also be registered as an investment adviser and may be a corporation or an individual.

    d. A broker dealer may only execute orders for its customers on an agency basis.

11. An investment adviser with $75,000,000 under management and registered with the state must typically keep records for:

    a. 2 years.

    b. 3 years.

    c. 5 years.

    d. 10 years.

12. A simplified registration is available for which of the following?

    a. A broker dealer in good standing with a securities regulator in Great Britain

    b. A broker dealer in a neighboring state

    c. A broker dealer in good standing with a Canadian regulator

    d. A broker dealer in good standing with FINRA/NYSE

13. An investment adviser who provides advisory services to individual investors may receive which of the following?

   I. A fee based on the customer's assets

   II. Commissions for executing transactions with certain broker dealers

   III. A percentage of the profits in the account

   IV. A profit on principal transactions

   a. I and II

   b. I and III

   c. I, II, and IV

   d. I, II, III, and IV

14. An agent may be denied a registration for all of the following reasons, EXCEPT:

   a. lack of training.

   b. failure to meet financial solvency requirements.

   c. a securities-related misdemeanor.

   d. a court injunction.

15. A broker dealer has been declared insolvent. Which of the following is true regarding the agents' registrations?

   a. The administrator holds all agents' registrations until the agents become employed by other firms.

   b. All agents' registrations are suspended.

   c. All agents' registrations are revoked.

   d. All agents' registrations are canceled.

16. An investment adviser without custody of funds is subject to all of the following, EXCEPT:

   a. filing fees.

   b. surprise audits.

   c. $35,000 surety bond.

   d. net capital requirements.

17. An investment adviser with no office in the state has given advice to nine individuals in the last 17 months. Which of the following is true?

    a. Because the investment adviser has no office in the state and has given advice to fewer than 10 people, it is not required to register.

    b. An investment adviser is always required to register prior to offering any advice to individuals.

    c. The investment adviser must be registered in this situation even though it has no office in the state.

    d. The investment adviser still qualifies for the *de minimis* exemption in this case.

18. Your client has just opened up a wrap account. Which of the following is true?

    a. The client will be charged one fee for advice and execution.

    b. The client must be given Form ADV Part 2.

    c. The client must be an accredited investor.

    d. The client must deposit at least $150,000 to open the account.

19. All registrations of firms, agents, and advisers:

    a. expire on December 31.

    b. expire after 24 months.

    c. expire after 12 months.

    d. are good for the life of the agent or firm.

Securities Registration, Exempt Securities, and Exempt Transactions

INTRODUCTION

In this section, we will review the various types of security registration, along with when the security is required to be registered. All securities that are sold to state residents must either be:

- Duly registered;

  or

- Exempt from registration;

  or

- Sold through an exemption transaction.

EXEMPT SECURITIES

Exempt securities are exempt from the registration requirements of the Securities Act of 1933. Exempt securities are not exempt from the antifraud provisions of the Uniform Securities Act (USA). Exempt securities are:

- Issued by exempt issuers, such as governments.
- Short-term debt instruments with less than 270 days to maturity.

SECURITIES REGISTRATION

Nonexempt securities become federally registered by submitting a registration statement to the Securities and Exchange Commission (SEC). Nonexempt securities must also register in the states in which the securities will be sold. The three methods of registering securities in a state are:

1. Coordination
2. Notice filing
3. Qualification

It is important to understand how the three types of securities registration differ and under what circumstances the different registration methods are used.

REGISTRATION OF IPOs THROUGH COORDINATION

When a company first sells stock to the public during an initial public offering (IPO), the company must file a registration statement with the SEC. The company must also file documents with the state securities administrator in the states where the issue will be sold. Most IPOs will register with the state securities administrator at the same time that they register with the SEC. This process of simultaneous registration is known as coordination. The following must be submitted to the administrator:

- Copies of the prospectus
- Any amendments to the prospectus
- The amount of the securities to be offered within the state
- A list of other states where the securities will be offered
- Consent to service of process
- Other information as required by the state securities administrator, including the corporate bylaws, articles of incorporation, specimen of the security, and indenture of any kind

If an amendment has been made to the federal registration, it must also be made to the state registration. A security's state registration will become effective at the time the federal registration becomes effective as long as no stop order has been issued and the documents have been on file with the state for the minimum number of days (usually 10–20 days). It is important to note that a state registration may not become effective prior to the security's federal registration becoming effective.

REGISTRATION THROUGH NOTICE FILING

The National Securities Market Improvement Act of 1996 withdrew the states' authority to require the registration of investment companies registered under the Investment Company Act of 1940. The states preserved the right to require investment companies to file a notice and pay a fee. When the issuer of a security notice files with the state securities administrator, the following must be submitted:

- Issuer's name and address
- Type of organization
- Description of the securities to be offered
- Copy of the prospectus
- Copy of documents filed with the SEC
- Consent to service of process
- State fee

Even though the state securities administrator no longer maintains jurisdiction over the registration process of the securities, the administrator still maintains broad investigative powers over any suspected fraudulent sales practices relating to the securities. The administrator may investigate the firms and agents who offer the securities for sale to investors within its state. Notice filing may also be used by other federally covered and federally registered securities that meet the minimum requirements. The administrator may require an issuer of a federally covered security trading on an exchange to file all information with the SEC and to submit a consent to service of process prior to offering any securities to state residents. A security that is federally registered and trading on the OTC Bulletin Board or on the pink sheets (Pink OTC Market) may be federally registered but may not meet the minimum criteria to notice file.

REGISTRATION OF NONESTABLISHED ISSUERS/
REGISTRATION THROUGH QUALIFICATION

Securities of issuers that do not meet the requirements for registering through notice filing and that are not an IPO must register through qualification.

Securities of issuers that will be sold only in one state through an intrastate offering will also be registered through qualification. Registration through qualification is the most complex method of registration. The issuer must file a statement containing all of the information required by the state securities administrator. It may include:

- Name and address of the issuer.
- Type of organization.
- Nature of the issuer's business.
- Description of industry.
- Description of issuer's assets.
- Biographical information on officers and directors, including name, address, compensation, and number of shares owned.
- Type of securities to be offered.
- Price of securities.
- Underwriter's discount.
- Issuer's capitalization and long-term debt.
- Audited balance sheet dated within 4 months of filing.
- Income statements for 3 years prior to date of balance sheet.
- Amount and use of proceeds.
- Copy of prospectus or offering circular.
- Copy of advertising and sales literature.
- Specimen of security to be offered.
- Any other information requested by the administrator.
- Consent to service of process.

A securities registration under qualification becomes effective when the administrator so orders.

The following apply to all types of securities registration:

- Registration is effective for up to 1 year from effective date or until all securities have been sold, whichever is longer.
- State securities administrators set filing fees.
- The registration statement may be amended after its effective date to increase the size of the offering so long as the price and underwriter's compensation remains unchanged.

- The administrator may not require the issuer to file reports more often than quarterly.
- The administrator may require the issuer to report on the progress of the sale of the securities.
- The person who files the registration statement with the state may be the issuer, a broker dealer, or a large stockholder selling shares as part of the offering.

The following apply to registration though coordination and qualification:

- State securities administrators may require that the proceeds from the offering be held in escrow until a certain amount has been sold.
- The administrator may require that the securities be sold on a specific subscription form.

EXEMPT SECURITIES/FEDERALLY COVERED EXEMPTIONS

The National Securities Market Improvement Act of 1996 provided federally covered exemptions for securities that have met the stringent listing requirements of any U.S. stock exchange, including the Nasdaq. An issuer whose common stock is listed on a centralized U.S. stock exchange such as the NYSE or the Nasdaq is provided an exemption for all of its securities, regardless of their type. An exemption from state registration is also provided to:

- Securities that are sold exclusively to qualified purchasers.
- Investment company securities.
- Securities and transactions exempt from federal registration.
- Debt securities with maturities of less than 270 days and sold in denominations of $50,000 or more.
- Exempt issuers.
- Employee benefit plans.
- Option contracts, both puts and calls on stocks and indexes.
- Equipment trust securities issued by a federally covered or exempt issuer.

Certain securities are exempt from state registration and sales literature requirements because the issuer is exempt. The following are examples of exempt issuers:

- U.S. government
- State and municipal governments
- Foreign national governments
- Canadian federal and municipal governments
- Insurance companies
- Banks and trusts
- Credit unions and savings and loans
- Common carriers (railroad, trucking, and airlines) that are subject to the Interstate Commerce Commission (the term *consolidated* is a key word)
- Religious and charitable organizations
- Public utility securities
- Securities issued by a cooperative

EXEMPT TRANSACTIONS

Sometimes a security that would otherwise have to register is exempt from state registration because of the type of transaction that is involved. The way in which the securities are sold removes the securities from the jurisdiction of the administrator. The following are all exempt transactions:

PRIVATE PLACEMENTS/
REGULATION D OFFERINGS

A private placement is a sale of securities that is made to a group of accredited investors and the securities are not offered to the general public. Accredited investors (and higher net worth individuals and institutions) include institutional investors and individuals who:

- Earn at least $200,000 per year if single;

   or

- Earn at least $300,000 jointly with a spouse;

or

- Have a net worth of at least $1,000,000, excluding the primary residence.

Sales to nonaccredited investors are limited to 10 in any 12-month period at the state level and 35 nonaccredited investors in any 12-month period at the federal level. No commission may be paid to representatives who sell a private placement to a nonaccredited investor. All investors in private placements must hold the securities fully paid for at least 6 months. The limits on the amount of money that may be raised under the various regulation D offerings are as follows:

- Regulation 504 D allows issuers to raise up to $5 million.
- Regulation 506 D allows issuers to raise an unlimited amount of capital.

RULE 144

Rule 144 regulates how control or restricted securities may be sold. Rule 144 designates:

- The holding period for the security.
- The amount of the security that may be sold.
- Filing procedures.
- Method of sale.

Control securities are owned by officers, directors, and owners of 10% or more of the company's outstanding stock. Control stock may be obtained by insiders through open-market purchases or through the exercise of company stock options. There is no holding period for control securities. However, insiders are not allowed to earn a short swing profit through the purchase and sale of control stock in the open market. If the securities were held less than 6 months, the insider must return any profit to the company. Restricted securities may be purchased by both insiders and investors through a private placement or be obtained through an offering other than a public sale. Securities obtained through a private placement or other nonpublic means need to be sold under Rule 144 in order to allow the transfer of ownership. Restricted stock must be held fully paid for 6 months. After 6 months, the securities may be freely sold by investors as long as the investors have not been affiliated with the issuer in the last 3 months. Rule 144 sets the following volume limits for both restricted and control stock during any 90-day period. The seller must file Form 144 at the time the order is entered and is limited to the greater of:

- The average weekly trading volume for the preceding 4 weeks,

  or

- 1% of the issuer's total outstanding stock.

For orders for 5,000 shares or less and that do not exceed $50,000, Form 144 does not need to be filed.

If the owner of restricted stock dies, their estate may sell the shares freely without regard to the holding period or volume limitations of Rule 144.

PRIVATE INVESTMENT IN A PUBLIC EQUITY (PIPE)

Public companies that wish to obtain additional financing without selling securities to the general public may sell securities to a group of accredited investors through a private placement. The accredited investors in most cases will be institutional investors who wish to invest a large amount of capital. Common stock, convertible or nonconvertible debt, and rights and warrants may all be sold to investors through a PIPE transaction. Obtaining capital through a PIPE transaction benefits the public company in a number of ways:

- Reduced transaction cost
- Term disclosure only upon completion of the transaction
- Increased institutional ownership
- Quick closing

Securities sold through a PIPE transaction are subject to Rule 144.

RULE 147 INTRASTATE OFFERING

Rule 147 pertains to offerings of securities that are limited to one state. Because the offering is being made only in one state, it is exempt from registration with the SEC and is subject to the jurisdiction of the state securities administrator. In order to qualify for an exemption from SEC registration, the issue must be organized and have its principal place of business in the state and meet at least one of the following business criteria:

- 80% of the issuer's income must be received in that state.
- 80% of the offering's proceeds must be used in that state.

- 80% of the issuer's assets must be located in that state.
- A majority of the issuer's employees are based in-state.

All purchasers must be located within the state and must agree not to resell the securities to an out-of-state resident for 6 months.

If the issuer is using an underwriter, the broker dealer must have an office in that state.

The SEC has also adopted Rule 147A, which is largely identical to Rule 147. However, Rule 147A allows companies that are incorporated or organized out of state to use the Rule 147 exemption. Rule 147A also allows out-of-state residents to purchase the securities.

REGULATION A OFFERINGS

As amended by the JOBS Act, a Regulation A offering, also known as a small business company offering, allows tier 1 issuers to raise up to $20 million and tier 2 issuers to raise up to $50 million in any 12 month period. Selling securities holders may not sell more than 30% of the shares being offered. This exemption from full registration allows smaller companies access to the capital markets without having to go through the expense of filing a full registration statement with the SEC. The issuer will instead file an abbreviated notice of sale or offering circular with the SEC and purchasers of the issue will be given a copy of the offering circular rather than a final prospectus. The same 20-day cooling-off period applies to Regulation A offerings.

TRANSACTIONS WITH FINANCIAL INSTITUTIONS

All transactions with financial institutions are exempt. The USA was designed to protect the individual investor, not the sophisticated financial institution. Financial institutions include:

- Banks.
- Insurance companies.
- Investment companies.
- Broker dealers.
- Pension plans with at least $1,000,000 in assets.

TRANSACTIONS WITH FIDUCIARIES

All transactions with fiduciaries are exempt from registration with the administrator. Transactions with any of the following are considered transactions with fiduciaries and are exempt:

- Trustees
- Executors

- Guardians
- Sheriffs/marshals
- Administrators
- Receivers

TRANSACTIONS WITH UNDERWRITERS

All transactions with underwriters of securities are exempt from state registration. For example, if XYZ Corporation is selling 10,000,000 shares of its common stock to its investment bank under a firm commitment underwriting agreement, the transaction is exempt from state registration.

UNSOLICITED ORDERS

All orders that are executed through a broker dealer at the sole request of the customer are considered unsolicited orders and the securities, if not registered within the state, are exempt from registration. The administrator may require proof that the order was unsolicited and may require that the customer sign an acknowledgment to that fact.

TRANSACTIONS IN MORTGAGE-BACKED SECURITIES

Because of the high quality of the collateral, transactions in mortgage-backed securities are exempt so long as the entire mortgage or deed of trust is sold as a unit in the transaction.

PLEDGES

Should a person pledge securities as collateral for a loan, the pledge does not constitute a sale. Additionally, should the borrower default on the loan, the person who now has ownership of the securities by way of default may sell those securities without being required to register the securities to recoup the losses.

OFFERS TO EXISTING SECURITIES HOLDERS

Transactions with existing holders of the following are exempt:

- Convertible securities
- Nontransferable warrants
- Transferable warrants exercisable within 90 days

These transactions with existing securities holders are all exempt provided no commission was paid directly or indirectly for soliciting the security holder.

PREORGANIZATION CERTIFICATES

Certain regulations may require that a corporation receive a minimum level of capital in order to be formed. A preorganization certificate is an agreement to purchase securities prior to the formation of a corporation. The offer or sale of the certificate is exempt if no commission was received for soliciting the sale. The number of subscribers may not exceed 10, and the subscriber may not make any payments.

ISOLATED NONISSUER TRANSACTIONS

An agent or a broker dealer may occasionally recommend a security to a client that is not registered in the client's state of residence as long as it is an isolated event. An isolated transaction means one or very few are performed per year per broker dealer. The number of transactions that qualifies as isolated transactions varies from state to state. An isolated nonissuer transaction may also include a transaction between two individuals without the use of a broker dealer. In this type of transaction, the owner of the securities may sell the securities to another interested party directly.

NONISSUER TRANSACTIONS

A nonissuer transaction is a transaction of publicly traded securities and is exempt if the issuer meets the following requirements:

- The issuer has securities registered under Section 12 of the Securities Exchange Act of 1934 and has been reporting for at least 180 days;

  or

- The issuer has securities registered under the Investment Company Act of 1940;

  or

- The issuer has filed the information required by the Securities Exchange Act of 1934 with the administrator for at least 180 days prior to the transaction.

Pretest

SECURITIES REGISTRATION, EXEMPT SECURITIES, AND EXEMPT TRANSACTIONS

1. An established issuer wants to register additional securities through filing. The issuer is most likely:

   a. a bank.

   b. an insurance company.

   c. an investment company.

   d. a large corporation raising money though an IPO.

2. A broker dealer sells a nonexempt unregistered security to an investment company. Which of the following is true?

   a. This is a prohibited practice.

   b. The broker dealer must offer rescission.

   c. This is an exempt transaction.

   d. This is a nonexempt transaction.

3. An exemption from registration that applies to a security sold to only residents of one state is offered under:

   a. Rule 144.

   b. Rule 147.

   c. Regulation D.

   d. Rule 145.

4. A registered representative may sell a nonexempt unregistered security in which of the following situations?

   a. An IPO
   b. A private placement
   c. A wash sale
   d. During arbitrage transactions only

5. Which of the following is an exempt transaction?

   a. A transaction involving $100,000 worth of Treasury bonds
   b. A transaction involving commercial paper
   c. A transaction involving an unsolicited order
   d. A transaction involving a common stock listed on the NYSE

6. Which of the following must apply for commercial paper to be considered an exempt security?

   I. It must be in denominations of less than $50,000.
   II. It must have denominations of more than $50,000.
   III. It must have a maturity of less than 270 days.
   IV. It must be issued by a bank.

   a. I, III, and IV
   b. II and III
   c. II, III, and IV
   d. II and IV

7. A large broker dealer has recommended a nonexempt unregistered security to three individual investors in the last 12 months. According to the USA, this is:

   a. a violation, and the broker dealer must offer rescission to the customers involved.
   b. a violation of both state and federal law, and the broker dealer may be fined, sanctioned, or both.
   c. an example of isolated nonissuer transactions, and the transactions are exempt.
   d. an example of unsolicited orders for government or municipal securities, and the securities are exempt from registration.

8. Which of the following is NOT a federally covered security?

   a. Stock listed on the NYSE

   b. Shares of an investment company

   c. Common stock that has been duly registered within the state through filing

   d. A Nasdaq GMS common stock

9. Under the USA, transactions with which of the following are NOT exempt?

   a. Wealthy investors

   b. Trustees

   c. Administrators

   d. Underwriters

10. All of the following are exempt from state registration, EXCEPT:

    a. common stock of Houston Power and Light Co.

    b. common stock of XYZ Consolidated.

    c. warrants of ALG Company, because ALG's common stock is listed on the NYSE.

    d. XYZ common stock, which is listed on the Vancouver Stock Exchange.

11. A securities state registration becomes effective under coordination after:

    a. 20 days.

    b. 30 days.

    c. 25 days.

    d. 10 days.

12. A broker dealer distributing a private placement may sell the offering to how many nonaccredited investors?

    a. No more than 35 in 12 months

    b. No more than 10 in 12 months

    c. No more than 15 in 12 months

    d. No more than 10 in 6 months

13. Which of the following becomes effective at the same time as the SEC registration?

    a. Qualification

    b. Coordination

    c. Application

    d. Notification

14. Which of the following is NOT an exempt transaction?

    a. A transaction involving $4,200 worth of securities executed at the customer's request

    b. Sales of unregistered securities to an investment company

    c. Recommendation to an individual investor to purchase 500 shares of XYZ, where XYZ is listed on the NYSE

    d. An issuer sells 5,000,000 shares of common stock to its underwriter

15. All of the following are ways to register a security within a state, EXCEPT:

    a. application.

    b. notification.

    c. qualification.

    d. coordination.

16. A federally covered security is:

    a. exempt from both SEC and state registration.

    b. only issued by exempt issuers.

    c. not required to register with the state securities administrator.

    d. issued with a maximum maturity of 270 days.

17. All of the following issuers are exempt from state registration, EXCEPT:

    a. the London Bridge and Tunnel Authority.

    b. New Mexico.

    c. Ontario.

    d. the Russian government.

18. An issuer whose registration has already become effective with the SEC will most likely register its securities with the state securities administrator through:

    a. coordination.

    b. application.

    c. notification.

    d. qualification.

19. The term *isolated nonissuer transactions* applies to transactions between state residents executed through which of the following?

    I. An underwriter

    II. A broker dealer

    III. A government

    IV. An investment adviser

    a. I and III

    b. II and IV

    c. III and IV

    d. I, II, III, and IV

20. Which of the following is an exempt transaction?

    a. Transactions with high net worth clients within the state

    b. Sale of 30-year Treasury bonds to the account of a conservative investor

    c. Transaction with a trust administrator

    d. The sale of a convertible bond to a long-term investor

State Securities Administrator: The Uniform Securities Act

INTRODUCTION

The state securities administrator has the authority to enforce all of the provisions of the Uniform Securities Act (USA) within its state. The state securities administrator may deny, revoke, or suspend the registration of a security, an agent, or a firm. The administrator may also revoke an exemption from registration, subpoena and investigate any registrant, and amend rules as required. The North American Securities Administrators Association (NASAA) is the oldest investor-protection organization in the country and represents the interest of all of the state securities administrators. NASAA also writes policies and administers the Series 63, 65, and 66 exams.

ACTIONS BY THE STATE SECURITIES ADMINISTRATOR

The North America Securities Administrators Association is a body of state regulators, each of whom is responsible for administering the provisions of the Uniform Securities Act within their state. Together they make up an advisory committee that refine and amend the Uniform Securities Act through the adoption of module rules and policy statements. NASAA is also responsible for creating the content tested on the Series 63, 65, and 66 exams. Among others, some of the more testable concepts relating to NASAA's model rules and policy statements include the following:

- Policy statement detailing dishonest and unethical business practices of broker dealers and agents
- Policy statement relating to dishonest sales practices relating to the sale of investment company products by broker dealers and agents
- Policy statement detailing requirements for broker dealers conducting business on the premises of other financial (banking) institutions
- Model Rule covering unethical business practices of investment advisers
- Model Rule detailing requirements for investment advisers who maintain custody of client funds

A state securities administrator may take action to bar, suspend, censure, or restrict the activities of a registrant if the administrator finds it in the public interest and the applicant or registrant does one or more of the following:

- Fails to pay filing fees
- Is insolvent
- Fails to supervise employees
- Willfully violates the securities or banking laws of another country or has had a foreign regulator deny, revoke, or suspend its registration within the last 5 years
- Violates federal securities or commodities laws
- Has been convicted of any felony within the last 10 years
- Has been convicted of a securities-related misdemeanor
- Willfully violates any provision of the USA
- Files an incomplete, false, or misleading application for registration
- Has been temporarily or permanently enjoined from the securities business by a court of law
- Has been subject to an order by a state securities administrator denying, revoking, or suspending its registration
- Is deemed unqualified due to a lack of experience, training, or knowledge
- Engages in unethical or dishonest business practices

The administrator deeming it in the public interest is not enough to take action. The applicant must have been involved in one or more of the activities listed above. If the administrator is going to take action against the applicant, it must notify the applicant promptly in writing of its intention and must provide a hearing for the applicant within 15 days of receiving the request for a hearing. An administrator may deny an applicant's registration based on lack of knowledge, training, or experience, but a lack of experience may not be the sole basis for the denial of a registration.

CANCELLATION OF A REGISTRATION

The administrator may cancel the registration of a broker dealer, investment adviser, or an agent if the registrant or applicant no longer exists, has ceased doing business, or cannot be located. If, for example, the administrator sends a notice to a registrant and the notice is returned to the administrator as undeliverable with no known forwarding address, the administrator would have reasonable grounds for canceling the registration. Additionally, an individual's registration may be canceled if he or she has been deemed mentally incompetent by a court of law. The cancellation of a registration by the administrator is not a disciplinary or punitive action; it is more clerical in nature.

WITHDRAWAL OF A REGISTRATION

A broker dealer, investment adviser, or an agent may request that its registration with the state be withdrawn. The withdrawal will become effective 30 days after the administrator receives the request if no revocation or suspension proceedings are in process. The administrator has up to 1 year after the withdrawal of an applicant's registration to take action against the applicant to suspend or revoke their registration.

ACTIONS AGAINST AN ISSUER OF SECURITIES

The administrator may deny, revoke, or suspend the registration of a security if it deems it is in the public interest and:

- Any officer or director has been convicted of a securities crime.
- The registration statement is false, misleading, or incomplete.

- The security is subject to a court injunction.
- Promoter's fees or offering expenses are excessive or unreasonable.
- The offering is fraudulent.

The administrator may also revoke a security's exemption from registration if it is in the public interest and the exemption was based on a false, misleading, fraudulent, or unethical practice or statement. An administrator may, without prior notice, revoke the exempt status of a securities transaction.

RULE CHANGES

An administrator may change or amend rules as he or she deems necessary. All rules enacted by the administrator will have the same force and effect as rules enacted under the USA. An administrator's order may be appealed to the court system within 60 days by any aggrieved party. The appeal will not act as a temporary stay to the administrator's order unless first so ordered by a court. A rule enacted by the administrator applies to all registrants in the administrator's state.

ADMINISTRATIVE ORDERS

If the state securities administrator issues an order, that order will be enforced against a specific registrant or activity. For example, if a broker dealer was engaging in sales practices that violated the USA, the administrator may issue an order suspending that broker dealer's registration with the state for 60 days. Any affected party may challenge an administrator's order within 60 days of issuance by filing a written petition. During the time that the challenge is pending the order will remain in effect. If the administrator determines that the order is no longer required or a court determines that the order is no longer required, the administrator's order will be vacated. A stop order is an administrative order taken against an issuer or security that stops the security from being sold in the administrator's state. If the issuer cures or corrects the deficiency or problem with the security, the stop order will be lifted and the security will be allowed to be sold. A cease and desist order is an order against a person or firm who is engaging in or about to engage in an activity the administrator deems unacceptable.

TAKENOTE!

If the administrator suspends the registration of a firm, all of the individuals who are registered with the firm will have their registrations placed in suspense status. After the term of suspension has been completed, all registrations will be reactivated. If the firm's registration had been revoked, all individuals whose registrations were not revoked would be required to find a new firm to become associated with.

INTERPRETIVE OPINIONS

A person who is actively engaged in the securities business may from time to time seek the opinion of the state securities administrator to ensure that the business that he or she is conducting is in line with the rules of the USA as amended within the state. In response to the request, the administrator may issue an opinion regarding the activity, issue a no action letter, or elect not to issue an opinion. If the administrator issues an interpretive opinion, the administrator may charge a fee for the interpretation of its rules.

ADMINISTRATIVE RECORDS

The state securities administrator will maintain all records relating to the business of the state securities administrator and will make the records available upon request. The administrator will provide certified copies if specifically requested. The administrator may charge a reasonable fee for the production and delivery of the records. The records to be maintained include:

- All applications for broker dealer registration.
- All applications for investment adviser registration.
- All applications for agent registration for broker dealers and investment advisers.
- All applications for registrations of securities and registration statements.
- All orders, actions, and interpretive opinions entered.
- All written claims for exemptions from registration.

The records may be maintained electronically, on microfilm, or on any other device the administrator may elect.

INVESTIGATIONS

A state securities administrator may investigate a broker dealer, an investment adviser, or an agent in any state if it feels that a violation has taken or may take place. The administrator may also subpoena people, books, and records in any state and may administer oaths to compel people to testify. Anyone who displays contempt for the administrator's order is guilty of contumacy and may be found in contempt of court if the administrator asks the court to enforce its orders.

CIVIL AND CRIMINAL PENALTIES

A state securities administrator may issue a cease and desist order without a prior hearing or notice. The administrator may appoint a receiver to oversee the assets of violators and may require them to make restitution. Anyone who is found to have criminally violated the laws of the USA is subject to a $5,000 fine and/or 3 years in prison. People who criminally violate the Investment Advisers Act of 1940 are subject to a $10,000 fine and/or 5 years in prison. The statute of limitations for an administrator taking action is 5 years.

An investor who sues for a violation of the USA is entitled to receive:

- The value paid for the securities minus any income received during the holding period (e.g., dividends).
- Interest on the money for the holding period.
- Court costs.

Civil actions may be taken against:

- An agent.
- A firm.
- The agent's supervisor.

If an investment adviser violates the provisions of the USA, clients may sue to recover:

- Advisory fees.
- Losses.
- Interest on the money.
- Attorney fees and court costs, minus any income received as a result of the advice.

JURISDICTION OF THE STATE SECURITIES ADMINISTRATOR

Although the USA sets forth model legislation for state securities laws, it is the responsibility of the state securities administrator to administer the laws within the state.

The powers granted to the administrator under the Uniform Securities Act include the ability to:

- Cancel, deny, suspend, or revoke a registration of an agent, firm, or security.
- Cancel, deny, suspend, or revoke an exemption from registration of an agent, firm, or security.
- Conduct investigations.
- Issue subpoenas.
- Issue cease and desist orders.
- Seek injunctions.
- Amend, make, and rescind rules and orders.

The only time that a state securities administrator has any authority to investigate a federally registered investment adviser is if the adviser's principal office is located within the administrator's state. The principal office is where the executive and C-level directors maintain offices.

ADMINISTRATOR'S JURISDICTION OVER SECURITIES TRANSACTIONS

State securities administrators have jurisdiction over securities transactions that:

- Originated within their state.
- Are directed into their state.
- Are accepted in their state.

If a client draws a check on an out-of-state bank or has securities sent to another state, that does not give the securities administrator in that state jurisdiction.

The offer and acceptance of a security constitutes a transaction or the sale of a security. It is the actual conveyance of the ownership of the security for value.

● TEST**FOCUS!**

Mr. Jones, a resident of Texas, receives a call from his investment representative, Bob, in New York. Bob recommends that Mr. Jones purchase 500 shares of XYZ based on his company's research and in line with Mr. Jones's investment objectives. Mr. Jones accepts the recommendation and purchases the 500 shares at the market.

In this case, the securities administrators from both Texas and New York have jurisdiction over the transaction. The state securities administrator from Texas can review the transaction because the sale was directed and accepted in Texas. Additionally, the state securities administrator from New York may review the transaction because the transaction originated from the representative's office within the state.

If, in this case, Mr. Jones tells his representative that he'll think about it and then calls his representative in New York the next day from his summer home in California and purchases XYZ, the transaction would be subject to the jurisdiction of three state securities administrators:

1. The administrator from New York—because that is where the sale originated.

2. The administrator from Texas—because that is where the sale was directed.

3. The administrator from California—because that is where the sale was accepted.

State securities administrators also have jurisdiction over offers of securities that:

- Originated within their state.
- Are directed into their state.

An offer is considered to have been made in the state in which it originated, as well as the state to which it is directed.

If, in our example, Bob, the representative in New York, directs the offer of XYZ to Mr. Jones in Texas and Mr. Jones elects not to purchase the stock, the offer would be subject to the jurisdiction of the securities administrators in both New York and Texas. The state securities administrator in New York would have jurisdiction because that is where the representative was sitting when he made the offer. The administrator in Texas would have jurisdiction because that is where the offer was directed.

An offer or sale of a security that may be converted or exchanged into another security also constitutes an offer or sale of the security into which the original security may be converted.

State securities administrators may:

- Investigate securities-related business within their borders.
- Issue subpoenas for people, books, and records from any state.
- Compel witnesses to testify.
- Issue cease and desist orders and seek injunctions.
- Deny, suspend, or revoke registrations, licenses, and exemptions.
- Adopt and amend rules.

State securities administrators may investigate complaints and alleged violations both in and out of their home state. The investigation may be conducted publicly or in private. During the course of the investigation, the administrator may subpoena people, books, and records from any state and may compel witnesses to testify under oath or to give a written sworn statement.

Individuals brought before the administrator may not invoke their Fifth Amendment right against self-incrimination. The administrator may force them to testify about the matter being investigated. However, a person who is forced to testify may not be prosecuted based on the testimony that he or she was compelled to offer. Thus, a witness in this situation is given partial immunity.

If the administrator finds that a person has engaged in or is about to engage in any activity that would violate the USA, the administrator may issue a cease and desist order. A cease and desist order may be issued without a hearing. The administrator has the power to prevent violations before they take place. However, only a court of law has the authority to force compliance with the order and to prescribe penalties for violating the order.

The state securities administrator may not:

- Establish requirements for broker dealers that exceed federal requirements.
- Establish requirements for investment advisers that exceed the requirements of the adviser's home state.
- Require the registration of federally covered advisers.

RADIO, TELEVISION, AND NEWSPAPER DISTRIBUTION

An advertisement, offer, or solicitation will not have been made and will be outside the jurisdiction of a state securities administrator if the following conditions are met:

- The television broadcast originated outside the administrator's state.
- The radio broadcast originated outside the administrator's state.
- The newspaper or periodical was published outside the administrator's state.
- The newspaper or periodical was published inside the state but two-thirds of its circulation is outside of the state of publication.

In the last case, the circulation numbers are based on the preceding year. If the conditions are met, the state securities administrator in the state of publication will not have jurisdiction because the advertisement, offer, or solicitation is not deemed to be made in the state where the publication originated.

RIGHT OF RESCISSION

If the seller of a security determines that the sale of securities has violated any provision of the USA, the seller may offer the affected parties rescission. All offers of rescission must be in writing and include an agreement to repurchase the securities at the original purchase price and must include interest for the time period that the money was invested. If the buyer does not accept the offer of rescission within 30 days, the seller has no further liability with regard to the sale of those securities, and the buyer forfeits the right to sue. An investor's acknowledgment that a sale is in violation of the USA is never valid.

EXAMPLE

A customer with an investment objective of speculation convinces his representative to sell him an interest in a private placement that will pay the representative a commission and is in violation of the USA. The investor is a nonaccredited investor and signs a letter stating that he recognizes that the investment is in violation of the USA and that he will not sue or otherwise hold the representative or his firm responsible for any losses.

This acknowledgment by the client is neither valid nor enforceable and in no way protects the representative or the firm.

Investment advisers that breach their fiduciary duty or are found to have made unsuitable transactions based on a client's investment objectives can be held liable for:

- The amount of the loss.

- Interest on the amount invested.

- Reasonable legal costs.

- The cost of the advice.

Minus any income received as a result of the advice.

STATUTE OF LIMITATIONS

If a buyer of a security finds that the sale of the security violates any of the provisions of the USA, the purchaser has 2 years from the discovery of the violation or 3 years from the purchase date, whichever comes first, to take action.

Pretest

STATE SECURITIES ADMINISTRATOR: THE UNIFORM SECURITIES ACT

1. A state securities administrator may require all of the following, EXCEPT:

   a. securities to be sold under a specific subscription form.

   b. an agent to take an oral exam.

   c. an issuer to file monthly financial reports.

   d. a specimen of the security.

2. A recent college graduate has just passed the Series 66 exam. The state securities administrator may deny the registration based solely on which of the following?

   I. Lack of experience

   II. Public interest

   III. Lack of training

   IV. A felony conviction 2 years ago prior to the application for registration

   a. I and III

   b. III and IV

   c. I, II, and III

   d. II, III, and IV

3. A New York agent calls a customer, who is a New Jersey resident, at his hotel where he is vacationing in Florida. The representative recommends that the client purchase 1,000 shares of ABC. The customer informs the representative that he will call him when he returns to New Jersey the following morning. On his return, the customer calls his representative and elects to purchase the 1,000 shares of ABC. Which state administrators have jurisdiction over this transaction?

   a. New York and Florida

   b. New Jersey and New York

   c. New York, New Jersey, and Florida

   d. New York

4. A state securities administrator takes action against the principal of a firm for failing to supervise the actions of one of the firm's agents. Which of the following is true?

   I. The administrator may take action against the firm's registration.

   II. The administrator may not take action against the firm's registration.

   III. The agent's registration may be subject to action by the administrator.

   IV. Because the administrator has taken action against the supervisor, it may not take action against the agent.

   a. I and II

   b. I and III

   c. II and III

   d. II and IV

5. A state securities administrator has sent a notice of its intention to revoke a firm's registration. The firm requests a hearing in writing. The hearing will be held within:

   a. 30 days.

   b. 15 days.

   c. 45 days.

   d. 60 days.

6. Which of the following is true regarding actions taken by the administrator?

    I. An administrator may issue subpoenas.

    II. An administrator may suspend a pending registration.

    III. An administrator may issue a stop order without a hearing.

    IV. An individual who displays contempt for the administrator's order may be found in contempt of court.

    a. I and II

    b. II and IV

    c. II, III, and IV

    d. I, II, III, and IV

7. An administrator may do all of the following, EXCEPT:

    a. require the production of documents.

    b. administer oaths.

    c. compel testimony.

    d. order injunctions.

8. The Uniform Securities Act was designed to be enforced by:

    a. the SEC.

    b. FINRA.

    c. the states.

    d. the federal government.

9. Which of the following are true with regard to an investor's right of rescission?

    I. The investor has 30 days to accept the offer.

    II. The offer may be made verbally.

    III. The offer must include an offer to pay interest.

    IV. The investor may receive punitive damages.

    a. I and II

    b. I and III

    c. I, II, and IV

    d. I, II, III, and IV

10. An agent who willfully violates the antifraud provision of the USA may be subject to which of the following?

    I. 3 years in prison

    II. A $5,000 fine

    III. 5 years in prison

    IV. A $10,000 fine

    a. I and II

    b. II only

    c. III and IV

    d. IV only

11. A client who determines that a firm has violated the USA by selling certain securities has how long to take action against the firm under the USA?

    a. 6 years

    b. 2 years from the discovery or 3 years from the triggering event, whichever occurs first

    c. 5 years

    d. There is no statute of limitations for violations of the USA.

12. Which of the following is NOT a violation of the USA?

    a. Buying warrants and selling the issuer's common stock short

    b. Making market predictions

    c. Telling a customer that she cannot lose money by purchasing Treasury bonds because the principal is guaranteed by the U.S. government

    d. Printing "FINRA" in large letters on the firm's business card

13. Which of the following is a violation of the USA?

    a. Cold calling customers in a neighboring state

    b. Explaining to a customer that securities listed on the NYSE are safer than nonlisted securities

    c. Mailing 150 form letters to potential customers

    d. Failing to withhold capital gains taxes on the sale of a security

14. An agent may be denied a registration for all of the following reasons, EXCEPT:

    a. the agent is being taken to arbitration by a number of clients for allegedly mishandling their accounts.

    b. the agent has a securities-related misdemeanor.

    c. the agent was convicted of fraud 8 1/2 years ago.

    d. It is solely deemed to be in the public's best interest.

15. A client who takes action against an investment adviser is entitled to all of the following under the USA, EXCEPT:

    a. reimbursement of fees.

    b. attorney's fees.

    c. treble damages.

    d. interest on money.

16. An agent has displayed a pattern of abusive activity. The administrator may take action against which of the following?

    I. The agent

    II. The principal of the firm

    III. The firm

    IV. Industry regulators for failing to supervise the firm

    a. I only

    b. I and III

    c. I, II, and III

    d. I, II, III, and IV

17. A customer who has rejected a broker dealer's offer of rescission may do which of the following under the USA?

    a. Reserve the right to accept the offer at a later date.

    b. Sue the firm in court.

    c. Take the firm to arbitration.

    d. Nothing; the customer has given up the right of recovery.

18. A state securities administrator may take action against an issuer for all of the following reasons, EXCEPT:

    a. the promoter's fees are excessive.

    b. the registration statement is incomplete.

    c. the prospects for the issuer's industry are not strong.

    d. the issuer has relied on an exemption from registration based on a misleading application.

19. A broker dealer has withdrawn its state registration. Its request to withdraw the registration will become effective in:

    a. 45 days.

    b. 30 days.

    c. 60 days.

    d. 90 days.

20. An offer of securities is subject to the jurisdiction of all of the following state securities administrators, EXCEPT:

    a. the state where the offer originated.

    b. the state where the issuer is headquartered.

    c. the state were the offer was directed.

    d. the state where the offer was accepted.

Answer Keys

CHAPTER 1: DEFINITION OF TERMS

1. (C) A minor is not considered a person because a minor may not enter into a legally binding contract.

2. (C) The pledge of securities as collateral for a margin loan is not considered a sale. All of the other choices constitute a sale, including a bonus security attached to another security, such as a warrant.

3. (D) A qualified purchaser must have at least $5,000,000 in assets. A family-owned business with $5,000,000 in investments is also a qualified purchaser.

4. (C) All of the choices listed are institutional investors except an employee benefit plan with $800,000 in assets. In order for the plan to be an institutional investor, it must have more than $5,000,000 in assets.

5. (B) A trust indenture is a contract between a corporate issuer of debt securities and a trustee. It is not a security.

6. (D) A gift of assessable stock is considered to be a sale of securities. Assessable stock can require the owner to make additional payments.

7. (A) The publisher of a market report based on market conditions is considered to be an investment adviser.

8. (D) A family-owned business with at least $5,000,000 in assets is a qualified purchaser.

9. (B) XYZ is a federally covered security and is given an exemption from state registration because it trades on a U.S. exchange.

10. (D) An interest in any of the items listed is a security.

11. (B) Only the company and the publisher of the market letter are investment advisers. Individuals are investment adviser representatives.

12. (D) The promise of a profit is not one of the requirements of the Howey test.

13. (D) A broker is a "person" that executes an order for its own account or for the accounts of others. Under the USA, a person is any entity that can enter into a legally binding contract.

14. (D) An offer of securities is made through a prospectus.

15. (C) A corporation that issues securities or simply proposes to issue securities is considered an issuer.

16. (D) An individual representing an out-of-state broker dealer is required to register as an agent. None of the other individuals are considered agents.

17. (A) A broker dealer with no office in the state that only conducts business with customers who do not reside in that state or who are in that state for less than 30 days and an out-of-state broker dealer that only conducts business with other broker dealers are not considered broker dealers in that state.

18. (D) An OTC BB stock is not a federally covered security. Only Nasdaq securities are given the federally covered exemption.

19. (C) A guarantee of interest or principal may be issued by all of those listed except an investment adviser.

20. (C) An offer has been made when a representative has made a recommendation.

CHAPTER 2: SECURITIES INDUSTRY RULES AND REGULATIONS

1. (D) The Securities Exchange Act of 1934 regulates the secondary market.

2. (C) The SEC is the ultimate industry authority in regulating conduct. The SEC is a direct government body, and both the NYSE and FINRA answer to the SEC.

3. (A) All of the choices listed must be included, except for the name of the principal who approved the ad for use.

4. (D) The Maloney Act of 1938 was an amendment to the Securities Exchange Act of 1934 and established the NASD as the SRO for the OTC market. The NASD is now part of FINRA.

5. (C) All of the choices listed would be retail communications if any part of the communication is seen by even a single retail investor.

6. (B) Brokerage firms must maintain their advertising for at least 3 years.

7. (D) Generic advertising may not contain information about past recommendations.

8. (D) All of the items listed must appear in a tombstone ad published prior to the issue's registration becoming effective.

CHAPTER 3: ECONOMIC FUNDAMENTALS

1. (C) During an inflationary period, the price of a treasury bond will fall the most. The fixed income security with the longest maturity will change the most in price as interest rates change.

2. (D) Rising interest rates are bearish for the stock market.

3. (B) The main theory of economics is one of supply and demand; if the supply outpaces the demand, the price of the goods will fall.

4. (D) The discount rate is the rate that is actually controlled by the Federal Reserve Board. All of the other rates are adjusted in the marketplace by the lenders as a result of a change in the discount rate.

5. (C) Falling inventories are a sign of a pick up in the economy.

6. (A) A bank may borrow money from another bank to meet their reserve requirement and it will pay the other bank the federal funds rate.

7. (A) The two tools of the government are monetary policy, which is controlled by the Federal Reserve Board and controls the money supply, and fiscal policy, which is determined by the president and Congress and controls government spending and taxation.

8. (D) Fiscal policy is controlled by the president and Congress.

9. (C) The Federal Reserve sets all of those except government spending.

10. (A) A decline in the gross domestic product must last at least 2 quarters or 6 months to be considered a recession.

CHAPTER 4: CUSTOMER RECOMMENDATIONS, PROFESSIONAL CONDUCT, AND TAXATION

1. (B) This is known as painting the tape, matched purchases, or matched sales.

2. (D) An industrial revenue bond may subject some wealthy investors to the AMT.

3. (B) Of all the investments listed, only the Ginnie Mae pass-through certificate will provide income. Ginnie Mae pass-through certificates pay monthly interest and principal payments.

4. (D) This client is concerned about legislative risk; that is, the risk that the government will do something that adversely affects an investment.

5. (A) The investor has a large position in a thinly traded stock; as a result, the investor is subject to a large amount of liquidity risk.

6. (B) An investor who is concerned with the changes in interest rates would be least likely to purchase long-term bonds. As interest rates change, the price of the long-term bonds will fluctuate the most.

7. (B) A 90-day T bill is considered a risk-free investment. Bankers' acceptances are money market instruments and are short term. Series HH government bonds can only be exchanged for mature series EE bonds. Convertible preferred stock also has risk.

8. (D) Using the pending dividend to create urgency on the part of the investor to purchase this stock is a perfect example of this violation, and the results are listed in answers A, B, and C.

9. (D) An investor in a low tax bracket seeking current income would be best suited for a corporate bond fund.

10. (B) Entering an order with advance notice of a pending research report is a violation known as trading ahead.

11. (B) Of all the choices listed, only the Treasury bond pays interest. Commercial paper and bankers' acceptances are issued at a discount. An income bond will only pay interest if the company has enough income to do so.

12. (D) The greatest risk when purchasing a CMO is the risk of early refinancing or prepayment risk.

13. (C) Treasury STRIPS are government-issued zero-coupon bonds. They are issued at a discount and mature at par or $1,000. For the exam, they are the best answer for college expense planning if the question is asking for an investment recommendation, not the type of account that it is deposited into.

14. (D) Showing a client the past performance for a mutual fund that has only been around for 3 years is in line with the regulations. All of the other choices are violations.

15. (A) If an investor may lose part or all of his capital, it is called capital risk.

16. (C) A money market fund is the best recommendation for investors who will need access to their funds in the next few years.

CHAPTER 5: VARIABLE ANNUITIES, RETIREMENT PLANS, AND LIFE INSURANCE

1. (D) Investors may always make contributions to their IRAs as long as they have earned income. In this case the person may contribute $6,000.

2. (A) If the separate account earns less than the assumed interest rate, the monthly payment as well as the value of the annuity unity will go down.

3. (C) This is a nonqualified plan, meaning that the money is deposited after taxes. Therefore, the retiree will only pay taxes on the growth, or $7,000.

4. (D) The maximum amount that a couple may contribute to their IRAs at any one time is 400% of the annual contribution limit. Between January 1 and April 15, a contribution may be made for the prior year, the current year, or both. $6,000 × 2 × 2 = $24,000.

5. (C) The retirement account is qualified, which means that the investors have deposited the money pre-tax. Therefore, all of the money is taxed as ordinary income when it is withdrawn.

6. (A) A 529 plan would allow the investor to make a lump sum deposit.

7. (A) The money has been deposited in a Roth IRA after taxes. It is allowed to grow tax-deferred. If the investor is over 59-1/2 and the money has been in the IRA for at least 5 years, then it may all be withdrawn without paying taxes on the growth.

8. (B) A fixed annuity does not provide protection from inflation. If inflation rises, the holder of a fixed annuity may end up worse off due to the loss of value of the dollar.

9. (D) The maximum contribution for a SEP IRA is the lesser of 25% of the post-contribution income or $57,000.

CHAPTER 6: REGISTRATION OF BROKER DEALERS, INVESTMENT ADVISERS, AND AGENTS

1. (D) A broker dealer may not employ anyone as an agent unless it is duly registered.

2. (C) A broker dealer that meets the SEC's net capital requirement is exempt from the $35,000 surety bond requirement.

3. (C) An investment adviser is limited to giving advice to five or fewer clients during a 12-month period under the *de minimis* exemption.

4. (D) All of the partners must register because they all act in a sales capacity by managing portfolios at the time the firm initially registered. Partners who do not act in a sales capacity are not required to register.

5. (C) An investment adviser with between $100,000,000 and $110,000,000 may select either federal or state registration, depending on the prospects for receiving additional funds.

6. (D) At the time a client enters into a new advisory relationship all of the choices must be disclosed except the representative's compensation.

7. (A) An agent is exempt from registration if the agent represents an exempt issuer, such as a municipality or the government of Brazil. A Canadian corporation is not an exempt issuer. An agent who represents a broker dealer is always required to register.

8. (D) A pension consultant who advises clients with $214,00,000 in assets must register as an investment adviser with the SEC.

9. (D) When an agent changes employment, the old employer, the new employer, and the agent all must notify the administrator. This is all done in most cases through Form U5 when an agent leaves a firm and through Form U4 when the agent joins a new firm.

10. (C) A broker dealer may also be registered as an investment adviser and may be a corporation or an individual.

11. (C) An investment adviser must keep books and records for 5 years.

12. (C) A Canadian broker dealer in good standing with a Canadian securities regulator can register through a simplified registration process.

13. (C) An investment adviser may receive all of the choices listed except a percentage of the customer's profits as long as it is all disclosed to the customer.

14. (B) An agent is not required to meet any financial solvency requirements.

15. (D) If a firm becomes insolvent, all agents' registrations are canceled.

16. (C) An investment adviser who does not have custody of client funds is not subject to the $35,000 requirement. An adviser without custody must have $10,000 in net capital.

17. (C) The investment adviser must register in this case. An exemption is given to advisers who have given advice to five or fewer individuals in 12 months.

18. (A) Investors who open wrap accounts will be charged one fee for advice and execution. The investor must receive Schedule H at the time the account is opened.

19. (A) All registrations expire on December 31.

CHAPTER 7: SECURITIES REGISTRATION, EXEMPT SECURITIES, AND EXEMPT TRANSACTIONS

1. (C) An issuer registering its securities through filing is most likely an investment company.

2. (C) This is an example of an exempt transaction. All transactions with financial institutions are exempt regardless of the security involved.

3. (B) Rule 147 offers an exemption from registration to issuers who sell securities only to residents of one state. Rule 147 is an intrastate offering.

4. (B) A registered representative may sell an unregistered nonexempt security through a private placement.

5. (C) All unsolicited orders are exempt transactions. An unsolicited order is placed by the customer without any advice from the representative. The question is asking about an exempt transaction, not an exempt security or an exempt issuer, as are detailed in the other choices.

6. (B) Commercial paper must be issued in denominations exceeding $50,000 with a maturity of less than 270 days.

7. (C) These are examples of isolated nonissuer transactions. The broker dealer has recommended the securities to three investors over the course of 1 year. A broker dealer is allowed to execute a few isolated nonissuer transactions in a security over a 12-month period.

8. (C) Securities given a federally covered exemption are exempt from state registration. This choice had to register because it was not a federally covered security.

9. (A) Transactions with wealthy investors are not exempt transactions. Transactions with all of the other choices listed would be exempt.

10. (D) A security listed on a foreign exchange is not an exempt security. All of the other choices are exempt.

11. (D) A state registration becomes effective after 10 days provided no stop order has been issued. A security's state registration may not become effective before its federal registration.

12. (B) A private placement may be sold to no more than 10 nonaccredited investors in a 12-month period under the USA.

13. (B) State registration through coordination becomes effective at the same time as the federal registration.

14. (C) A recommendation to an investor involving a NYSE-listed security is not an exempt transaction.

15. (A) A security is not registered by application. A security may be registered with the state through notification, qualification, or coordination.

16. (C) A federally covered security is not required to register at the state level.

17. (A) Political subdivisions of foreign countries (except Canada) are not given an exemption from registration.

18. (C) A security whose registration statement has already become effective with the SEC would most likely register through notification or notice filing.

19. (B) An isolated nonissuer transaction must be executed through a broker dealer or an investment adviser.

20. (C) A transaction with a trust administrator is an exempt transaction.

CHAPTER 8: STATE SECURITIES ADMINISTRATOR: THE UNIFORM SECURITIES ACT

1. (C) A state securities administrator may not require an issuer to file reports more than quarterly.

2. (B) An agent may be denied a registration based on lack of training or a criminal record. An agent may not be denied a registration solely based on the public interest or lack of experience.

3. (C) All three administrators would have jurisdiction over this transaction. New York because that is where the offer originated, Florida because that is where the offer was directed, and New Jersey because that is where the client accepted the offer.

4. (B) The administrator may take action against both the firm and the agent.

5. (B) The administrator must hold a hearing within 15 days of receiving a written request.

6. (D) An administrator may do all of the choices listed, and an individual may be found in contempt of court for displaying contumacy.

7. (D) An administrator may not order an injunction. Only a court may order an injunction. The administrator may ask a court for an injunction, but the court must order it.

8. (C) The USA was designed to be enforced and administered by the states.

9. (B) If an investor has been offered rescission, the investor must accept it within 30 days and the offer must pay the investor interest for the time that the money was invested.

10. (A) An individual who willfully violates the USA may be fined $5,000, sentenced to up to 3 years in prison, or both.

11. (B) An investor who discovers a violation has 2 years from the discovery or 3 years from the triggering event, whichever occurs first, to take action.

12. (A) All of the choices listed are violations except buying warrants and selling the issuer's common stock short. This is an example of an arbitrage transaction.

13. (B) Implying that one security is safer than another due to its exchange listing is a violation.

14. (D) An agent may not be denied a registration solely on the basis of the public interest.

15. (C) A client is not entitled to treble damages. The client is entitled to attorney's fees, reimbursement of advisory fees, and interest on the money that was invested.

16. (C) It is highly unlikely that an administrator would try to take action against another regulator due to the actions of an agent. If the administrator takes action against the principal of the firm for the actions of an agent, the administrator may take action against the firm as well.

17. (D) A customer who has rejected an offer of rescission has forfeited all rights of recovery.

18. (C) An administrator may not take action against an issuer's registration because it does not think that the industry has good prospects for the issuer.

19. (B) The withdrawal of a registration will become effective after 30 days, as long as no action is being taken against the broker dealer.

20. (B) An offer of securities is not subject to the jurisdiction of the administrator in the state where the issuer is headquartered.

Glossary of Exam Terms

A

AAA/Aaa The highest investment-grade rating for bond issuers awarded by Standard & Poor's and Moody's ratings agencies.

acceptance waiver and consent (AWAC) A process used when a respondent does not contest an allegation made by FINRA. The respondent accepts the findings without admitting any wrongdoing and agrees to accept any penalty for the violation.

account executive (AE) An individual who is duly licensed to represent a broker dealer in securities transactions or investment banking business. Also known as a registered representative.

accredited investor Any individual or institution that meets one or more of the following: (1) a net worth exceeding \$1 million, excluding the primary residence, or (2) is single and has an annual income of \$200,000 or more or \$300,000 jointly with a spouse.

accretion An accounting method used to step up an investor's cost base for a bond purchased at a discount.

accrued interest The portion of a debt securities future interest payment that has been earned by the seller of the security. The purchaser must pay this amount of accrued interest to the seller at the time of the transaction's settlement. Interest accrues from the date of the last interest payment date up to, but not including, the transaction's settlement date.

accumulation stage The period during which an annuitant is making contributions to an annuity contract.

accumulation unit A measure used to determine the annuitant's proportional ownership interest in the insurance company's separate account during the accumulation stage. During the accumulation stage, the number of accumulation units owned by the annuitant changes and their value varies.

acid-test ratio	A measure of corporate liquidity found by subtracting inventory from current assets and dividing the result by the current liabilities.
ACT	*See* Automated Comparison Transaction (ACT) service.
ad valorem tax	A tax based on the value of the subject property.
adjusted basis	The value assigned to an asset after all deductions or additions for improvements have been taken into consideration.
adjusted gross income (AGI)	An accounting measure employed by the IRS to help determine tax liability. AGI = earned income + investment income (portfolio income) + capital gains + net passive income.
administrator	(1) An individual authorized to oversee the liquidation of an intestate decedent's estate. (2) An individual or agency that administers securities' laws within a state.
ADR/ADS	*See* American depositary receipt (ADR).
advance/decline line	Measures the health of the overall market by calculating advancing issues and subtracting the number of declining issues.
advance refunding	The early refinancing of municipal securities. A new issue of bonds is sold to retire the old issue at its first available call date or maturity.
advertisement	Any material that is distributed by a broker dealer or issuer for the purpose of increasing business or public awareness for the firm or issuer. The broker dealer or issuer must distribute advertisements to an audience that is not controlled. Advertisements are distributed through any of the following: newspapers/magazines, radio, TV, billboards, telephone.
affiliate	An individual who owns 10% or more of the company's voting stock. In the case of a direct participation program (DPP), this is anyone who controls the partnership or is controlled by the partnership.
agency issue	A debt security issued by any authorized entity of the U.S. government. The debt security is an obligation of the issuing entity, not an obligation of the U.S. government (with the exception of Ginnie Mae and the Federal Import Export Bank issues).
agency transaction	A transaction made by a firm for the benefit of a customer. The firm merely executes a customer's order and charges a fee for the service, which is known as a commission.
agent	A firm or an individual who executes securities transactions for customers and charges a service fee known as a commission. Also known as a broker.

aggregate indebtedness	The total amount of the firm's customer-related debts.
allied member	An owner-director or 5% owner of an NYSE member firm. Allied members may not trade on the floor.
all-or-none (AON) order	A non-time-sensitive order that stipulates that the customer wants to buy or sell all of the securities in the order.
all-or-none underwriting	A type of underwriting that states that the issuer wants to sell all of the securities being offered or none of the securities being offered. The proceeds from the issue will be held in escrow until all securities are sold.
alpha	A measure of the projected change in the security's price as a result of fundamental factors relating only to that company.
alternative minimum tax (AMT)	A method used to calculate the tax liability for some high-income earners that adds back the deductions taken for certain tax preference items.
AMBAC Indemnity Corporation	Insures the interest and principal payments for municipal bonds.
American depositary receipt (ADR)/ American depositary security (ADS)	A receipt representing the beneficial ownership of foreign securities being held in trust overseas by a foreign branch of a U.S. bank. ADRs/ADSs facilitate the trading and ownership of foreign securities and trade in the United States on an exchange or in the over-the-counter markets.
American Stock Exchange (AMEX)	An exchange located in New York using the dual-auction method and specialist system to facilitate trading in stocks, options, exchange-traded funds, and portfolios. AMEX was acquired by the NYSE Euronext and is now part of NYSE Alternext.
amortization	An accounting method that reduces the value of an asset over its projected useful life. Also the way that loan principal is systematically paid off over the life of a loan.
annual compliance review	All firms must hold at least one compliance meeting per year with all of its agents.
annuitant	An individual who receives scheduled payments from an annuity contract.
annuitize	A process by which an individual converts from the accumulation stage to the payout stage of an annuity contract. This is accomplished by exchanging accumulation units for annuity units. Once a payout option is selected, it cannot be changed.
annuity	A contract between an individual and an insurance company that is designed to provide the annuitant with lifetime income in exchange for either a lump sum or periodic deposits into the contract.

annuity unit	An accounting measure used to determine an individual's proportionate ownership of the separate account during the payout stage of the contract. The number of annuity units owned by an individual remains constant, and their value, which may vary, is used to determine the amount of the individual's annuity payment.
appreciation	An asset's increase in value over time.
arbitrage	An investment strategy used to profit from market inefficiencies.
arbitration	A forum provided by both the NYSE and FINRA to resolve disputes between two parties. Only a public customer may not be forced to settle a dispute through arbitration. The public customer must agree to arbitration in writing. All industry participants must settle disputes through arbitration.
ask	*See* offer.
assessed value	A base value assigned to property for the purpose of determining tax liability.
assessment	An additional amount of taxes due as a result of a municipal project that the homeowner benefits from. Also an additional call for capital by a direct participation program.
asset	Anything of value owned by an individual or a corporation.
asset allocation fund	A mutual fund that spreads its investments among different asset classes (i.e., stocks, bonds, and other investments) based on a predetermined formula.
assignee	A person to whom the ownership of an asset is being transferred.
assignment	(1) The transfer of ownership or rights through a signature. (2) The notification given to investors who are short an option that the option holder has exercised its right and they must now meet their obligations as detailed in the option contract.
associated person	Any individual under the control of a broker dealer, issuer, or bank, including employees, officers, and directors, as well as those individuals who control or have common control of a broker dealer, issuer, or bank.
assumed interest rate (AIR)	(1) A benchmark used to determine the minimum rate of return that must be realized by a variable annuity's separate account during the payout phase in order to keep the annuitant's payments consistent. (2) In the case of a variable life insurance policy, the minimum rate of return that must be achieved in order to maintain the policy's variable death benefit.
at-the-close order	An order that stipulates that the security is to be bought or sold only at the close of the market, or as close to the close as is reasonable, or not at all.
at the money	A term used to describe an option when the underlying security price is equal to the exercise price of the option.

at-the-opening order	An order that stipulates that the security is to be bought or sold only at the opening of the market, or as close to the opening as is reasonable, or not at all.
auction market	The method of trading employed by stock exchanges that allows buyers and sellers to compete with one another in a centralized location.
authorized stock	The maximum number of shares that a corporation can sell in an effort to raise capital. The number of authorized shares may only be changed by a vote of the shareholders.
Automated Comparison Transaction (ACT) service	ACT is the service that clears and locks Nasdaq trades.
average cost	A method used to determine the cost of an investment for an investor who has made multiple purchases of the same security at different times and prices. An investor's average cost may be used to determine a cost base for tax purposes or to evaluate the profitability of an investment program, such as dollar-cost averaging. Average cost is determined by dividing the total dollars invested by the number of shares purchased.
average price	A method used to determine the average price paid by an investor for a security that has been purchased at different times and prices, such as through dollar-cost averaging. An investor's average price is determined by dividing the total of the purchase prices by the number of purchases.

B

BBB/Baa	The lowest ratings assigned by Standard & Poor's and Moody's for debt in the investment-grade category.
back-end load	A mutual fund sales charge that is assessed upon the redemption of the shares. The amount of the sales charge to be assessed upon redemption decreases the longer the shares are held. Also known as a contingent deferred sales charge.
backing away	The failure of an over-the-counter market maker to honor firm quotes. It is a violation of FINRA rules.
balanced fund	A mutual fund whose investment policy requires that the portfolio's holdings are diversified among asset classes and invested in common and preferred stock, bonds, and other debt instruments. The exact asset distribution among the asset classes will be predetermined by a set formula that is designed to balance out the investment return of the fund.
balance of payments	The net balance of all international transactions for a country in a given time.

balance of trade	The net flow of goods into or out of a country for a given period. Net exports result in a surplus or credit; net exports result in a deficit or net debit.
balance sheet	A corporate report that shows a company's financial condition at the time the balance sheet was created.
balance sheet equation	Assets = liabilities + shareholders equity.
balloon maturity	A bond maturity schedule that requires the largest portion of the principal to be repaid on the last maturity date.
bankers' acceptance (BA)	A letter of credit that facilitates foreign trade. BAs are traded in the money market and have a maximum maturity of 270 days.
basis	The cost that is assigned to an asset.
basis book	A table used to calculate bond prices for bonds quoted on a yield basis and to calculate yields for bonds quoted on a price basis.
basis point	Measures a bond's yield; 1 basis point is equal to 1/100 of 1%.
basis quote	A bond quote based on the bond's yield.
bearer bond	A bond that is issued without the owner's name being registered on the bond certificate or the books of the issuer. Whoever has possession of (bears) the certificate is deemed to be the rightful owner.
bearish	An investor's belief that prices will decline.
bear market	A market condition that is characterized by continuing falling prices and a series of lower lows in overall prices.
best efforts underwriting	A type of underwriting that does not guarantee the issuer that any of its securities will be sold.
beta	A measure of a security's or portfolio's volatility relative to the market as a whole. A security or portfolio whose beta is greater than 1 will experience a greater change in price than overall market prices. A security or portfolio with a beta of less than 1 will experience a price change that is less than the price changes realized by the market as a whole.
bid	A price that an investor or broker dealer is willing to pay for a security. It is also a price at which an investor may sell a security immediately and the price at which a market maker will buy a security.
blind pool	A type of direct participation program where less than 75% of the assets to be acquired have been identified.
block trade	A trade involving 10,000 shares or market value of over $200,000.
blotter	A daily record of broker dealer transactions.
blue chip stock	Stock of a company whose earnings and dividends are stable regardless of the economy.

Blue List	A daily publication of municipal bond offerings and secondary market interest.
blue sky	A term used to describe the state registration process for a security offering.
blue-sky laws	Term used to describe the state-based laws enacted under the Uniform Securities Act.
board broker	*See* order book official.
board of directors	A group of directors elected by the stockholders of a corporation to appoint and oversee corporate management.
Board of Governors	The governing body of FINRA. The board is made up of 27 members elected by FINRA's membership and the board itself.
bona fide quote	*See* firm quote.
bond	The legal obligation of a corporation or government to repay the principal amount of debt along with interest at a predetermined schedule.
bond anticipation note	Short-term municipal financing sold in anticipation of long-term financing.
bond buyer indexes	A group of yield-based municipal bond indexes published daily in the *Daily Bond Buyer*.
bond counsel	An attorney for the issuer of municipal securities who renders the legal opinion.
bond fund	A fund whose portfolio is made up of debt instruments issued by corporations, governments, and/or their agencies. The fund's investment objective is usually current income.
bond interest coverage ratio	A measure of the issuer's liquidity. It demonstrates how many times the issuer's earnings will cover its bond interest expense.
bond quotes	Corporate and government bond quotes are based on a percentage of par. Municipal bonds are usually quoted on a yield-to-maturity basis.
bond rating	A rating that assesses the financial soundness of issuers and their ability to make interest and principal payments in a timely manner. Standard & Poor's and Moody's are the two largest ratings agencies. Issuers must request and pay for the service to rate their bonds.
bond ratio	A measure used to determine how much of the corporation's capitalization was obtained through the issuance of bonds.
bond swap	The sale and purchase of two different bonds to allow the investor to claim a loss on the bond being sold without violating wash sale rules.
book entry	Securities that are issued in book entry form do not offer any physical certificates as evidence of ownership. The owner's name is registered on the books of the issuer, and the only evidence of ownership is the trade confirmation.

book value	A corporation's book value is the theoretical liquidation value of the company. Book value is in theory what someone would be willing to pay for the entire company.
book value per bond	A measure used to determine the amount of the corporation's tangible value for each bond issued.
book value per share	Used to determine the tangible value of each common share. It is found by subtracting intangible assets and the par value of preferred stock from the corporation's total net worth and dividing that figure by the number of common shares outstanding.
branch office	A branch office of a member firm is required to display the name of the member firm and is any office in which the member conducts securities business outside of its main office.
breadth	A measure of the broad market's health. It measures how many stocks are increasing and how many are declining.
breakdown	A technical term used to describe the price action of a security when it falls below support to a lower level and into a new trading range.
breakeven point	The point at which the value of a security or portfolio is exactly equal to the investor's cost for that security or portfolio.
breakout	A technical term used to describe the price action of a security when it increases past resistance to a higher level and into a new trading range.
breakpoint sale	The practice of selling mutual fund shares in dollar amounts that are just below the point where an investor would be entitled to a sales charge reduction. A breakpoint sale is designed for the purpose of trying to earn a larger commission. This is a violation of the Rules of Fair Practice and should never be done.
breakpoint schedule	A breakpoint schedule offers mutual fund investors reduced sales charges for larger dollar investments.
broad-based index	An index that represents a large cross-section of the market as a whole. The price movement of the index reflects the price movement of a large portion of the market, such as the S&P 500 or the Wilshire 5000.
broker	*See* agent.
broker dealer	A person or firm who buys and sells securities for its own account and for the accounts of others. When acting as a broker or agent for a customer, the broker dealer is merely executing the customer's orders and charging the customer a fee known as a commission. When acting as a dealer or principal, the broker dealer is trading for its own account and participating in the customer's transaction by taking the other side of the trade and charging the customer

a markup or markdown. A firm also is acting as a principal or dealer when it is trading for its own account and making markets in OTC securities.

broker's broker	(1) A municipal bond dealer who specializes in executing orders for other dealers who are not active in the municipal bond market. (2) A specialist on the exchange executing orders for other members or an OTC market.
bullish	An investor who believes that the price of a security or prices as a whole will rise is said to be bullish.
bull market	A market condition that is characterized by rising prices and a series of higher highs.
business cycle	The normal economic pattern that is characterized by four stages: expansion, peak, contraction, and trough. The business cycle constantly repeats itself and the economy is always in flux.
business day	The business day in the securities industry is defined as the time when the financial markets are open for trading.
buyer's option	A settlement option that allows the buyer to determine when the transaction will settle.
buy in	An order executed in the event of a customer's or firm's failure to deliver the securities it sold. The buyer repurchases the securities in the open market and charges the seller for any loss.
buying power	The amount of money available to buy securities.
buy stop order	A buy stop order is used to protect against a loss or to protect a profit on a short sale of stock.

C

call	(1) A type of option that gives the holder the right to purchase a specified amount of the underlying security at a stated price for a specified period of time. (2) The act of exercising a call option.
callable bond	A bond that may be called in or retired by the issuer prior to its maturity date.
callable preferred	A preferred share issued with a feature allowing the issuing corporation to retire it under certain conditions.
call date	A specific date after which the securities in question become callable by the issuer.
call feature	A condition attached to some bonds and preferred stocks that allows the issuer to call in or redeem the securities prior to their maturity date and according to certain conditions.

call price	The price that will be paid by the issuer to retire the callable securities in question. The call price is usually set at a price above the par value of the bond or preferred stock, which is the subject of the call.
call protection	A period of time, usually right after the securities' issuance, when the securities may not be called by the issuer. Call protection usually ranges from 5 to 10 years.
call provision	*See* call feature.
call risk	The risk borne by the owner of callable securities that may require that the investor accept a lower rate of return once the securities have been called. Callable bonds and preferred stock are more likely to be called when interest rates are low or are falling.
call spread	An option position consisting of one long and one short call on the same underlying security with different strike prices, expirations, or both.
call writer	An investor who has sold a call.
capital	Money and assets available to use in an attempt to earn more money or to accumulate more assets.
capital appreciation	An increase in an asset's value over time.
capital assets	Tangible assets, including securities, real estate, equipment, and other assets, owned for the long term.
capital gain	A profit realized on the sale of an asset at a price that exceeds its cost.
capitalization	The composition of a company's financial structure. It is the sum of paid-in capital + paid-in surplus + long-term debt + retained earnings.
capital loss	A loss realized on the sale of an asset at a price that is lower than its cost.
capital market	The securities markets that deal in equity and debt securities with more than 1 year to maturity.
capital risk	The risk that the value of an asset will decline and cause an investor to lose all or part of the invested capital.
capital stock	The sum of the par value of all of a corporation's outstanding common and preferred stock.
capital structure	*See* capitalization.
capital surplus	The amount of money received by an issuer in excess of the par value of the stock at the time of its initial sale to the public.
capped index option	An index option that trades like a spread and is automatically exercised if it goes 30 points in the money.
capping	A manipulative practice of selling stock to depress the price.

carried interest	A sharing arrangement for an oil and gas direct participation program where the general partner shares in the tangible drilling costs with the limited partners.
cash account	An account in which the investor must deposit the full purchase price of the securities by the fourth business day after the trade date. The investor is not required by industry regulations to sign anything to open a cash account.
cash assets ratio	The most liquid measure of a company's solvency. The cash asset ratio is found by dividing cash and equivalents by current liabilities.
cash dividend	The distribution of corporate profits to shareholders of record. Cash dividends must be declared by the company's board of directors.
cash equivalent	Short-term liquid securities that can quickly be converted into cash. Money market instruments and funds are the most common examples.
cash flow	A company's cash flow equals net income plus depreciation.
cashiering department	The department in a brokerage firm that is responsible for the receipt and delivery of cash and securities.
cash management bill	Short-term federal financing issued in minimum denominations of $10 million.
cash settlement	A transaction that settles for cash requires the delivery of the securities from the seller as well as the delivery of cash from the buyer on the same day of the trade. A trade done for cash settles the same day.
catastrophe call	The redemption of a bond by an issuer due to the destruction of the facility that was financed by the issue. Issuers will carry insurance to cover such events and to pay off the bondholders.
certificate of deposit (CD)	An unsecured promissory note issued as evidence of ownership of a time deposit that has been guaranteed by the issuing bank.
certificates of accrual on Treasury securities	Zero-coupon bonds issued by brokerage firms and collateralized by Treasury securities.
change	The difference between the current price and the previous day's closing price.
Chicago Board of Trade (CBOT)	A commodity exchange that provides a marketplace for agricultural and financial futures.
Chicago Board Options Exchange (CBOE)	The premier option exchange in the United States for listed options.
Chinese wall	The physical separation that is required between investment banking and trading and retail divisions of a brokerage firm. Now known as a firewall.

churning	Executing transactions that are excessive in their frequency or size in light of the resources of the account for the purpose of generating commissions. Churning is a violation of the Rules of Fair Practice.
class A share	A mutual fund share that charges a front-end load.
class B share	A mutual fund share that charges a back-end load.
class C share	A mutual fund share that charges a level load.
class D share	A mutual fund share that charges a level load and a back-end load.
classical economics	A theory stating that the economy will do the best when the government does not interfere.
clearing firm	A firm that carries its customers' cash and securities and/or provides the service to customers of other firms.
clearinghouse	An agency that guarantees and settles futures and option transactions.
close	The last price at which a security traded for the day.
closed-end indenture	A bond indenture that will not allow additional bonds to be issued with the same claim on the issuer's assets.
closed-end investment company	A management company that issues a fixed number of shares to investors in a managed portfolio and whose shares are traded in the secondary market.
closing date	The date when sales of interest in a direct participation plan will cease.
closing purchase	An order executed to close out a short option position.
Code of Arbitration Procedure	The FINRA bylaw that provides for a forum for dispute resolution relating to industry matters. All industry participants must arbitrate in public and the customer must agree to arbitration in writing.
Code of Procedure	The FINRA bylaw that sets guidelines for the investigation of trade practice complaints and alleged rule violations.
coincident indicator	An economic indicator that moves simultaneously with the movement of the underlying economy.
collateral	Assets pledged to a lender. If the borrower defaults, the lender will take possession of the collateral.
collateral trust certificate	A bond backed by the pledge of securities the issuer owns in another entity.
collateralized mortgage obligation (CMO)	A corporate debt security that is secured by an underlying pool of mortgages.
collection ratio	A measure of a municipality's ability to collect the taxes it has assessed.
collect on delivery (COD)	A method of trade settlement that requires the physical delivery of the securities to receive payment.

combination	An option position with a call and put on the same underlying security with different strike prices and expiration months on both.
combination fund	A mutual fund that tries to achieve growth and current income by combining portfolios of common stock with portfolios of high-yielding equities.
combination preferred stock	A preferred share with multiple features, such as cumulative and participating.
combination privileges	A feature offered by a mutual fund family that allows an investor to combine two simultaneous purchases of different portfolios in order to receive a reduced sales charge on the total amount invested.
combined account	A margin account that contains both long and short positions.
commercial paper	Short-term unsecured promissory notes issued by large financially stable corporations to obtain short-term financing. Commercial paper does not pay interest and is issued at a discount from its face value. All commercial paper matures in 270 days or less and matures at its face value.
commingling	A FINRA violation resulting from the mixing of customer and firm assets in the same account.
commission	A fee charged by a broker or agent for executing a securities transaction.
commission house broker	A floor broker who executes orders for the firm's account and for the accounts of the firm's customers on an exchange.
common stock	A security that represents the ownership of a corporation. Common stockholders vote to elect the board of directors and to institute major corporate policies.
common stock ratio	A measure of how much of a company's capitalization was obtained through the sale of common stock. The ratio is found by summing the par value of the common stock, excess paid in capital, and retained earnings, and then dividing that number by the total capitalization.
competitive bid underwriting	A method of underwriter selection that solicits bids from multiple underwriters. The underwriter submitting the best terms will be awarded the issue.
compliance department	The department of a broker dealer that ensures that the firm adheres to industry rules and regulations.
concession	The amount of an underwriting discount that is allocated to a syndicate member or a selling group member for selling new securities.
conduct rules	The Rules of Fair Practice.
conduit theory	The IRS classification that allows a regulated investment company to avoid paying taxes on investment income it distributes to its shareholders.

confirmation	The receipt for a securities transaction that must be sent to all customers either on or before the completion of a transaction. The confirmation must show the trade date, settlement date, and total amount due to or from the customer. A transaction is considered to be complete on settlement date.
consolidated tape	The consolidated tape A displays transactions for NYSE securities that take place on the NYSE, all regional exchanges, and the third markets. The consolidated tape B reports transactions for AMEX stocks that take place on the American Stock Exchange, all regional exchanges, and in the third market.
consolidation	A chart pattern that results from a narrowing of a security's trading range.
constant dollar plan	An investment plan designed to keep a specific amount of money invested in the market regardless of the market's condition. An investor will sell when the value of the account rises and buy when the value of the account falls.
constant ratio plan	An investment plan designed to keep the investor's portfolio invested at a constant ratio of equity and debt securities.
construction loan note	A short-term municipal note designed to provide financing for construction projects.
constructive receipt	The time when the IRS determines that the taxpayer has effectively received payment.
consumer price index (CPI)	A price-based index made up of a basket of goods and services that are used by consumers in their daily lives. An increase in the CPI indicates a rise in overall prices, while a decline in the index represents a fall in overall prices.
consumption	A term used to describe the purchase of newly produced household goods.
contemporaneous trader	A trader who enters an order on the other side of the market at the same time as a trader with inside information enters an order. Contemporaneous traders can sue traders who act on inside information to recover losses.
contingent deferred sales charge	*See* back-end load.
contraction	A period of declining economic output. Also known as a recession.
contractual plan	A mutual fund accumulation plan under which the investor agrees to contribute a fixed sum of money over time. If the investor does not complete or terminates the contract early, the investor may be subject to penalties.
control	The ability to influence the actions of an organization or individual.
control person	A director or officer of an issuer or broker dealer or a 10% stockholder of a corporation.
control stock	Stock that is acquired or owned by an officer, director, or person owning 10% or more of the outstanding stock of a company.

conversion price	The set price at which a convertible security may be exchanged for another security.
conversion privilege	The right offered to a mutual fund investor that allows the investor to move money between different portfolios offered by the same mutual fund family without paying another sales charge.
conversion ratio	The number of shares that can be received by the holder of a convertible security if it were converted into the underlying common stock.
convertible bond	A bond that may be converted or exchanged for common shares of the corporation at a predetermined price.
convertible preferred stock	A preferred stock that may be converted or exchanged for common shares of the corporation at a predetermined price.
cooling-off period	The period of time between the filing of a registration statement and its effective date. During this time, the SEC is reviewing the registration statement and no sales may take place. The cooling-off period is at least 20 days.
coordination	A method of securities registration during which a new issue is registered simultaneously at both the federal and state levels.
corporate account	An investment account for the benefit of a company that requires a corporate resolution listing the names of individuals who may transact business in the company's name.
corporate bond	A legally binding obligation of a corporation to repay a principal amount of debt along with interest at a predetermined rate and schedule.
corporation	A perpetual entity that survives after the death of its officers, directors, and stockholders. It is the most common form of business entity.
correspondent broker dealer	A broker dealer who introduces customer accounts to a clearing broker dealer.
cost basis	The cost of an asset, including any acquisition costs. It is used to determine capital gains and losses.
cost depletion	A method used to determine the tax deductions for investors in oil and gas programs.
cost of carry	All costs incurred by an investor for maintaining a position in a security, including margin interest and opportunity costs.
coterminous	Municipalities that share the same borders and have overlapping debt.
coupon bond	*See* bearer bond.
coupon yield	*See* nominal yield.
covenant	A promise made by an issuer of debt that describes the issuer's obligations and the bondholders' rights.

covered call	The sale of a call against a long position in the underlying security.
covered put	The sale of a put against a short position in the underlying security or against cash that will allow the person to purchase the security if the put is exercised.
CPI	*See* consumer price index (CPI).
credit agreement	The portion of the margin agreement that describes the terms and conditions under which credit will be extended to the customer.
credit balance	The cash balance in a customer's account.
credit department	*See* margin department.
credit risk	The risk that the issuer of debt securities will default on its obligation to pay interest or principal on a timely basis.
credit spread	An option position that results in a net premium or credit received by the investor from the simultaneous purchase and sale of two calls or two puts on the same security.
crossed market	A market condition that results when a broker enters a bid for a stock that exceeds the offering price for that stock. Also a condition that may result when a broker enters an offer that is lower than the bid price for that stock.
crossing stock	The pairing off of two offsetting customer orders by the same floor broker. The floor broker executing the cross must first show the order to the crowd for possible price improvement before crossing the orders.
crossover point	The point at which all tax credits have been used up by a limited partnership; results in a tax liability for the partners.
cum rights	A stock that is the subject of a rights offering and is trading with the rights attached to the common stock.
cumulative preferred stock	A preferred stock that entitles the holder to receive unpaid dividends prior to the payment of any dividends to common stockholders. Dividends that accumulate in arrears on cumulative issues are always the first dividends to be paid by a corporation.
cumulative voting	A method of voting that allows stockholders to cast all of their votes for one director or to distribute them among the candidates they wish to vote for. Cumulative voting favors smaller investors by allowing them to have a larger say in the election of the board of directors.
current assets	Cash, securities, accounts receivable, and other assets that can be converted into cash within 12 months.
current liabilities	Corporate obligations, including accounts payable, that must be paid within 12 months.

current market value (CMV)/current market price (CMP)	The present value of a marketable security or of a portfolio of marketable securities.
current ratio	A measure of a corporation's short-term liquidity found by dividing its current assets by its current liabilities.
current yield	A relationship between a securities annual income relative to its current market price. Determined by dividing annual income by the current market price.
CUSIP (Committee on Uniform Securities Identification Procedures)	A committee that assigns identification numbers to securities to help identify them.
custodial account	An account operated by a custodian for the benefit of a minor.
custodian	A party responsible for managing an account for another party. In acting as a custodian, the individual or corporation must adhere to the prudent man rule and only take such actions as a prudent person would do for him- or herself.
customer	Any individual or entity that maintains an account with a broker dealer.
customer agreement	An agreement signed by a customer at the time the account is opened, detailing the conditions of the customer's relationship with the firm. The customer agreement usually contains a predispute arbitration clause.
customer ledger	A ledger that lists all customer cash and margin accounts.
customer protection rule	Rule 15C3-3 requires that customer assets be kept segregated from the firm assets.
cyclical industry	An industry whose prospects fluctuate with the business cycle.

D

Daily Bond Buyer	A daily publication for the municipal securities industry that publishes information related to the municipal bond market and official notices of sales.
dated date	The day when interest starts to accrue for bonds.
dealer	(1) A person or firm who transacts securities business for its own account. (2) A brokerage firm acting as a principal when executing a customer's transaction or making markets over the counter.
dealer paper	Commercial paper sold to the public by a dealer, rather than placed with investors directly by the issuer.
debenture	An unsecured promissory note issued by a corporation backed only by the issuer's credit and promise to pay.

debit balance	The amount of money a customer owes a broker dealer.
debit spread	An option position that results in a net premium paid by the investor from the simultaneous purchase and sale of two calls or two puts on the same security.
debt securities	A security that represents a loan to the issuer. The owner of a debt security is a creditor of the issuing entity, be it a corporation or a government.
debt service	The scheduled interest payments and repayment of principal for debt securities.
debt service account	An account set up by a municipal issuer to pay the debt service of municipal revenue bonds.
debt service ratio	Indicates the issuer's ability to pay its interest and principal payments.
debt-to-equity ratio	A ratio that shows how highly leveraged the company is. It is found by dividing total long-term debt by total shareholder equity.
declaration date	The day chosen by the board of directors of a corporation to pay a dividend to shareholders.
deduction	An adjustment taken from gross income to reduce tax liability.
default	The failure of an issuer of debt securities to make interest and principal payments when they are due.
default risk	*See* credit risk.
defeasance	Results in the elimination of the issuer's debt obligations by issuing a new debt instrument to pay off the outstanding issue. The old issue is removed from the issuer's balance sheet and the proceeds of the new issue are placed in an escrow account to pay off the now-defeased issue.
defensive industry	A term used to describe a business whose economic prospects are independent from the business cycle. Pharmaceutical companies, utilities, and food producers are examples of defensive industries.
deferred annuity	A contract between an individual and an insurance company that delays payments to the annuitant until some future date.
deferred compensation plan	A contractual agreement between an employer and an employee under which the employee elects to defer receiving money owed until after retirement. Deferred compensation plans are typically unfunded, and the employee could lose all the money due under the agreement if the company goes out of business.
deficiency letter	A letter sent to a corporate issuer by the SEC, requesting additional information regarding the issuer's registration statement.
defined benefit plan	A qualified retirement plan established to provide a specific amount of retirement income for the plan participants. Unlike a defined contribution plan, the individual's retirement benefits are known prior to reaching retirement.

defined contribution plan	A qualified retirement plan that details the amount of money that the employer will contribute to the plan for the benefit of the employee. This amount is usually expressed as a percentage of the employee's gross annual income. The actual retirement benefits are not known until the employee reaches retirement, and the amount of the retirement benefit is a result of the contributions to the plan, along with the investment experience of the plan.
deflation	The economic condition that is characterized by a persistent decline in overall prices.
delivery	As used in the settlement process, results in the change of ownership of cash or securities.
delivery vs. payment	A type of settlement option that requires that the securities be physically received at the time payment is made.
delta	A measure of an option's price change in relation to a price change in the underlying security.
demand deposit	A deposit that a customer has with a bank or other financial institution that will allow the customer to withdraw the money at any time or on demand.
Department of Enforcement	The FINRA committee that has original jurisdiction over complaints and violations.
depletion	A tax deduction taken for the reduction in the amount of natural resources (e.g., gas, gold, oil) available to a business or partnership.
depreciation	A tax deduction taken for the reduction of value in a capital asset.
depreciation expense	A noncash expense that results in a reduction in taxable income.
depression	An economic condition that is characterized by a protracted decline in economic output and a rising level of unemployment.
derivative	A security that derives its value in whole or in part based on the price of another security. Options and futures are examples of derivative securities.
designated order	An order entered by an institution for a new issue of municipal bonds that states what firm and what agent is going to get the sales credit for the order.
devaluation	A significant fall in the value of a country's currency relative to other currencies. Devaluation could be the result of poor economic prospects in the home country. In extreme circumstances, it can be the result of government intervention.
developmental drilling program	An oil or gas program that drills for wells in areas of proven reserves.
developmental fee	A fee paid to organizers of a direct participation plan for the development of plans, obtaining financing or zoning authorizations, and other services.

diagonal spread	A spread that is created through the simultaneous purchase and sale of two calls or two puts on the same underlying security that differ in both strike price and expiration months.
dilution	A reduction in a stockholder's proportional ownership of a corporation as a result of the issuance of more shares. Earnings per share may also be diluted as a result of the issuance of additional shares.
direct debt	The total amount of a municipality's debt that has been issued by the municipality for its own benefit and for which the municipality is responsible to repay.
direct paper	Commercial paper sold to investors directly from the issuer without the use of a dealer.
direct participation program (DPP)	An entity that allows all taxable events to be passed through to investors, including limited partnerships and subchapter S corporations.
discount	The amount by which the price of a security is lower than its par value.
discount bond	A bond that is selling for a price that is lower than its par value.
discount rate	The rate that is charged to Federal Reserve member banks on loans directly from the Federal Reserve. This rate is largely symbolic, and member banks only borrow directly from the Federal Reserve as a last resort.
discretion	Authorization given to a firm or a representative to determine which securities are to be purchased and sold for the benefit of the customer without the customer's prior knowledge or approval.
discretionary account	An account where the owner has given the firm or the representative authority to transact business without the customer's prior knowledge or approval. All discretionary accounts must be approved and monitored closely by a principal of the firm.
disintermediation	The flow of money from traditional bank accounts to alternative higher yielding investments. This is more likely to occur as the Federal Reserve tightens monetary policy and interest rates rise.
disposable income	The sum of money an individual has left after paying taxes and required expenditures.
disproportional allocation	A method used by FINRA to determine if a free-riding violation has occurred with respect to a hot issuer. A firm is only allowed to sell up to 10% of a new issue to conditionally approved purchasers.
disproportionate sharing	An oil and gas sharing arrangement where the general partner pays a portion of the cost but receives a larger portion of the program's revenues.
distribution	Cash or property sent to shareholders or partners.

distribution stage	The period of time during which an annuitant is receiving payments from an annuity contract.
diversification	The distribution of investment capital among different investment choices. By purchasing several different investments, investors may be able to reduce their overall risk by minimizing the impact of any one security's adverse performance.
diversified fund/ diversified management company	A mutual fund that distributes its investment capital among a wide variety of investments. In order for a mutual fund to market itself as a diversified mutual fund it must meet the 75-5-10 rule: 75% of the fund's assets must be invested in securities issued by other entities, no more than 5% of the fund's assets may be invested in any one issuer, and the fund may own no more than 10% of any one company's outstanding securities.
dividend	A distribution of corporate assets to shareholders. A dividend may be paid in cash, stock, or property or product.
dividend department	The department in a brokerage firm that is responsible for the collecting of dividends and crediting them to customer accounts.
dividend disbursement agent	An agent of the issuer who pays out the dividends to shareholders of record.
dividend payout ratio	The amount of a company's earnings that were paid out to shareholders relative to the total earnings that were available to be paid out to shareholders. It can be calculated by dividing dividends per share by earnings per share.
dividend yield	Also known as a stock's current yield. It is a relationship between the annual dividends paid to shareholders relative to the stock's current market price. To determine a stock's dividend yield, divide annual dividends by the current market price.
DJIA	*See* Dow Jones Industrial Average.
doctrine of mutual reciprocity	An agreement that the federal government would not tax interest income received by investors in municipal bonds and that reciprocally the states would not tax interest income received by investors in federal debt obligations.
dollar bonds	A term issue of municipal bonds that are quoted as a percentage of par rather than on a yield basis.
dollar-cost averaging	A strategy of investing a fixed sum of money on a regular basis into a fluctuating market price. Over time an investor should be able to achieve an average cost per share that is below the average price per share. Dollar-cost averaging is a popular investment strategy with mutual fund investors.
donor	A person who gives a gift of cash or securities to another person. Once the gift has been made, the donor no longer has any rights or claim to the security. All gifts to a minor are irrevocable.

do not reduce (DNR)	An order qualifier for an order placed under the market that stipulates that the price of the order is not to be reduced for the distribution of ordinary dividends.
don't know (DK)	A term used to describe a dealer's response to a confirmation for a trade they "don't know" doing.
Dow Jones Composite Average	An index composed of 65 stocks that is used as an indicator of market performance.
Dow Jones Industrial Average (DJIA)	An index composed of 30 industrial companies. The Dow Jones is the most widely quoted market index.
Dow Jones Transportation Average	An index composed of 20 transportation stocks.
Dow Jones Utility Average	An index composed of 15 utility stocks.
Dow theory	A theory that believes that the health both of the market and of the economy may be predicted by the performance of the Dow Jones Industrial Average.
dry hole	A term used to describe a nonproducing well.
dual-purpose fund	A mutual fund that offers two classes of shares to investors. One class is sold to investors seeking income and the other class is sold to investors seeking capital appreciation.

E

early withdrawal penalty	A penalty tax charged to an investor for withdrawing money from a qualified retirement plan prior to age 59-1/2, usually 10% on top of ordinary income taxes.
earned income	Money received by an individual in return for performing services.
earnings per share	The net amount of a corporation's earnings available to common shareholders divided by the number of common shares outstanding.
earnings per share fully diluted	The net amount of a corporation's earnings available to common shareholders after taking into consideration the potential conversion of all convertible securities.
eastern account	A type of syndicate account that requires all members to be responsible for their own allocation as well as for their proportional share of any member's unsold securities.
economic risk	The risk of loss of principal associated with the purchase of securities.
EE savings bonds	Nonmarketable U.S. government zero-coupon bonds that must be purchased from the government and redeemed to the government.

effective date	The day when a new issue's registration with the SEC becomes effective. Once the issue's registration statement has become effective, the securities may then be sold to investors.
efficient market theory	A theory that states that the market operates and processes information efficiently and prices in all information as soon as it becomes known.
Employee Retirement Income Security Act of 1974 (ERISA)	The legislation that governs the operation of private-sector pension plans. Corporate pension plans organized under ERISA guidelines qualify for beneficial tax treatment by the IRS.
endorsement	The signature on the back of a security that allows its ownership to be transferred.
EPS	*See* earnings per share.
equipment leasing limited partnership	A limited partnership that is organized to purchase equipment and lease it to corporations to earn lease income and to shelter passive income for investors.
equipment trust certificate	A bond backed by a pledge of large equipment, such as airplanes, railroad cars, and ships.
equity	A security that represents the ownership in a corporation. Both preferred and common equity holders have an ownership interest in the corporation.
equity financing	The sale of common or preferred equity by a corporation in an effort to raise capital.
equity option	An option to purchase or sell common stock.
ERISA	*See* Employee Retirement Income Security Act of 1974.
erroneous report	A report of an execution given in error to a client. The report is not binding on the firm or on the agent.
escrow agreement	Evidence of ownership of a security provided to a broker dealer as proof of ownership of the underlying security for covered call writers.
Eurobond	A bond issued in domestic currency of the issuer but sold outside of the issuer's country.
Eurodollar	A deposit held outside of the United States denominated in U.S. dollars.
Eurodollar bonds	A bond issued by a foreign issuer denominated in U.S. dollars.
Euroyen bonds	Bonds issued outside of Japan but denominated in yen.
excess equity (EE)	The value of an account's equity in excess of Regulation T.
exchange	A market, whether physical or electronic, that provides a forum for trading securities through a dual-auction process.
exchange distribution	A distribution of a large block of stock on the floor of the exchange that is crossed with offsetting orders.

exchange privilege	The right offered by many mutual funds that allows an investor to transfer or move money between different portfolios offered through the same fund company. An investor may redeem shares of the fund, which is being sold at the NAV, and purchase shares of the new portfolio at the NAV without paying another sales charge.
ex date/ex-dividend date	The first day when purchasers of a security will no longer be entitled to receive a previously declared dividend.
executor/executrix	An individual with the authority to manage the affairs of a decedent's estate.
exempt security	A security that is exempt from the registration requirements of the Securities Act of 1933.
exempt transaction	A transaction that is not subject to state registration.
exercise	An investor's election to take advantage of the rights offered through the terms of an option, a right, or a warrant.
exercise price	The price at which an option investor may purchase or sell a security. Also the price at which an investor may purchase a security through a warrant or right.
existing property program	A type of real estate direct participation program that purchases existing property for the established rental income.
expansion	A period marked by a general increase in business activity and an increase in gross domestic product.
expansionary policy	A monetary policy enacted through the Federal Reserve Board that increases money supply and reduces interest rates in an effort to stimulate the economy.
expense ratio	The amount of a mutual fund's expenses relative to its assets. The higher the expense ratio, the lower the investor's return. A mutual fund's expense ratio tells an investor how efficiently a mutual fund operates, not how profitable the mutual fund is.
expiration cycle	A 4-month cycle for option expiration: January, April, July, and October; February, May, August, and November; or March, June, September, and December.
expiration date	The date on which an option ceases to exist.
exploratory drilling program	A direct participation program that engages in the drilling for oil or gas in new areas seeking to find new wells.
exploratory well	Also known as wildcatting. The drilling for oil or gas in new areas in an effort to find new wells.
ex rights	The common stock subject to a rights offering trade without the rights attached.

ex rights date	The first day when the common stock is subject to a rights offering trade without the rights attached.
ex warrants	Common trading without the warrants attached.

F

face-amount certificate company (FAC)	A type of investment company that requires an investor to make fixed payments over time or to deposit a lump sum, and that will return to the investor a stated sum known as the face amount on a specific date.
face amount/face value	*See* par.
fail to deliver	An event where the broker on the sell side of the transaction fails to deliver the security.
fail to receive	An event where the broker on the buy side of the transaction fails to receive the security from the broker on the sell side.
Fannie Mae	*See* Federal National Mortgage Association.
Farm Credit Administrator	The agency that oversees all of the activities of the banks in the Federal Farm Credit System.
Federal Deposit Insurance Corporation (FDIC)	The government insurance agency that provides insurance for bank depositors in case of bank failure.
Federal Farm Credit System	An organization of banks that is designed to provide financing to farmers for mortgages, feed and grain, and equipment.
federal funds rate	The rate banks charge each other on overnight loans.
Federal Home Loan Mortgage Corporation (FHLMC; Freddie Mac)	A publicly traded for-profit corporation that provides liquidity to the secondary mortgage market by purchasing pools of mortgages from lenders and, in turn, issues mortgage-backed securities.
Federal Intermediate Credit Bank	Provides short-term financing to farmers for equipment.
Federal National Mortgage Association (FNMA; Fannie Mae)	A publicly traded for-profit corporation that provides liquidity to the secondary mortgage market by purchasing pools of mortgages and issuing mortgage-backed securities.
Federal Open Market Committee (FOMC)	The committee of the Federal Reserve Board that makes policy decisions relating to the nation's money supply.

Federal Reserve Board	A seven-member board that directs the policies of the Federal Reserve System. The members are appointed by the President and approved by Congress.
Federal Reserve System	The nation's central banking system, the purpose of which is to regulate money supply and the extension of credit. The Federal Reserve System is composed of 12 central banks and 24 regional banks, along with hundreds of national and state chartered banks.
fictitious quote	A quote that is not representative of an actual bid or offer for a security.
fidelity bond	A bond that must be posted by all broker dealers to ensure the public against employee dishonesty.
fill or kill (FK)	A type of order that requires that all of the securities in the order be purchased or sold immediately or not at all.
final prospectus	The official offering document for a security that contains the security's final offering price along with all information required by law for an investor to make an informed decision.
firm commitment underwriting	Guarantees the issuer all of the money right away. The underwriters purchase all of the securities from the issuer regardless of whether they can sell the securities to their customers.
firm quote	A quote displayed at which the dealer is obligated to buy or sell at least one round lot at the quoted price.
fiscal policy	Government policy designed to influence the economy through government tax and spending programs. The President and Congress control fiscal policy.
5% markup policy	FINRA's guideline that requires all prices paid by customers to be reasonably related to a security's market price. The 5% policy is a guideline, not a rule, and it does not apply to securities sold through a prospectus.
fixed annuity	An insurance contract where the insurance company guarantees fixed payments to the annuitant, usually until the annuitant's death.
fixed assets	Assets used by a corporation to conduct its business, such as plant and equipment.
flat	A term used to describe a bond that trades without accrued interest, such as a zero-coupon bond or a bond that is in default.
floor broker	An individual member of an exchange who may execute orders on the floor.
floor trader	Members of the exchange who trade for their own accounts. Members of the NYSE may not trade from the floor for their own accounts.
flow of funds	A schedule of expenses and interested parties that prioritizes how payments will be made from the revenue generated by a facility financed by a municipal revenue bond.

forced conversion	The calling in of convertible bonds at a price that is less than the market value of the underlying common stock into which the bonds may be converted.
foreign currency	Currency of another country.
foreign currency option	An option to purchase or sell a specified amount of another country's currency.
Form 10-K	An annual report filed by a corporation detailing its financial performance for the year.
Form 10-Q	A quarterly report filed by a corporation detailing its financial performance for the quarter.
form letter	A letter sent out by a brokerage firm or a registered representative to more than 25 people in a 90-day period. Form letters are subject to approval and recordkeeping requirements.
forward pricing	The way in which open-end mutual funds are valued for investors who wish to purchase or redeem shares of the fund. Mutual funds usually price their shares at the end of the business day. The price to be paid or received by the investor will be the price that is next calculated after the fund receives the order.
401K	A qualified retirement plan offered by an employer.
403B	A qualified retirement plan offered to teachers and employees of nonprofit organizations.
fourth market	A transaction between two large institutions without the use of a broker dealer.
fractional share	A portion of a whole share that represents ownership of an open-end mutual fund.
fraud	Any attempt to gain an unfair advantage over another party through the use of deception, concealment, or misrepresentation.
free credit balance	Cash reserves in a customer's account that have not been invested. Customers must be notified of their free credit balances at least quarterly.
free look	A privilege offered to purchasers of contractual plans and insurance policies that will allow the individual to cancel the contract within the free-look period, usually 45 days.
freeriding	The purchase and sale of a security without depositing the money required to cover the purchase price as required by Regulation T.
freeriding and withholding	The withholding of new issue securities offered by a broker dealer for the benefit of the brokerage firm or an employee.
front-end load	(1) A sales charge paid by investors in open-end mutual funds that is paid at the time of purchase. (2) A contractual plan that seeks to assess sales

charges in the first years of the plan and may charge up to 50% of the first year's payments as sales charges.

frozen account	An account where the owner is required to deposit cash or securities up front, prior to any purchase or sale taking place. An account is usually frozen as a result of a customer's failure to pay or deliver securities.
full power of attorney	A type of discretionary authority that allows a third party to purchase and sell securities as well as to withdraw cash and securities without the owner's prior consent or knowledge. This type of authority is usually reserved to trustees and attorneys.
fully registered bonds	A type of bond issuance where the issuer has a complete record of the owners of the bonds and who is entitled to receive interest and principal payments. The owners of fully registered bonds are not required to clip coupons.
functional allocation	An arrangement for oil and gas programs where the general partner pays the tangible drilling costs and the limited partner absorbs the intangible drilling costs.
fundamental analyst	A method of valuing the company that takes into consideration the financial performance of the corporation, the value of its assets, and the quality of its management.
funded debt	Long-term debt obligations of corporations or municipalities.
fungible	Easily exchangeable items with the same conditions.

G

general account	An insurance company's account that holds the money and investments for fixed contracts and traditional life insurance policies.
general obligation bond	A municipal bond that is backed by the taxing power of the state or municipality.
general partner	The partner in a general partnership who manages the business and is responsible for any debt of the program.
general securities principal	An individual who has passed the Series 24 exam and may supervise the activities of the firm and its agents.
generic advertising	Advertising designed to promote name recognition for a firm and securities as investments, but does not recommend specific securities.
good 'til cancel (GTC)	An order that remains on the books until it is executed or canceled.
goodwill	An intangible asset of a corporation, such as its name recognition and reputation, that adds to its value.

Government National Mortgage Association (GNMA; Ginnie Mae)	A government corporation that provides liquidity to the mortgage markets by purchasing pools of mortgages that have been insured by the Federal Housing Administration and the Veterans Administration. Ginnie Mae issues pass-through certificates to investors backed by the pools of mortgages.
government security	A security that is an obligation of the U.S. government and that is backed by the full faith and credit of the U.S. government, such as Treasury bills, notes, and bonds.
grant anticipation note (GAN)	Short-term municipal financing issued in anticipation of receiving a grant from the federal government or one of its agencies.
greenshoe option	An option given to an underwriter of common stock that will allow it to purchase up to an additional 15% of the offering from the issuer at the original offering price to cover over-allotments for securities that are in high demand.
gross domestic product (GDP)	The value of all goods and services produced by a country within a period of time. GDP includes government purchases, investments, and exports minus imports.
gross income	All income received by a taxpayer before deductions for taxes.
gross revenue pledge	A flow-of-funds pledge for a municipal revenue bond that states that debt service will be paid first.
growth fund	A fund whose objective is capital appreciation. Growth funds invest in common stocks to achieve their objective.
growth stock	The stock of a company whose earnings grow at a rate that is faster than the growth rate of the economy as a whole. Growth stocks are characterized by increased opportunities for appreciation and little or no dividends.
guardian	An individual who has a fiduciary responsibility for another, usually a minor.

H

halt	A temporary stop in the trading of a security. If a common stock is halted, all derivatives and convertibles will be halted as well.
head and shoulders	A chart pattern that indicates a reversal of a trend. A head-and-shoulders top indicates a reversal of an uptrend and is considered bearish. A head-and-shoulders bottom is the reversal of a downtrend and is considered bullish.
hedge	A position taken in a security to offset or reduce the risk associated with the risk of another security.
HH bond	A nonmarketable government security that pays semiannual interest. Series HH bonds are issued with a $500 minimum value and may only be

purchased by trading matured series EE bonds; they may not be purchased with cash.

high — The highest price paid for a security during a trading session or during a 52-week period.

holder — An individual or corporation that owns a security. The holder of a security is also known as being long the security.

holding period — The length of time during which an investor owns a security. The holding period is important for calculating tax liability.

hold in street name — The registration of customer securities in the name of the broker dealer. Most customers register securities in the name of the broker dealer to make the transfer of ownership easier.

horizontal spread — Also known as a calendar spread. The simultaneous purchase and sale of two calls or two puts on the same underlying security with the same exercise price but with different expiration months.

hot issue — A new issue of securities that trades at an immediate premium to its offering price in the secondary market.

HR 10 plan — *See* Keogh plan.

hypothecation — The customer's pledge of securities as collateral for a margin loan.

I

immediate annuity — An annuity contract purchased with a single payment that entitles the holder to receive immediate payments from the contract. The annuitant purchases annuity units and usually begins receiving payments within 60 days.

immediate family — An individual's immediate family includes parents, parents-in-law, children, spouse, and any relative financially dependent upon the individual.

immediate or cancel (IOC) — An order that is to be executed as fully as possible immediately and whatever is not executed will be canceled.

income bond — A highly speculative bond that is issued at a discount from par and only pays interest if the issuer has enough income to do so. The issuer of the income bond only promises to pay principal at maturity. Income bonds trade flat without accrued interest.

income fund — A mutual fund whose investment objective is to achieve current income for its shareholders by investing in bonds and preferred stocks.

income program — A type of oil and gas program that purchases producing wells to receive the income received from the sale of the proven reserves.

income statement	A financial statement that shows a corporation's revenue and expenses for the time period in question.
indefeasible title	A record of ownership that cannot be challenged.
index	A representation of the price action of a given group of securities. Indexes are used to measure the condition of the market as a whole, such as with the S&P 500, or can be used to measure the condition of an industry group, such as with the Biotech index.
index option	An option on an underlying financial index. Index options settle in cash.
indication of interest	An investor's expression of a willingness to purchase a new issue of securities after receiving a preliminary prospectus. The investor's indication of interest is not binding on either the investor or the firm.
Individual Retirement Account (IRA)	A self-directed retirement account that allows individuals with earned income to contribute the lesser of 100% of earned income or the annual maximum per year. The contributions may be made with pre- or after-tax dollars, depending on the individual's level of income and whether he or she is eligible to participate in an employer's sponsored plan.
industrial development bond	A private-purpose municipal bond whose proceeds are used to build a facility that is leased to a corporation. The debt service on the bonds is supported by the lease payments.
inflation	The persistent upward pressure on the price of goods and services over time.
initial margin requirement	The initial amount of equity that a customer must deposit to establish a position. The initial margin requirement is set by the Federal Reserve Board under Regulation T.
initial public offering (IPO)	The first offering of common stock to the general investing public.
in part call	A partial call of a bond issue for redemption.
inside information	Information that is not known to people outside of the corporation. Information becomes public only after it is released by the corporation through a recognized media source. Inside information may be both material and immaterial. It is only illegal to trade on inside material information.
inside market	The highest bid and the lowest offer for a security.
insider	A company's officers, directors, large stockholders of 10% or more of the company, and anyone who is in possession of nonpublic material information, along with the immediate family members of the same.

Insider Trading and Securities Fraud Enforcement Act of 1988	Federal legislation that made the penalties for people trading on material nonpublic information more severe. Penalties for insider traders are up to the greater of 300% of the amount of money made or the loss avoided or $1 million and up to 5 years in prison. People who disseminate inside information may be imprisoned and fined up to $1 million.
INSTINET	A computer network that facilitates trading of large blocks of stocks between institutions without the use of a broker dealer.
institutional account	An account in the name of an institution but operated for the benefit of others (i.e., banks and mutual funds). There is no minimum size for an institutional account.
institutional communication	Any communication that is distributed exclusively to institutional investors. Institutional communication does not require the preapproval of a principal but must be maintained for 3 years by the firm.
institutional investor	An investor who trades for its own account or for the accounts of others in large quantities and is covered by fewer protective laws.
insurance covenant	The promise of an issuer of revenue bonds to maintain insurance on the financed project.
intangible asset	Nonphysical property of a corporation, such as trademarks and copyrights.
intangible drilling cost (IDC)	Costs for an oil and gas program that are expensed in the year in which they are incurred for such things as wages, surveys, and well casings.
interbank market	An international currency market.
interest	The cost for borrowing money, usually charged at an annual percentage rate.
interest rate option	An option based on U.S. government securities. The options are either rate-based or priced-based options.
interest rate risk	The risk borne by investors in interest-bearing securities, which subjects the holder to a loss of principal should interest rates rise.
interlocking directorate	Corporate boards that share one or more directors.
Intermarket Trading System/ Computer-Assisted Execution System (ITS/CAES)	A computer system that links the third market for securities with the exchanges.
Internal Revenue Code (IRC)	The codes that define tax liabilities for U.S. taxpayers.

interpositioning	The placing of another broker dealer in between the customer and the best market. Interpositioning is prohibited unless it can be demonstrated that the customer received a better price because of it.
interstate offering	A multistate offering of securities that requires that the issuer register with the SEC as well as with the states in which the securities will be sold.
in the money	A relationship between the strike price of an option and the underlying security's price. A call is in the money when the strike price is lower than the security's price. A put is in the money when the strike price is higher than the security's price.
intrastate offering	*See* Rule 147.
intrinsic value	The amount by which an option is in the money.
introducing broker	*See* correspondent broker dealer.
inverted yield curve	A yield curve where the cost of short-term financing exceeds the cost of long-term financing.
investment adviser	Anyone who charges a fee for investment advice or who holds himself out to the public as being in the business of giving investment advice for a fee.
Investment Advisers Act of 1940	The federal legislation that sets forth guidelines for business requirements and activities of investment advisers.
investment banker	A financial institution that is in the business of raising capital for companies and municipalities by underwriting securities.
investment company	A company that sells undivided interests in a pool of securities and manages the portfolio for the benefit of the investors. Investment companies include management companies, unit investment trusts, and face-amount companies.
Investment Company Act of 1940	Federal legislation that regulates the operation and registration of investment companies.
investment-grade security	A security that has been assigned a rating in the highest rating tier by a recognized ratings agency.
investment objective	An investor's set of goals as to how he or she is seeking to make money, such as capital appreciation or current income.
investor	The purchaser of a security who seeks to realize a profit.
IRA rollover	The temporary distribution of assets from an IRA and the subsequent reinvestment of the assets into another IRA within 60 days. An IRA may be rolled over only once per year and is subject to a 10% penalty and ordinary income taxes if the investor is under 59-1/2 and if the assets are not deposited in another qualified account within 60 days.

IRA transfer	The movement of assets from one qualified account to another without the account holder taking possession of the assets. Investors may transfer an IRA as often as they like.
issued stock	Stock that has actually been sold to the investing public.
issuer	Any entity that issues or proposes to issue securities.

J

joint account	An account that is owned by two or more parties. Joint accounts allow either party to enter transactions for the account. Both parties must sign a joint account agreement. All joint accounts must be designated as joint tenants in common or with rights of survivorship.
joint tenants in common (JTIC)	A joint account where the assets of a party who has died transfer to the decedent's estate, not the other tenant.
joint tenants with rights of survivorship (JTWROS)	A joint account where the assets of a party who has died transfer to the surviving party, not the decedent's estate.
joint venture	An interest in an operation shared by two or more parties. The parties have no other relationship beyond the joint venture.
junk bond	A bond with a high degree of default risk that has been assigned a speculative rating by the ratings agencies.
junk bond fund	A speculative bond fund that invests in high-yield bonds in order to achieve a high degree of current income.

K

Keogh plan	A qualified retirement account for self-employed individuals. Contributions are limited to the lesser of 20% of their gross income or $51,000.
Keynesian economics	An economic theory that states that government intervention in the marketplace helps sustain economic growth.
know-your-customer rule	Industry regulation that requires a registered representative to be familiar with the customer's financial objectives and needs prior to making a recommendation; also known as Rule 405.

L

lagging indicator	A measurement of economic activity that changes after a change has taken place in economic activity. Lagging indicators are useful confirmation tools when determining the strength of an economic trend. Lagging indicators include corporate profits, average duration of unemployment, and labor costs.
last in, first out (LIFO)	An accounting method used that states that the last item that was produced is the first item sold.
leading indicator	A measurement of economic activity that changes prior to a change in economic activity. Leading economic indicators are useful in predicting a coming trend in economic activity. Leading economic indicators include housing permits, new orders for durable goods, and the S&P 500.
LEAPS (long-term equity anticipation securities)	A long-term option on a security that has an expiration of up to 39 months.
lease rental bonds	A municipal bond that is issued to finance the building of a facility that will be rented out. The lease payments on the facility will support the bond's debt service.
legal list	A list of securities that have been approved by certain state securities regulators for purchase by fiduciaries.
legal opinion	An opinion issued by a bond attorney stating that the issue is a legally binding obligation of the state or municipality. The legal opinion also contains a statement regarding the tax status of the interest payments received by investors.
legislative risk	The risk that the government may do something that adversely affects an investment.
letter of intent (LOI)	A letter signed by the purchaser of mutual fund shares that states the investor's intention to invest a certain amount of money over a 13-month period. By agreeing to invest this sum, the investor is entitled to receive a lower sales charge on all purchases covered by the letter of intent. The letter of intent may be backdated up to 90 days from an initial purchase. Should the investor fail to invest the stated sum, a sales charge adjustment will be charged.
level load	A mutual fund share that charges a flat annual fee, such as a 12B-1 fee.
level one	A Nasdaq workstation service that allows the agent to see the inside market only.
level two	A Nasdaq workstation service that allows the order-entry firm to see the inside market, to view the quotes entered by all market makers, and to execute orders.

level three	A Nasdaq workstation service that allows market-making firms to see the inside market, to view the quotes entered by all market makers, to execute orders, and to enter their own quotes for the security. This is the highest level of Nasdaq service.
leverage	The use of borrowed funds to try to obtain a rate of return that exceeds the cost of the funds.
liability	A legal obligation to pay a debt either incurred through borrowing or through the normal course of business.
life annuity/straight life	An annuity payout option that provides payments over the life of the annuitant.
life annuity with period certain	An annuity payout option that provides payments to the annuitant for life or to the annuitant's estate for the period certain, whichever is longer.
life contingency	An annuity payout option that provides a death benefit in case the annuitant dies during the accumulation stage.
limit order	An order that sets a maximum price that the investor will pay in the case of a buy order or the minimum price the investor will accept in the case of a sell order.
limited liability	A protection afforded to investors in securities that limits their liability to the amount of money invested in the securities.
limited partner	A passive investor in a direct participation program who has no role in the project's management.
limited partnership (LP)	An association of two or more partners with at least one partner being the general partner who is responsible for the management of the partnership.
limited partnership agreement	The foundation of all limited partnerships. The agreement is the contract between all partners, and it spells out the authority of the general partner and the rights of all limited partners.
limited power of attorney/limited trading authorization	Legal authorization for a representative or a firm to effect purchases and sales for a customer's account without the customer's prior knowledge. The authorization is limited to buying and selling securities and may not be given to another party.
limited principal	An individual who has passed the Series 26 exam and may supervise Series 6 limited representatives.
limited representative	An individual who has passed the Series 6 exam and may represent a broker dealer in the sale of mutual fund shares and variable contracts.
limited tax bond	A type of general obligation bond that is issued by a municipality that may not increase its tax rate to pay the debt service of the issue.

liquidity	The ability of an investment to be readily converted into cash.
liquidity risk	The risk that an investor may not be able to sell a security when needed or that selling a security when needed will adversely affect the price.
listed option	A standardized option contract that is traded on an exchange.
listed security	A security that trades on one of the exchanges. Only securities that trade on an exchange are known as listed securities.
loan consent agreement	A portion of the margin agreement that allows the broker dealer to loan out the customer's securities to another customer who wishes to borrow them to sell the security short.
locked market	A market condition that results when the bid and the offer for a security are equal.
LOI	*See* letter of intent.
London Interbank Offered Rate (LIBOR)	The interbank rates for dollar-denominated deposits in England.
long	A term used to describe an investor who owns a security.
long market value	The total long market value of a customer's account.
long-term gain	A profit realized through the sale of a security at a price that is higher than its purchase price after a being held for more than 12 months.
long-term loss	A loss realized through the sale of a security at a price that is lower than its purchase price after being held for more than 12 months.
loss carry forward	A capital loss realized on the sale of an asset in 1 year that is carried forward in whole or part to subsequent tax years.
low	The lowest price at which a security has traded in any given period, usually measured during a trading day or for 52 weeks.

M

M1	The most liquid measure of the money supply. It includes all currency and demand and NOW deposits (checking accounts).
M2	A measure of the money supply that includes M1 plus all time deposits, savings accounts, and noninstitutional money market accounts.
M3	A measure of the money supply that includes M2 and large time deposits, institutional money market funds, short-term repurchase agreements, and other large liquid assets.

maintenance call	A demand for additional cash or collateral made by a broker dealer when a margin customer's account equity has fallen below the minimum requirement of the NYSE or that is set by the broker dealer.
maintenance covenant	A promise made by an issuer of a municipal revenue bond to maintain the facility in good repair.
Major Market Index (XMI)	An index created by the Amex to AMEX 15 of the 30 largest stocks in the Dow Jones Industrial Average.
Maloney Act of 1938	An amendment to the Securities Exchange Act of 1934 that gave the NASD (now part of FINRA) the authority to regulate the over-the-counter market.
managed underwriting	An underwriting conducted by a syndicate led by the managing underwriter.
management company	A type of investment company that actively manages a portfolio of securities in order to meet a stated investment objective. Management companies are also known as mutual funds.
management fee	(1) The fee received by the lead or managing underwriter of a syndicate. (2) The fee received by a sponsor of a direct participation program.
managing partner	The general partner in a direct participation program.
managing underwriter	The lead underwriter in a syndicate who is responsible for negotiating with the issuer, forming the syndicate, and settling the syndicate account.
margin	The amount of customer equity that is required to hold a position in a security.
margin account	An account that allows the customer to borrow money from the brokerage firm to buy securities.
margin call	A demand for cash or collateral mandated by the Federal Reserve Board under Regulation T.
margin department	The department in a broker dealer that calculates money owed by the customer or money due the customer.
margin maintenance call	*See* maintenance call.
mark to the market	The monitoring of a the current value of a position relative to the price at which the trade was executed for securities purchased on margin or on a when-issued basis.
markdown	The profit earned by a dealer on a transaction when purchasing securities for its own account from a customer.
marketability	The ability of an investment to be exchanged between two investors. A security with an active secondary market has a higher level of marketability than one whose market is not as active.

market arbitrage	A type of arbitrage that consists of purchasing a security in one marketplace and selling it in another to take advantage of price inefficiencies.
market letter	A regular publication, usually issued by an investment adviser, that offers information and/or advice regarding a security, market conditions, or the economy as a whole.
market maker	A Nasdaq firm that is required to quote a continuous two-sided market for the securities in which it trades.
market not held	A type of order that gives the floor broker discretion over the time and price of execution.
market on close	An order that will be executed at whatever price the market is at, either on the closing print or just prior to the closing print.
market on open	An order that will be executed at whatever price the market is at, either on the opening print or just after the opening print.
market order	A type of order that will be executed immediately at the best available price once it is presented to the market.
market-out clause	A clause in an underwriting agreement that gives the syndicate the ability to cancel the underwriting if it finds a material problem with the information or condition of the issuer.
market risk/ systematic risk	The risk inherent in any investment in the market that states an investor may lose money simply because the market is going down.
market value	The value of a security that is determined in the marketplace by the investors who enter bids and offers for a security.
markup	The compensation paid to a securities dealer for selling a security to a customer from its inventory.
markup policy	FINRA's guideline that states that the price that is paid or received by an investor must be reasonably related to the market price for that security. FINRA offers 5% as a guideline for what is reasonable to charge investors when they purchase or sell securities.
material information	Information that would affect a company's current or future prospects or an investor's decision to invest in the company.
maturity date	The date on which a bond's principal amount becomes payable to its holders.
member	A member of FINRA or one of the 1,366 members of the NYSE.
member firm	A firm that is a member of the NYSE, FINRA, or another self-regulatory organization.
member order	A retail order entered by a member of a municipal bond syndicate for which the member will receive all of the sales credit.

mini maxi underwriting	A type of best efforts underwriting that states that the offering will not become effective until a minimum amount is sold and sets a maximum amount that may be sold.
minimum death benefit	The minimum guaranteed death benefit that will be paid to the beneficiaries if the holder of a variable life insurance policy dies.
minus tick	A trade in an exchange-listed security that is at a price that is lower than the previous trade.
modern portfolio theory	An investing approach that looks at the overall return and risk of a portfolio as a whole, not as a collection of single investments.
modified accelerated cost recovery system (MACRS)	An accounting method that allows the owner to recover a larger portion of the asset's value in the early years of its life.
monetarist theory	A theory that states that the money supply is the driving force in the economy and that a well-managed money supply will benefit the economy.
monetary policy	Economic policy that is controlled by the Federal Reserve Board and controls the amount of money in circulation and the level of interest rates.
money market	The secondary market where short-term highly liquid securities are traded. Securities traded in the money market include T-bills, negotiable CDs, bankers' acceptances, commercial paper, and other short-term securities with less than 12 months to maturity.
money market mutual fund	A mutual fund that invests in money market instruments to generate monthly interest for its shareholders. Money market mutual funds have a stable NAV that is equal to $1, but it is not guaranteed.
money supply	The total amount of currency, loans, and credit in the economy. The money supply is measured by M1, M2, M3, and L.
moral obligation bond	A type of municipal revenue bond that will allow the state or municipality to vote to cover a shortfall in the debt service.
multiplier effect	The ability of the money supply to grow simply through the normal course of banking. When banks and other financial institutions accept deposits and subsequently loan out those deposits to earn interest, the amount of money in the system grows.
municipal bond	A bond issued by a state or political subdivision of a state in an effort to finance its operations. Interest earned by investors in municipal bonds is almost always free from federal income taxes.
municipal bond fund	A mutual fund that invests in a portfolio of municipal debt in an effort to produce income that is free from federal income taxes for its investors.

Municipal Bond Investors Assurance Corp. (MBIA)	An independent insurance company that will, for a fee received from the issuer, insure the interest and principal payments on a municipal bond.
municipal note	A short-term municipal issue sold to manage the issuer's cash flow, usually in anticipation of the offering of long-term financing.
Municipal Securities Rulemaking Board (MSRB)	The self-regulatory organization that oversees the issuance and trading of municipal bonds. The MSRB's rules are enforced by other industry SROs.
Munifacts	A service that provides real-time secondary market quotes. Munifacts is now known as Thomson Muni Market Monitor.
mutual fund	An investment company that invests in and manages a portfolio of securities for its shareholders. Open-end mutual funds sell their shares to investors on a continuous basis and must stand ready to redeem their shares upon the shareholder's request.
mutual fund custodian	A qualified financial institution that maintains physical custody of a mutual fund's cash and securities. Custodians are usually banks, trust companies, or exchange member firms.

N

naked	The sale of a call option without owning the underlying security or the sale of a put option without being short the stock or having cash on deposit that is sufficient to purchase the underlying security.
narrow-based index	An index that is based on a market sector or a limited number of securities.
NASD (National Association of Securities Dealers)	The industry self-regulatory agency that was authorized by the Maloney Act of 1938 and empowered to regulate the over-the-counter market. The NASD is now part of FINRA.
NASD bylaws	The rules that define the operation of the NASD and how it regulates the over-the-counter market. The four major bylaws are the Rules of Fair Practice, the Uniform Practice Code, the Code of Procedure, and the Code of Arbitration. Now known as FINRA bylaws.
NASD Manual	An NASD publication that outlines the rules and regulations of NASD membership. Now known as the FINRA Manual.
National Securities Clearing Corporation (NSCC)	The clearing intermediary through which clearing member firms reconcile their securities accounts.

NAV (net asset value)	The net value of a mutual fund after deducting all its liabilities. A mutual fund must calculate its NAV at least once per business day. To determine NAV per share, simply divide the mutual fund's NAV by the total number of shares outstanding.
negotiability	The ability of an investment to be freely exchanged between noninterested parties.
negotiable certificate of deposit	A certificate issued by a bank for a time deposit in excess of $100,000 that can be exchanged between parties prior to its maturity date. FDIC insurance only covers the first $250,000 of the principal amount should the bank fail.
NOW (negotiable order of withdrawal) Account	A type of demand deposit that allows the holder to write checks against an interest-bearing account.
net change	The difference between the previous day's closing price and the price of the most recently reported trade for a security.
net current assets per share	A calculation of the value per share that excludes fixed assets and intangibles.
net debt per capita	A measure of a municipal issuer's ability to meet its obligations. It measures the debt level of the issuer in relation to the population.
net debt to assessed valuation	A measure of the issuer's ability to meet its obligations and to raise additional revenue through property taxes.
net direct debt	The total amount of general obligation debt, including notes and short-term financing, issued by a municipality or state.
net interest cost (NIC)	A calculation that measures the interest cost of a municipal issue over the life of all bonds. Most competitive underwritings for municipal securities are awarded to the syndicate that submits the bid with the lowest NIC.
net investment income	The total sum of investment income derived from dividend and interest income after subtracting expenses.
net revenue pledge	A pledge from a revenue bond that pays maintenance and operation expenses first, then debt service.
net total debt	The total of a municipality's direct debt plus its overlapping debt.
net worth	The value of a corporation after subtracting all of its liabilities. A corporation's net worth is also equal to shareholder's equity.
new account form	Paperwork that must be filled out and signed by the representative and a principal of the firm prior to the opening of any account being opened for a customer.

new construction program	A real estate program that seeks to achieve capital appreciation by building new properties.
new housing authority (NHA)	A municipal bond issued to build low-income housing. NHA bonds are guaranteed by the U.S. government and are considered the safest type of municipal bonds. NHA bonds are not considered to be double-barreled bonds.
new issue	*See* initial public offering (IPO).
New York Stock Exchange (NYSE)	A membership organization that provides a marketplace for securities to be exchanged in one centralized location through a dual-auction process.
no-load fund	A fund that does not charge the investor a sales charge to invest in the fund. Shares of no-load mutual funds are sold directly from the fund company to the investor.
nominal owner	An individual or entity registered as the owner of record of securities for the benefit of another party.
nominal quote	A quote given for informational purposes only. A trader who identifies a quote as being nominal cannot be held to trading at the prices that were clearly identified as being nominal.
nominal yield	The yield that is stated or named on the security. The nominal yield, once it has been set, never changes, regardless of the market price of the security.
noncompetitive bid	A bid submitted for Treasury bills where the purchaser agrees to accept the average of all yields accepted at the auction. Noncompetitive tenders are always the first orders filled at the auction.
noncumulative preferred	A type of preferred stock whose dividends do not accumulate in arrears if the issuer misses the payment.
nondiscrimination	A clause that states that all eligible individuals must be allowed to participate in a qualified retirement plan.
nondiversification	An investment strategy that concentrates its investments among a small group of securities or issuers.
nondiversified management company	An investment company that concentrates its investments among a few issuers or securities and does not meet the diversification requirements of the Investment Company Act of 1940.
nonfixed UIT	A type of UIT that allows changes in the portfolio and traditionally invests in mutual fund shares.
nonqualified retirement plan	A retirement plan that does not allow contributions to be made with pre-tax dollars; that is, the retirement plan does not qualify for beneficial tax treatment from the IRS for its contributions.
nonsystematic risk	A risk that is specific to an issuer or an industry.

note	An intermediate-term interest-bearing security that represents an obligation of its issuer.
not-held (NH) order	An order that gives the floor broker discretion as to the time and price of execution.
numbered account	An account that has been designated a number for identification purposes in order to maintain anonymity for its owner. The owner must sign a statement acknowledging ownership.

O

odd lot	A transaction that is for less than 100 shares of stock or for less than 5 bonds.
odd lot differential	An additional fee that may be charged to an investor for the handling of odd lot transactions (usually waived).
odd lot theory	A contrarian theory that states that small investors will invariably buy and sell at the wrong time.
offer	A price published at which an investor or broker dealer is willing to sell a security.
offering circular	The offering document that is prepared by a corporation selling securities under a Regulation A offering.
office of supervisory jurisdiction (OSJ)	An office identified by the broker dealer as having supervisory responsibilities for agents. It has final approval of new accounts, makes markets, and structures offerings.
Office of the Comptroller of the Currency	An office of the U.S. Treasury that is responsible for regulating the practices of national banks.
official notice of sale	The notice of sale published in the *Daily Bond Buyer* by a municipal issuer that is used to obtain an underwriter for municipal bonds.
official statement	The offering document for a municipal issuer that must be provided to every purchaser if the issuer prepares one.
oil and gas direct participation program	A type of direct participation program designed to invest in oil and gas production or exploration.
oil depletion allowance	An accounting method used to reduce the amount of reserves available from a producing well.
omnibus account	An account used by an introducing member to execute and clear all of its customers' trades.
open-end covenant	A type of bond indenture that allows for the issuance of additional bonds with the same claim on the collateral as the original issue.

open-end investment company	*See* mutual fund.
option	A contract between two investors to purchase or sell a security at a given price for a certain period of time.
option agreement	A form that must be signed and returned by an option investor within 15 days of the account's approval to trade options.
option disclosure document	A document that must be furnished to all option investors at the time the account is approved for options trading. It is published by the Options Clearing Corporation (OCC), and it details the risks and features of standardized options.
Options Clearing Corporation (OCC)	The organization that issues and guarantees the performance of standardized options.
order book official (OBO)	Employees of the CBOE who are responsible for maintaining a fair and orderly market in the options assigned to them and for executing orders that have been left with them.
order department	The department of a broker dealer that is responsible for routing orders to the markets for execution.
order memorandum/ order ticket	The written document filled out by a registered representative that identifies, among other things, the security, the amount, the customer, and the account number for which the order is being entered.
original issue discount (OID)	A bond that has been issued to the public at a discount to its par value. The OID on a corporate bond is taxed as if it was earned annually. The OID on a municipal bond is exempt from taxation.
OTC market	*See* over-the-counter (OTC) market.
out of the money	The relationship of an option's strike price to the underlying security's price when exercising the option would not make economic sense. A call is out of the money when the security's price is below the option's strike price. A put is out of the money when the security's price is above the option's strike price.
outstanding stock	The total amount of a security that has been sold to the investing public and that remains in the hands of the investing public.
overlapping debt	The portion of another taxing authority's debt that a municipality is responsible for.
overriding royalty interest	A type of sharing arrangement that offers an individual with no risk a portion of the revenue in exchange for something of value, such as the right to drill on the owner's land.
over-the-counter (OTC) market	An interdealer market that consists of a computer and phone network through which broker dealers trade securities.

P

par	The stated principal amount of a security. Par value is of great importance for fixed-income securities such as bonds or preferred stock. Par value for bonds is traditionally $1,000, whereas par for a preferred stock is normally $100. Par value is of little importance when looking at common stock.
parity	A condition that results when the value of an underlying common stock to be received upon conversion equals the value of the convertible security.
partial call	A call of a portion of an issuer's callable securities.
participation	The code set forth in the Employee Retirement Income Security Act of 1974 that states who is eligible to participate in an employer sponsored retirement plan.
passive income	Income received by an individual for which no work was performed, such as rental income received from a rental property.
passive loss	A loss realized on an investment in a limited partnership or rental property that can be used to offset passive income.
pass-through certificate	A security that passes through income and principal payments made to an underlying portfolio of mortgages. Ginnie Mae is one of the biggest issuers of this type of security.
payment date	The day when a dividend will actually be sent to investors. The payment date is set by the corporation's board of directors at the time when they initially declare the dividend.
payout stage	The period during which an annuitant receives payments from an annuity contract.
payroll deduction plan	A nonqualified retirement plan where employees authorize the employer to take regular deductions from their paychecks to invest in a retirement account.
pension plan	A contractual retirement plan between an employee and an employer that is designed to provide regular income for the employee after retirement.
percentage depletion	An accounting method that allows for a tax deduction for the reduction of reserves.
periodic payment plan	A contract to purchase mutual fund shares over an extended period of time, usually in exchange for the fund company waiving its minimum investment requirement.
person	Any individual or entity that can enter into a legally binding contract for the purchase and sale of securities.

personal income	Income earned by an individual from providing services and through investments.
phantom income	(1) A term used to describe the taxable appreciation on a zero-coupon bond. (2) The term used to describe taxable income generated by a limited partnership that is not producing positive cash flow.
Philadelphia Automated Communication Execution System (PACE)	The computerized order-routing system for the Philadelphia Stock Exchange.
pink sheets	An electronic quote service containing quotes for unlisted securities that is published by the National Quotation Bureau; operated as the PINK over-the-counter market.
placement ratio	A ratio that details the percentage of municipal bonds sold, relative to the number of bonds offered in the last week, published by the *Daily Bond Buyer*.
plus tick	A transaction in an exchange-listed security that is higher than the previous transaction.
point	An increment of change in the price of a security: 1 bond point equals 1% of par or 1% of $1,000, or $10.
POP	*See* public offering price (POP).
portfolio income	Interest and dividends earned through investing in securities.
portfolio manager	An entity that is hired to manage the investment portfolios of a mutual fund. The portfolio manager is paid a fee that is based on the net assets of the fund.
position	The amount of a security in which an investor has an interest by either being long (owning) or short (owing) the security.
power of substitution	*See* stock power.
preemptive right	The right of a common stockholder to maintain proportional ownership interest in a security. A corporation may not issue additional shares of common stock without first offering those shares to existing stockholders.
preferred stock	An equity security issued with a stated dividend rate. Preferred stockholders have a higher claim on a corporation's dividends and assets than common holders.
preferred stock ratio	A ratio detailing the amount of an issuer's total capitalization that is made up of preferred stock. The ratio is found by dividing the total par value of preferred stock by the issuer's total capitalization.

preliminary prospectus/red herring	A document used to solicit indications of interest during the cooling-off period for a new issue of securities. All of the information in the preliminary prospectus is subject to revision and change. The cover of a preliminary prospectus must have a statement saying that the securities have not yet become registered and that they may not be sold until the registration becomes effective. This statement is written in red ink, and this is where the term *red herring* comes from.
price-earnings ratio (PE)	A measure of value used by analysts. It is calculated by dividing the issuer's stock price by its earnings per share.
price spread	A term used to describe an option spread where the long and short options differ only in their exercise prices.
primary earnings per share	The amount of earnings available per common share prior to the conversion of any outstanding convertible securities.
prime rate	The interest rate that banks charge their best corporate customers on loans.
principal	(1) The face amount of a bond. (2) A broker dealer trading for its own account. (3) An individual who has successfully completed a principal exam and may supervise representatives.
principal transaction	A transaction where a broker dealer participates in a trade by buying or selling securities for its own account.
priority	The acceptance of bids and offers for exchange-listed securities on a first-come, first-served (FCFS) basis.
private placement	The private sale of securities to a limited number of investors. Also known as a Regulation D offering.
profit sharing plan	A plan that allows the employer to distribute a percentage of its profits to its employees at a predetermined rate. The money may be paid directly to the employee or deposited into a retirement account.
progressive tax	A tax structure where the tax rate increases as the income level of the individual or entity increases.
project note	A municipal bond issued as interim financing in anticipation of the issuance of new housing authority bonds.
prospectus	*See* final prospectus.
proxy	A limited authority given by stockholders to another party to vote their shares in a corporate election. The stockholder may specify how the votes are cast or may give the party discretion.
proxy department	The department in a brokerage firm that is responsible for forwarding proxies and financial information to investors whose stock is held in street name.

prudent man rule	A rule that governs investments made by fiduciaries for the benefit of a third party. The rule states that the investments must be similar to those that a prudent person would make for him- or herself.
public offering	The sale of securities by an issuer to public investors.
public offering price (POP)	The price paid by an investor to purchase open-end mutual fund shares. Also the price set for a security the first time it is sold to the investing public.
put	An option contract that allows the buyer to sell a security at a set price for a specific period of time. The seller of a put is obligated to purchase the security at a set price for a specific period of time, should the buyer exercise the option.
put buyer	A bearish investor who pays a premium for the right to sell a security at a set price for a certain period of time.
put spread	An option position created by the simultaneous purchase and sale of two put options on the same underlying security that differ in strike prices, expiration months, or both.
put writer	A bullish investor who sells a put option in order to receive the option premium. The writer is obligated to purchase the security if the buyer exercises the option.

Q

qualified legal opinion	A legal opinion containing conditions or reservations relating to the issue. A legal opinion is issued by a bond counsel for a municipal issuer.
qualified retirement plan	A retirement plan that qualifies for favorable tax treatment by the IRS for contributions made into the plan.
quick assets	A measure of liquidity that subtracts the value of a corporation's unsold inventory from its current assets.
quick ratio	*See* acid-test ratio.
quote	A bid and offer broadcast from the exchange or through the Nasdaq system that displays the prices at which a security may be purchased and sold and in what quantities.

R

range	The price difference between the high and low for a security.

rate covenant	A promise in the trust indenture of a municipal revenue bond to keep the user fees high enough to support the debt service.
rating	A judgment of an issuer's ability to meet its credit obligations. The higher the credit quality of the issuer is, the higher the credit rating. The lower the credit quality is, the lower the credit rating, and the higher the risk associated with the securities.
rating service	Major financial organizations that evaluate the credit quality of issuers. Issuers have to request and pay for the service. Standard and Poor's, Moody's, and Fitch are the most widely followed rating services.
raw land program	A type of real estate limited partnership that invests in land for capital appreciation.
real estate investment trust (REIT)	An entity that is organized to invest in or manage real estate. REITs offer investors certain tax advantages that are beyond the scope of the exam.
real estate limited partnership	A type of direct participation program that invests in real estate projects to produce income or capital appreciation.
real estate mortgage investment conduit (REMIC)	An organization that pools investors' capital to purchase portfolios of mortgages.
realized gain	A profit earned on the sale of a security at a price that exceeds its purchase price.
realized loss	A loss recognized by an investor by selling a security at a price that is less than its purchase price.
reallowance	A sales concession available to dealers who sell securities subject to an offering who are not syndicate or selling group members.
recapture	An event that causes a tax liability on a previously taken deduction, such as selling an asset above its depreciated cost base.
recession	A decline in GDP that lasts for at least 6 months but not longer than 18 months.
reclamation	The right of a seller to demand or claim any loss from the buying party due to the buyer's failure to settle the transaction.
record date	A date set by a corporation's board of directors that determines which shareholders will be entitled to receive a declared dividend. Shareholders must be owners of record on this date in order to collect the dividend.
recourse loan	A loan taken out by a limited partnership that allows the lender to seek payment from the limited partners in the case of the partnership's failure to pay.
redeemable security	A security that can be redeemed by the issuer at the investor's request. Open-end mutual funds are an example of redeemable securities.

redemption	The return of an investor's capital by an issuer. Open-end mutual funds must redeem their securities within 7 days of an investor's request.
red herring	*See* preliminary prospectus.
registered	A term that describes the level of owner information that is recorded by the security's issuer.
registered as to principal only	A type of bond registration that requires the investor to clip coupons to receive the bond's interest payments. The issuer will automatically send the investor the bond's principal amount at maturity.
registered options principal (ROP)	An individual who has passed the Series 4 exam.
registered principal	A supervisor of a member firm who has passed the principal examination.
registered representative	An individual who has successfully completed a qualified examination to represent a broker dealer or issuer in securities transactions.
registrar	An independent organization that accounts for all outstanding stock and bonds of an issuer.
registration statement	The full disclosure statement that nonexempt issuers must file with the SEC prior to offering securities for sale to the public. The Securities Act of 1933 requires that a registration statement be filed.
regressive tax	A tax that is levied on all parties at the same rate, regardless of their income. An example of a regressive tax is a sales tax. A larger percentage of a low-income earner's income is taken away by the tax.
regular-way settlement	The standard number of business days in which a securities transaction is completed and paid for. Corporate securities and municipal bonds settle the regular way on the second business day after the trade date with payment due on the fourth business day. Government securities settle the next business day.
regulated investment company	An investment company that qualifies as a conduit for net investment income under Internal Revenue Code subchapter M, so long as it distributes at least 90% of its net investment income to shareholders.
Regulation A	A small company offering that allows a company to raise up to $5 million in any 12-month period, without filing a full registration.
Regulation D	A private placement or sale of securities that allows for an exemption from registration under the Securities Act of 1933. A private placement may be sold to an unlimited number of accredited investors but may only be sold to 35 nonaccredited investors in any 12-month period.
Regulation G	Regulates the extension of credit for securities purchases by other commercial lenders.

Regulation T	Regulates the extension of credit by broker dealers for securities purchases.
Regulation U	Regulates the extension of credit by banks for securities purchases.
Regulation X	Regulates the extension of credit by overseas lenders for securities purchases.
Rehypothecation	The act of a broker dealer repledging a customer's securities as collateral at a bank to obtain a loan for the customer.
REIT	*See* real estate investment trust (REIT).
rejection	The act of a buyer of a security refusing delivery.
reorganization department	The department in a brokerage firm that handles changes in securities that result from a merger or acquisition or calls.
repurchase agreement (REPO)	A fully collateralized loan that results in a sale of securities to the lender, with the borrower agreeing to repurchase them at a higher price in the future. The higher price represents the lender's interest.
reserve maintenance fund	An account set up to provide additional funds to maintain a revenue-producing facility financed by a revenue bond.
reserve requirement	A deposit required to be placed on account with the Federal Reserve Board by banks. The requirement is a percentage of the bank's customers' deposits.
resistance	A price level to which a security appreciates and attracts sellers. The new sellers keep the security's price from rising any higher.
restricted account	(1) A long margin account that has less than 50% equity but more than 25% or a short margin account that has equity of less than 50% but more than 30%. (2) A customer account that has been subject to a sellout.
restricted stock	A nonexempt unregistered security that has been obtained by means other than a public offering.
retail communication	Any communication that may be seen in whole or in part by an individual investor. Retail communication must be approved by a principal prior to first use and maintained by the firm for 3 years.
retained earnings	The amount of a corporation's net income that has not been paid out to shareholders as dividends.
retention	The amount of a new issue that an underwriter allocates to its own clients.
retention requirement	The amount of equity that must be left in a restricted margin account when withdrawing securities.
return on equity	A measure of performance found by dividing after-tax income by common stockholders' equity.
return on investment (ROI)	The profit or loss realized by an investor from holding a security expressed as a percentage of the invested capital.
revenue anticipation note	A short-term municipal issue that is sold to manage an issuer's cash flow in anticipation of other revenue in the future.

reverse repurchase agreement	A fully collateralized loan that results in the purchase of securities with the intention of reselling them to the borrower at a higher price. The higher price represents the buyer's/lender's interest.
reverse split	A stock split that results in fewer shares outstanding, with each share being worth proportionally more.
reversionary working interest	A revenue-sharing arrangement where the general partner shares none of the cost and receives none of the revenue until the limited partners have received their payments back, plus any predetermined amount of return.
right	A short-term security issued in conjunction with a shareholder's preemptive right. The maximum length of a right is 45 days, and it is issued with a subscription price, which allows the holder to purchase the underlying security at a discount from its market price.
rights agent	An independent entity responsible for maintaining the records for rights holders.
rights of accumulation	A right offered to mutual fund investors that allows them to calculate all past contributions and growth to reach a breakpoint to receive a sales charge discount on future purchases.
rights offering	The offering of new shares by a corporation that is preceded by the offering of the new shares to existing shareholders.
riskless simultaneous transaction	The purchase of a security on a principal basis by a brokerage firm for the sole purpose of filling a customer's order that the firm has already received. The markup on riskless principal transactions has to be based on the firm's actual cost for the security.
rollover	The distribution of assets from a qualified account to an investor for the purpose of depositing the assets in another qualified account within 60 days. An investor may only roll over an IRA once every 12 months.
round lot	A standard trading unit for securities. For common and preferred stock, a round lot is 100 shares. For bonds, it is 5 bonds.
Rule 144	SEC rule that regulates the sale of restricted and control securities requiring the seller to file Form 144 at the time the order is entered to sell. Rule 144 also regulates the number of securities that may be sold.
Rule 145	SEC rule that requires a corporation to provide stockholders with full disclosure relating to reorganizations and to solicit proxies.
Rule 147	An intrastate offering that provides an exemption from SEC registration.
Rule 405	The NYSE rule that requires that all customer recommendations must be suitable and that the representative must "know" the customer.

S

sale	*See* sell.
sales charge	*See* commission.
sales literature	Written material distributed by a firm to a controlled audience for the purpose of increasing business. Sales literature includes market letters, research reports, and form letters sent to more than 25 customers.
sales load	The amount of commission charged to investors in open-end mutual funds. The amount of the sales load is added to the net asset value of the fund to determine the public offering price of the fund.
satellite office	An office not identified to the public as an office of the member, such as an agent's home office.
savings bond	A nonnegotiable U.S. government bond that must be purchased from the government and redeemed to the government. These bonds are generally known as Series EE and HH bonds.
scale	A list of maturities and yields for a new serial bond issue.
Schedule 13D	A form that must be filed with the SEC by any individual or group of individuals acquiring 5% or more of a corporation's nonexempt equity securities. Form 13D must be filed within 10 days of the acquisition.
scheduled premium policy	A variable life insurance policy with fixed premium payments.
SEC	*See* Securities and Exchange Commission (SEC).
secondary distribution	A distribution of a large number of securities by a large shareholder or group of large shareholders. The distribution may or may not be done under a prospectus.
secondary offering	An underwriting of a large block of stock being sold by large shareholders. The proceeds of the issue are received by the selling shareholders, not the corporation.
secondary market	A marketplace where securities are exchanged between investors. All transactions that take place on an exchange or on the Nasdaq are secondary market transactions.
sector fund	A mutual fund that invests in companies within a specific business area in an effort to maximize gains. Sector funds have larger risk-reward ratios because of the concentration of investments.
Securities Act of 1933	The first major piece of securities industry legislation. It regulates the primary market and requires that nonexempt issuers file a registration statement

with the SEC. The act also requires that investors in new issues be given a prospectus.

Securities Act Amendments of 1975	Created the Municipal Securities Rulemaking Board (MSRB).
Securities Exchange Act of 1934	Regulates the secondary market and all broker dealers and industry participants. It created the Securities and Exchange Commission, the industry's ultimate authority. The act gave the authority to the Federal Reserve Board to regulate the extension of credit for securities purchases through Regulation T.
Securities and Exchange Commission	The ultimate securities industry authority. The SEC is a direct government body, not a self-regulatory organization. The commissioners are appointed by the U.S. President and must be approved by Congress.
Securities Investor Protection Corporation (SIPC)	The industry's nonprofit insurance company that provides protection for investors in case of broker dealer failure. All member firms must pay dues to SIPC based upon their revenue. SIPC provides coverage for each separate customer for up to $500,000, of which a maximum of $250,000 may be cash. The Securities Investor Protection Act of 1970 created SIPC.
security	Any investment that can be exchanged for value between two parties that contains risk. Securities include stocks, bonds, mutual funds, notes, rights, warrants, and options, among others.
segregation	The physical separation of customer and firm assets.
self-regulatory organization (SRO)	An industry authority that regulates its own members. FINRA, the NYSE, and the CBOE are all self-regulatory organizations that regulate their own members.
sell	The act of conveying the ownership of a security for value to another party. A sale includes any security that is attached to another security, as well as any security which the security may be converted or exchanged into.
seller's option	A type of settlement option that allows the seller to determine when delivery of the securities and final settlement of the trade will occur.
selling away	Any recommendation to a customer that involves an investment product that is not offered through the employing firm without the firm's knowledge and consent. This is a violation of industry regulations and may result in action being taken against the representative.
selling concession	*See* concession.
selling dividends	The act of using a pending dividend to create urgency for the customer to purchase a security. This is a violation and could result in action being taken against the representative.

selling group	A group of broker dealers who may sell a new issue of securities but who are not members of the syndicate and who have no liability to the issuer.
sell out	A transaction executed by a broker dealer when a customer fails to pay for the securities.
sell-stop order	An order placed beneath the current market for a security to protect a profit, to guard against a loss, or to establish a short position.
separate account	The account established by an insurance company to invest the pooled funds of variable contract holders in the securities markets. The separate account must register as either an open-end investment company or as a unit investment trust.
separate trading of registered interest and principal securities (STRIPS)	A zero-coupon bond issued by the U.S. government. The principal payment due in the future is sold to investors at a discount and appreciates to par at maturity. The interest payment component is sold to other investors who want some current income.
serial bonds	A bond issue that has an increasing amount of principal maturing in successive years.
Series EE bond	A nonmarketable U.S. government zero-coupon bond that is issued at a discount and matures at its face value. Investors must purchase the bonds from the U.S. government and redeem them to the government at maturity.
Series HH bond	A nonmarketable U.S. government interest-bearing bond that can only be purchased by trading in matured Series EE bonds. Series HH bonds may not be purchased with cash and are issued with a $500 minimum denomination.
settlement	The completion of a securities transaction. A transaction settles and is completed when the security is delivered to the buyer and the cash is delivered to the seller.
settlement date	The date when a securities ownership changes. Settlement dates are set by FINRA's Uniform Practice Code.
75-5-10 diversification	The diversification test that must be met by mutual funds under the Investment Company Act of 1940 in order to market themselves as a diversified mutual fund: 75% of the fund's assets must be invested in other issuer's securities, no more than 5% of the fund's assets may be invested in any one company, and the fund may own no more than 10% of an issuer's outstanding securities.
shareholder's equity	*See* net worth.
share identification	The process of identifying which shares are being sold at the time the sale order is entered in order to minimize an investor's tax liability.

shelf offering	A type of securities registration that allows the issuer to sell the securities over a 2-year period. Well-known seasoned issuers may sell securities over a 3-year period.
short	A position established by a bearish investor that is created by borrowing the security and selling in the hopes that the price of the security will fall. The investor hopes to be able to repurchase the security at a lower price, thus replacing it cheaply. If the security's price rises, the investor will suffer a loss.
short against the box	A short position established against an equal long position in the security to roll tax liabilities forward. Most of the benefits of establishing a short against the box position have been eliminated.
short straddle	The simultaneous sale of a call and a put on the same underlying security with the same strike price and expiration. A short straddle would be established by an investor who believes that the security price will move sideways.
simplified arbitration	A method of resolving disputes of $50,000 or less. There is no hearing; one arbitrator reads the submissions and renders a final decision.
Simplified Employee Pension (SEP)	A qualified retirement plan created for small employers with 25 or fewer employees that allows the employees' money to grow tax-deferred until retirement.
single account	An account operated for one individual. The individual has control of the account, and the assets go to the individual's estate in the case of his or her death.
sinking fund	An account established by an issuer of debt to place money for the exclusive purpose of paying bond principal.
special assessment bond	A municipal bond backed by assessments from the property that benefits from the improvements.
specialist	Member of an exchange responsible for maintaining a fair and orderly market in the securities that he or she specializes in and for executing orders left with him or her.
specialist book	A book of limit orders left with the specialist for execution.
special situation fund	A fund that seeks to take advantage of unusual corporate developments, such as take mergers and restructuring.
special tax bond	A type of municipal revenue bond that is supported only by revenue from certain taxes.
speculation	An investment objective where the investor is willing to accept a high degree of risk in exchange for the opportunity to realize a high return.
split offering	An offering where a portion of the proceeds from the underwriting goes to the issuer and a portion goes to the selling shareholders.

spousal account	An IRA opened for a nonworking spouse that allows a full contribution to be made for the nonworking spouse.
spread	(1) The difference between the bid and ask for a security. (2) The simultaneous purchase and sale of two calls or two puts on the same underlying security.
spread load plan	A contractual plan that seeks to spread the sales charge over a longer period of time, as detailed in the Spread Load Plan Act of 1970. The maximum sales charge over the life of the plan is 9%, while the maximum sales charge in any one year is 20%.
stabilizing	The only form of price manipulation allowed by the SEC. The managing underwriter enters a bid at or below the offering price to ensure even distribution of shares.
standby underwriting	An underwriting used in connection with a preemptive rights offering. The standby underwriter must purchase any shares not subscribed to by existing shareholders.
statutory disqualification	A set of rules that prohibit an individual who has been barred or suspended or convicted of a securities-related crime from becoming registered.
statutory voting	A method of voting that requires investors to cast their votes evenly for the directors they wish to elect.
stock ahead	A condition that causes an investor's order not to be executed, even though the stock is trading at a price that would satisfy the customer's limit order, because other limit orders have been entered prior to the customer's order.
stock certificate	Evidence of equity ownership.
stock or bond power	A form that, when signed by the owner and attached to a security, makes the security negotiable.
stock split	A change in the number of outstanding shares, the par value, and the number of authorized shares that has been approved through a vote of the shareholders. Forward-stock splits increase the number of shares outstanding and reduce the stock price in order to make the security more attractive to individual investors.
stop limit order	An order that becomes a limit order to buy or sell the stock when the stock trades at or through the stop price.
stop order	An order that becomes a market order to buy or sell the stock when the stock trades at or through the stop price.
stopping stock	A courtesy offered by a specialist to public customers, whereby the specialist guarantees a price but tries to obtain a better price for the customer.
straddle	The simultaneous purchase or sale of a call and a put on the same security with the same strike price and expiration.

straight line depreciation	An accounting method that allows an owner to take equal tax deductions over the useful life of the asset.
strangle	The purchase or sale of a call and a put on either side of the current market price. The options have the same expiration months but different strike prices.
stripped bond	A bond that has had its coupons removed by a broker dealer and that is selling at a deep discount to its principal payment in the future.
stripper well	An oil well that is in operation just to recover a very limited amount of reserves.
subchapter S corporation	A business organization that allows the tax consequences of the organization to flow through to the owners.
subscription agreement	An application signed by the purchaser of an interest in a direct participation plan. An investor in a limited partnership does not become an investor until the general partner signs the subscription agreement.
subscription right	*See* right.
suitability	A determination that the characteristics of a security are in line with an investor's objectives, financial profile, and attitudes.
Super Display Book System (SDBK)	The electronic order-routing system used by the NYSE to route orders directly to the trading post.
supervise	The actions of a principal that ensure that the actions of a firm and its representatives are in compliance with industry regulations.
support	The price to which a security will fall and attract new buyers. As the new buyers enter the market, it keeps the price from falling any lower.
surplus fund	An account set up for funds generated by a project financed by a municipal revenue bond to pay a variety of expenses.
syndicate	A group of underwriters responsible for underwriting a new issue.
systematic risk	A risk inherent in any investment in the market. An investor may lose money simply because the market is going down.

T

takedown	The price at which a syndicate purchases a new issue of securities from the issuer.
tax and revenue anticipation note	A short-term note sold by a municipal issuer as interim financing in anticipation of tax and other revenue.

tax anticipation note (TAN)	A short-term note sold by a municipal issuer as interim financing in anticipation of tax revenue.
tax-deferred annuity	A nonqualified retirement account that allows an investor's money to grow tax deferred. A tax-deferred annuity is a contract between an insurance company and an investor.
tax equivalent yield	The interest rate that must be offered by a taxable bond of similar quality in order to be equal to the rate that is offered by a municipal bond.
tax-exempt bond fund	A bond fund that seeks to produce investment income that is free from federal tax by investing in a portfolio of municipal bonds.
tax liability	The amount of money that is owed by an investor after realizing a gain on the sale of an investment or after receiving investment income.
tax preference item	An item that receives preferential tax treatment and must be added back into income when calculating an investor's alternative minimum tax.
tax-sheltered annuity (TSA)	A qualified retirement plan offered to employees of governments, school systems, or nonprofit organizations. Contributions to TSAs are made with pre-tax dollars.
technical analysis	A method of security analysis that uses past price performance to predict the future performance of a security.
Telephone Consumer Protection Act of 1991	Legislation that regulates how potential customers are contacted by phone at home.
tenants in common	*See* joint tenants in common.
tender offer	An offer to buy all or part of a company's outstanding securities for cash or cash and securities.
term bond	A bond issue that has its entire principal due on one date.
term maturity	A type of bond maturity that has all principal due on one date.
testimonial	The use of a recognized expert or leader to endorse the services of a firm.
third market	A transaction in an exchange-listed security executed over the Nasdaq workstation.
third-party account	An account that is managed for the benefit of a customer by another party, such as an investment adviser, a trustee, or an attorney.
30-day visible supply	The total par value of all new issue municipal bonds coming to market in the next 30 days.
time deposit	An account that is established by a bank customer where the customer agrees to leave the funds on deposit for an agreed upon amount of time.

time value	The value of an option that exceeds its intrinsic value or its in-the-money amount.
tombstone ad	An announcement published in financial papers advertising the offering of securities by a group of underwriters. Only basic information may be contained in the tombstone ad, and all offers must be made through the prospectus only.
top heavy rule	The rule that states the maximum salary for which a Keogh contribution may be based. This is in effect to limit the disparity between high- and low-salary employees.
trade confirmation	The printed notification of a securities transaction. A confirmation must be sent to a customer on or before the completion of a transaction. The completion of a transaction is considered to be the settlement date.
trade date	The day when an investor's order is executed.
tranche	A class of collateralized mortgage obligation (CMO) that has a predicted maturity and interest rate.
transfer agent	An independent entity that handles name changes, records the names of security holders of record, and ensures that all certificates are properly endorsed.
transfer and hold in safekeeping	A request by customers for the brokerage firm to transfer their securities into the firm's name and to hold them in safekeeping at the firm. A brokerage may charge a fee for holding a customer's securities that have been registered in its name.
transfer and ship	A request by customers for the brokerage firm to transfer their securities into their name and to ship them to their address of record.
Treasury bill	A U.S. government security that is issued at a discount and matures at par in 4, 13, 26, and 52 weeks.
Treasury bond	A long-term U.S. government security that pays semiannual interest and matures in 10 to 30 years.
Treasury note	An intermediate-term U.S. government security that pays semiannual interest and matures in 1 to 10 years.
Treasury receipt	A zero-coupon bond created by a brokerage firm that is backed by U.S. government securities. It is issued at a discount and matures at par.
treasury stock	Stock that has been issued by a corporation and that has subsequently been repurchased by the corporation. Treasury stock does not vote or receive dividends. It is not used in the calculation of earnings per share.
trendline	A line used to predict the future price movement for a security. Drawing a line under the successive lows or successive highs creates a trendline.

trough	The bottoming out of the business cycle just prior to an new upward movement in activity.
true interest cost (TIC)	A calculation for the cost of a municipal issuer's interest expense that includes the time value of money.
Trust Indenture Act of 1940	Regulates the issuance of corporate debt in excess of $5 million and with a term exceeding 1 year. It requires an indenture between the issuer and the trustee.
trustee	A person who legally acts for the benefit of another party.
12B-1 fee	An asset-based distribution fee that is assessed annually and paid out quarterly to cover advertising and distribution costs. All 12B-1 fees must be reasonable.
two-dollar broker	An independent exchange member who executes orders for commission house brokers and other customers for a fee.
type	A classification method for an option as either a call or a put.

U

uncovered	*See* naked.
underlying security	A security for which an investor has an option to buy or sell.
underwriting	The process of marketing a new issue of securities to the investing public. A broker dealer forwards the proceeds of the sale to the issuer minus its fee for selling the securities.
unearned income	Any income received by an individual from an investment, such as dividends and interest income.
uniform delivery ticket	A document that must be attached to every security delivered by the seller, making the security "good delivery."
Uniform Gifts to Minors Act (UGMA)	Sets forth guidelines for the gifting of cash and securities to minors and for the operation of accounts managed for the benefit of minors. Once a gift is given to a minor, it is irrevocable.
Uniform Practice Code	The FINRA bylaw that sets guidelines for how industry members transact business with other members. The Uniform Practice Code establishes such things as settlement dates, rules of good delivery, and ex-dividend dates.
Uniform Securities Act (USA)	The framework for state-based securities legislation. The act is a model that can be adapted to each state's particular needs.

Uniform Transfer to Minors Act (UTMA)	Legislation that has been adopted in certain states, in lieu of the Uniform Gifts to Minors Act. UTMA allows the custodian to determine the age at which the assets become the property of the minor. The maximum age for transfer of ownership is 25.
unit investment trust (UIT)	A type of investment company organized as a trust to invest in a portfolio of securities. The UIT sells redeemable securities to investors in the form of shares or units of beneficial interest.
unit of beneficial interest	The redeemable share issued to investors in a unit investment trust.
unit refund annuity	An annuity payout option that will make payments to the annuitant for life. If the annuitant dies prior to receiving an amount that is equal to his or her account value, the balance of the account will be paid to the annuitant's beneficiaries.
unqualified legal opinion	A legal opinion issued by a bond attorney for the issue where there are no reservations relating to the issue.
unrealized	A paper profit or loss on a security that is still owned.

V

variable annuity	A contract issued by an insurance company that is both a security and an insurance product. The annuitant's contributions are invested through the separate account into a portfolio of securities. The annuitant's payments depend largely on the investment results of the separate account.
variable death benefit	The amount of a death benefit paid to a beneficiary that is based on the investment results of the insurance company's separate account. This amount is over the contract's minimum guaranteed death benefit.
variable life insurance	A life insurance policy that provides for a minimum guaranteed death benefit, as well as an additional death benefit, based on the investment results of the separate account.
variable rate municipal security	Interim municipal financing issued with a variable rate.
vertical spread	The simultaneous purchase and sale of two calls or two puts on the same underlying security that differ only in strike price.
vesting	The process by which an employer's contributions to an employee's retirement account become the property of the employee.
visible supply	*See* 30-day visible supply.

| voluntary accumulation plan | A method, such as dollar-cost averaging, by which an investor regularly makes contributions to acquire mutual fund shares. |
| voting right | The right of a corporation's stockholders to cast their votes for the election of the corporation's board of directors as well as for certain major corporate issues. |

W

warrant	A long-term security that gives the holder the right to purchase the common shares of a corporation for up to 10 years. The warrant's subscription price is always higher than the price of the underlying common shares when the warrant is initially issued.
wash sale	The sale of a security at a loss and the subsequent repurchase of that security or of a security that is substantially the same within 30 days of the sale. The repurchase disallows the claim of the loss for tax purposes.
western account	A type of municipal security syndicate account where only the member with unsold bonds is responsible for the unsold bonds.
when-issued security	A security that has been sold prior to the certificates being available for delivery.
wildcatting	An exploratory oil- and gas-drilling program.
wire room	*See* order department.
withdrawal plan	The systematic removal of funds from a mutual fund account over time. Withdrawal plans vary in type and availability among fund companies.
workable indication	An indication of the prices and yields that a municipal securities dealer may be willing to buy or sell bonds.
working capital	A measure of a corporation's liquidity that is found by subtracting current liabilities from current assets.
working interest	An interest that requires the holder to bear the proportional expenses and allows the holder to share in the revenue produced by an oil or gas project in relation to the interest.
workout quote	A nonfirm quote that requires handling and settlement conditions to be worked out between the parties prior to the trade.
writer	An investor who sells an option to receive the premium income.
writing the scale	The procedure of assigning prospective yields to a new issuer of serial municipal bonds.

Y

Yellow Sheets
A daily publication published by the national quotation bureau providing quotes for corporate bonds.

yield
The annual amount of income generated by a security relative to its price; expressed as a percentage.

yield-based option
An interest rate option that allows the holder to receive the in-the-money amount in cash upon exercise or expiration.

yield curve
The rate at which interest rates vary among investments of similar quality with different maturities. Longer-term securities generally offer higher yields.

yield to call
An investor's overall return for owning a bond should it be called in prior to maturity by the issuer.

yield to maturity
An investor's overall return for owning a bond if the bond is held until maturity.

Z

zero-coupon bond
A bond that is issued at a discount from its par value and makes no regular interest payments. An investor's interest is reflected by the security's appreciation toward par at maturity. The appreciation is taxable each year even though it is not actually received by the investor (phantom income).

zero-minus tick
A trade in an exchange-listed security that occurs at the same price as the previous transaction, but at a price that is lower than the last transaction that was different.

zero-plus tick
A trade in an exchange-listed security that occurs at the same price as the previous transaction, but at a price that is higher than the last transaction that was different.

Index

Power Your Career
CFA® | FRM® | CMT® | CAIA® | FINRA® | CFP®
CIMA® | Investment Banking

5 Reasons Students Prefer Wiley

✔ Access Best-in-Class Content   ✔ Bite-Sized Lessons   ✔ Free Updates
✔ Learn with Top Instructors   ✔ Outcome Focused

Visit efficientlearning.com

WILEY